THE PROBLEM OF UNIVER
CONTEMPORARY PHILOS

CW01460173

Are there any universal entities? Or is the world populated only by particular things? The problem of universals is one of the most fascinating and enduring topics in the history of metaphysics, with roots in ancient and medieval philosophy. This collection of new essays provides an innovative overview of the contemporary debate on universals. Rather than focusing exclusively on the traditional opposition between realism and nominalism, the contributors explore the complexity of the debate and illustrate a broad range of positions within both the realist and the nominalist camps. Realism is viewed through the lens of the distinction between constituent and relational ontologies, while nominalism is reconstructed in light of the controversy over the notion of trope. The result is a fresh picture of contemporary metaphysics, in which traditional strategies of dealing with the problem of universals are both reaffirmed and called into question.

GABRIELE GALLUZZO is a lecturer in ancient philosophy in the Department of Classics and Ancient History at the University of Exeter.

MICHAEL LOUX is George N. Shuster Professor of Philosophy at the University of Notre Dame.

THE PROBLEM OF UNIVERSALS IN CONTEMPORARY PHILOSOPHY

EDITED BY

GABRIELE GALLUZZO

MICHAEL J. LOUX

CAMBRIDGE
UNIVERSITY PRESS

CAMBRIDGE
UNIVERSITY PRESS

University Printing House, Cambridge CB2 8BS, United Kingdom

One Liberty Plaza, 20th Floor, New York, NY 10006, USA

477 Williamstown Road, Port Melbourne, VIC 3207, Australia

314-321, 3rd Floor, Plot 3, Splendor Forum, Jasola District Centre, New Delhi - 110025, India

79 Anson Road, #06-04/06, Singapore 079906

Cambridge University Press is part of the University of Cambridge.

It furthers the University's mission by disseminating knowledge in the pursuit of education, learning and research at the highest international levels of excellence.

www.cambridge.org
Information on this title: www.cambridge.org/9781107498341

© Cambridge University Press 2015

First published 2015
First paperback edition 2018

A catalogue record for this publication is available from the British Library

Library of Congress Cataloging in Publication data
The problem of universals in contemporary philosophy / edited by Gabriele Galluzzo, Michael J. Loux.
pages cm
Includes bibliographical references and index.
ISBN 978-1-107-10089-3 (alk. paper)
1. Universals (Philosophy) I. Galluzzo, Gabriele, editor.
B105.U5P765   2015
111'.2 – dc23   2015003493

ISBN 978-1-107-10089-3 Hardback
ISBN 978-1-107-49834-1 Paperback

For Jonathan and Francesco

Contents

Contents

Contributors

GABRIELE GALLUZZO is a lecturer in ancient philosophy in the Department of Classics and Ancient History at the University of Exeter

ROBERT K. GARCIA is an assistant professor of philosophy at Texas A&M University

SOPHIE GIBB is a senior lecturer in philosophy at Durham University

JOHN HEIL is a professor of philosophy at Washington University in St Louis and an honorary research associate at Monash University

MICHAEL J. LOUX is George N. Shuster Professor of Philosophy at the University of Notre Dame

E. J. LOWE was a professor of philosophy at Durham University

FRASER MACBRIDE is a professor of philosophy at the University of Glasgow

ANNA-SOFIA MAURIN is a professor of theoretical philosophy at the University of Gothenburg

PETER VAN INWAGEN is John Cardinal O'Hara Professor of Philosophy at the University of Notre Dame

Acknowledgments

The chapters collected in this volume had their origin in a conference on the problem of universals in contemporary analytic philosophy held at the Scuola Normale Superiore in Pisa, Italy in July 2010. We wish first of all to thank the Scuola Normale Superiore for the financial support and for providing an ideal setting for philosophical discussion. Massimo Mugnai generously offered to co-organize the event and apply for funds. This is the place to express our sincere gratitude to him. Alex Oliver, Gonzalo Rodriguez-Pereyra, and Dean Zimmerman also presented papers at the conference and greatly contributed to discussion. We are very grateful to them for their suggestions, criticisms, and comments, which helped all the contributors to shape their views and improve the final versions of their papers. Thanks go also to Giulia Felappi, Michele Ginammi, Giorgio Lando, Laura Mari, Valentina Morotti, and Giacomo Turbanti, who helped with the organization of the conference and took an active part in the philosophical discussion. Most of all, they created a lively and intellectually stimulating environment, which added value to our proceedings. The conference attracted a number of visitors from Italy and beyond. We wish to thank all the participants for enriching the event with their active presence.

We are very grateful to Hilary Gaskin for taking an interest in this book and considering it for publication. Thanks go also to two anonymous referees for Cambridge University Press, who made a number of insightful comments on the chapters and greatly improved the quality of the volume.

While this volume was close to completion, we lost two dear friends and colleagues who greatly contributed to our project: E. J. Lowe and Francesco Del Punta. Besides being one of the contributors, Jonathan Lowe was also supposed to be co-editor of the volume. He conceived with us the initial idea of the project and constantly advised us on a number of philosophical and editorial matters. Most of all, however, he was a splendid person, a dear friend and a good example of how to do good metaphysics.

Francesco Del Punta, too, played a crucial role in our project. He was the first to entertain the bold idea of bringing together philosophers and historians of philosophy to talk about the problem of universals. He co-organized with us the 2010 conference and ever since he provided unceasing encouragement in our attempts to bring the volume to completion. He always remained for us a source of inspiration and a severe judge of the quality of our scientific enterprise. During the 2010 conference he said he would watch the end of our works from 'a rather comfortable cloud.' We do hope that the cloud is indeed comfortable. This volume is for Jonathan and Francesco.

Introduction

Gabriele Galluzzo and Michael J. Loux

All but one of the chapters in this volume had their origin in a conference on the problem of universals in contemporary analytic philosophy held at the Scuola Normale Superiore in Pisa, Italy in July 2010. The conference was part of a larger project under the direction of Francesco Del Punta on the problem of universals across the whole history of philosophy. The aim of the conference was to give a broad overview of the contemporary debate on universals, and to indicate the issues that promise to be crucial to future metaphysical investigation.

It is difficult to provide an entirely uncontroversial characterization of what exactly the problem of universals is. This is due to the undeniable fact that the problem intersects with a large number of philosophical areas, ranging from metaphysics to semantics and also including philosophy of mathematics and epistemology. In the history of philosophy the problem has occasionally been described in semantic terms as the question as to whether or not the general terms of natural language refer to and so introduce peculiar kinds of entities, universals, somehow distinct from the familiar particular objects of our everyday experience. Sometimes, philosophers in the past have also looked at the problem of universals as an eminently epistemic issue, mainly concerned with the nature of our concepts: do general concepts represent general or universal entities or do they simply represent particular entities in a general way? This volume is characterized by a distinctively *metaphysical* approach to the problem of universals. Contributors to the volume share the common assumption that the problem of universals is primarily a metaphysical and ontological issue, mainly concerned with how many categories of things we should introduce into our ontology: is the furniture of the world confined exclusively to particular entities? Or do we need to include in the catalogue of things that there are universals as well, i.e. entities that are shared or at least shareable by many particulars? To take this approach does not mean to deny that the problem of universals may be significantly linked with a number of central areas in semantics and epistemology. However, semantic and epistemic issues are here regarded as interesting consequences of a fundamentally metaphysical problem.

As the chapters indicate, this volume covers a broad range of topics on the nature and existence of universals and their relation to the particulars that exhibit them. Given the vastness of the contemporary debate on universals and the many ramifications of the problem itself, it would have been impossible to aim at absolute exhaustiveness and completeness. Nonetheless, we have tried to select those topics that have significantly shaped and continue to shape our understanding of one of the most enduring themes in the history of philosophy. In line with the spirit of the original conference we have also wished to present different philosophical traditions and orientations concerning the problem of universals. Our aim in doing so was to show that the traditional division between realists and nominalists conceals a wide variety of philosophical views, often difficult to accommodate within the traditional schemes. Realism and nominalism are in many respects divided fields, more so actually than philosophers are often prepared to acknowledge. The recognition of this and related facts has led some contributors to challenge and call into question the traditional categories we are used to employing in conceptualizing and phrasing disputes on universals. Finally, although our focus has mainly been on the problem of universals as such more than on some of its possible implications for neighboring areas in metaphysics, we have also included in the volume vivid examples of how the problem overlaps with a series of different but related metaphysical questions, such as the metaphysical foundation of natural laws and the controversial issue of the nature of states of affairs. Although the single contributions argue for a number of positive philosophical positions, they also give a flavor of the debate and so introduce the different options on the philosophical market. In the rest of this introduction, we wish to give a sense of the contents and articulation of the volume.

One topic that played a major role in the conference was the contrast between broadly Aristotelian and broadly Platonistic approaches to universals. Roughly, the contrast is that between theories that make universals in some sense immanent in the spatiotemporal world and those that construe universals as in some sense transcendent. The contrast is in many ways well known and traditional, but it has in recent years come to be entirely rethought and redesigned in light of new and more fine-grained conceptual categories.

One way this contrast gets fleshed out is in terms of the contrast between what have been called constituent and relational approaches to ontological issues. Both are attempts to deal with the character or qualitative nature of familiar concrete particulars; and both tell us that those particulars derive their character from entities – properties, attributes, natures – that have their own character non-derivatively. Constituent theories tell us that those underived sources of character are something like parts, components, or (as it is usually put) constituents of the particulars whose character they underwrite. So familiar particulars have a more fundamental, metaphysical structure than their commonsense mereological structure, and in virtue of that structure, they have the various forms of character they do. Relational approaches, by contrast, deny that the underived sources of character inhabit the spatiotemporal world. Nonetheless, familiar spatiotemporal particulars can enter into non-mereological relations or ties with those sources of character (they instantiate, exemplify, or exhibit them); and in virtue of doing so, those particulars have the different forms of character we associate with them.

In his chapter ('An Exercise in Constituent Ontology'), Michael J. Loux lays out this contrast and points out that in recent discussions of ontological issues the relational approach has been dominant. That dominance, he suggests, is rooted in the assumption that the constituent approach with its talk of constituents and ontological structure involves a kind of category mistake, the mistake of thinking that concrete particulars can have abstract entities (things like properties or attributes) as parts or ingredients. Loux argues that no compelling case against the constituent approach can be derived from this assumption, and he goes onto lay out the general contours of the constituent approach. He takes the traditional bundle theory (where familiar particulars are bundles of fully determinate first-order properties) as the entry point for constituent theorizing and points to four sets of difficulties for the theory, arguing that we can take alternative versions of the constituent approach to result from attempts to deal with those difficulties. Contending that no recent constituent theories are successful here, Loux points to Aristotle's hylemorphic theory as a constituent account that is successful in dealing with the four sets of difficulties.

In 'Against Ontological Structure' Peter van Inwagen agrees with the Aristotelian that we have no option but to endorse an ontology of universals, but he rejects the constituent theorist's account of the relation between universals and the familiar particulars that exhibit them. He takes universals to fall under a general category he calls "relation." The category includes propositions (O-adic relations), properties (monadic relations), and what are more commonly or properly called relations (dyadic, triadic, and more generally, n-adic members of the category). As he sees it, all the items in this general category are assertibles, things that can be asserted or said. Propositions are saturated assertibles: they can be said or asserted full stop; whereas properties and what are properly called relations are unsaturated assertibles: they are things that are asserted of or said of other things or n-tuples of other things. As van Inwagen sees it, assertibles, whether saturated or unsaturated, are nonphysical, non-spatial abstract entities; and while he concedes that properties and relations can enter into non-mereological relations or ties to the individuals that exhibit them, he denies, contra Loux, that they can, in any sense, be parts, ingredients, or components of concrete particulars. Indeed, he tells us that he simply does not understand what constituent theorists are saying when they speak of constituents, complexes, and ontological structure. Such talk, he insists, is meaningless.

In his contribution ('In Defense of Substantial Universals'), E. J. Lowe agrees with van Inwagen in rejecting the constituent approach; but unlike van Inwagen, who wants to endorse a Platonistic theory, Lowe construes himself as endorsing a broadly Aristotelian theory. He sees Aristotle as presenting two quite different ontological schemes. On the one hand, there is the hylemorphic theory of the *Physics* and the *Metaphysics*. That theory, Lowe concedes, is a constituent theory. He finds its talk of informed matter mystifying, and he insists that the theory fails to show how the hylemorphic complexes Aristotle wants to call substances constitute genuinely unified objects. But while rejecting the hylemorphic approach, Lowe points to Chapter 2 of the *Categories* as the source of a non-constituent theory whose broad outlines he wants to endorse. There, Aristotle presents what Lowe calls a four-category ontology. As he sees it, Aristotle distinguishes between two categories of universal – substance kinds and attributes – and two categories of individual – individual substances and their modes. Lowe goes on to defend Aristotle's distinction between substance kinds and attributes against those metaphysicians who want to lump all first-order universals together. He argues that we need substance kinds as a distinct category of universals if we are to deal with pressing metaphysical problems about individuation, instantiation, and the nature of laws.

Like Lowe, Gabriele Galluzzo ('A kind farewell to Platonism') wants to defend a distinction between substance kinds and other universals instantiated by individual substances – what Galluzzo calls properties. He sees the idea that there is a distinction here as independent of the contrast between constituent and relational theories, but he agrees with Lowe that the distinction fits most comfortably in an Aristotelian context. It is a distinction between two irreducibly different categories of first-order universal – what-universals and how-universals. Substance kinds are responsible for individual substances being *what* they are; whereas what Galluzzo calls properties underlie substances being *how* they are. The former are sortal universals: they mark out their members as countably distinct from each other and from things of other kinds, and they provide criteria of identity for the individuals falling under them.

Galluzzo concedes that for each substance kind, there is a cluster of properties that serves to explain phenomena idiosyncratic to the kind; he even concedes that such properties may be *de re* necessary to the individuals belonging to the kind; but he resists any attempt to reduce the kind to a conjunction of these properties. As he sees it, the kind is prior to the associated properties: it is because the individuals are members of the substance kind that they exhibit the associated properties and not vice versa. There remains the question of just which universals are genuine substance kinds; and while Galluzzo is himself sympathetic to a broadly Aristotelian account where the fully determinate biological kinds under which familiar living beings fall are taken to exhaust the basic or fundamental substance kinds, he insists that the framework of substances kinds is a flexible scheme that is amendable to a variety of metaphysical theories.

Another topic that played a major role in the conference from which this volume originated is trope theory, the constituent theory presented by D. C. Williams in the 1950s and since defended by an increasingly large number of metaphysicians. Trope theorists tell us that the underived sources of character are as individual or particular as the familiar particulars whose character they underwrite. They call these sources of character tropes, and they tell us that ordinary objects are bundles of tropes, and what we call universals, sets of resembling tropes. Over time, trope theories have progressively become more attractive and popular than austere nominalism, i.e. the view that there are no properties (whether tropes or universal properties) but only particular concrete objects. This is so because trope theories may appear to combine the advantages of both realism and nominalism: like realists, trope theories admit of the existence of properties; like nominalists, they provide a one-category ontology, being tropes as particular as the objects whose character they underwrite.

In 'Is trope theory a divided house?' Robert Garcia argues that there are two quite different things that have gone by the title "trope." Some theorists have construed tropes as characteristics or properties, and others have taken them to be propertied or charactered individuals. The former are things like the redness of a certain dress and the courage of Socrates; whereas the latter are maximally thinly charactered individuals like that red individual or that courageous individual. Garcia calls the former modifier tropes and the latter module tropes. He argues that we get two fundamentally different ontological theories from these two notions; and he tells us that both theories have their problems. If we construct a trope theory employing the notion of a module trope, we meet with serious difficulties in our attempts to identify universals with sets of tropes. On the other hand, if we construct a theory of tropes employing the concept of a modifier trope, we meet with difficulties in our attempts to construe familiar objects as bundles of tropes.

In 'Universals in a world of particulars' John Heil uses D.C. Williams' original version of trope theory as the jumping-off point for the construction of a quite different theory of character. Heil understands Williams' tropes as what Garcia calls module tropes. As he sees it, Williams had particular or individual properties in mind; but while Heil thinks that the idea of a particular property can play a role in our account of familiar objects, he wants to dissociate that idea from other themes at work in Williams' technical notion of a trope. In particular, he rejects Williams' bundle theoretic account of ordinary objects. He proposes instead that we apply the idea of a particular or individual property within the context of a substance/attribute ontology. He wants to deny that we can provide a reductive analysis of the concept of substance. Substances are irreducibly fundamental, but in giving an account of their character, we do not need to appeal to the universals of the realist. We can and should invoke the idea of particular properties. Heil wants to construe these properties as ways substances are, and he suggests that if we understand them in these terms, we should give up the idea that they are parts or components of substances. But while deviating from Williams in his account of familiar concrete objects, Heil accepts Williams' account of universals as sets of resembling particular properties and argues that it represents a theory that has all the virtues of traditional realism about universals without its ontological costs.

Realists about universals frequently claim that universals succeed while tropes and their ilk fail in grounding the generality of laws. Heil challenges this view. In her 'Tropes and the generality of laws' Sophie Gibb does as well. She argues that the realist has no advantage whatsoever over the trope theorist here. The realist's argument is that if we assume the numerical identity of a universal in its various instances, it is easy to explain how a law of the form 'Every F is G' should hold generally. We have, after all, a single universal 'F' at work here; but since that universal is identical in all its instances, it can assumed, *ceteris paribus*, to act in the same way in all those instances. Gibb argues that the realist's notion of identity of property provides no more plausible explanation of the generality at work here than does the trope theorist's notion of exact similarity. Just as a single property can be assumed to make the same causal contribution in similar circumstances, so can tropes that are exactly similar; and Gibb argues that this is true whether we understand properties in dispositional or categorical terms.

The last two chapters deal with a variety of topics central to discussions about universals and their relations to particulars. Besides their intrinsic merits in relation to the debates on universals, these two chapters are intended to show how far-reaching and ramified the problem of universals is, as it fruitfully intersects with a number of neighboring metaphysical issues. An important theme in early analytic philosophy is the defense of realism about universals. Russell argued for the existence of universals by arguing for the ineliminability and generality of relations. In 'On the origins of order: non-symmetric or only symmetric relations?' Fraser MacBride echoes this theme, arguing that non-symmetric relations are ineliminable. A non-symmetric relation is one for which there are different ways in which it applies to the things it relates. So if R is a binary non-symmetric relation, then, for appropriate x and y, there are two different ways in which it is capable of applying to x and y, either by its being the case that $x \, R \, y$ or its being the case that $y \, R \, x$. MacBride argues that we have to take this requirement on non-symmetric relations to be a primitive and non-eliminable fact about the world, a fact in no need of further explanation; and he goes on to attack recent attempts at reducing non-symmetric to symmetric relations. In so doing, MacBride rejects the Humean principle that there are no brute metaphysical necessities (i.e. necessities that call for no further explanation), and argues for the importance of grounding metaphysical discourse on some metaphysically primitive assumptions.

One influential version of constituent ontology tells us that in addition to particulars and properties we need to posit complexes called states of affairs. The argument goes as follows: to explain how it could be that a particular, x, could exemplify a property, F, we need more than the existence of x and F since both could exist without its being the case that x is F. To get the result that x is F, we need to posit a new item – the state of affairs consisting in x's being F. In 'States of affairs and the relation regress' Anna-Sofia Maurin explores this line of argument. She argues that the postulation of the relevant state of affairs succeeds in giving us the result that x is F only if the items in that state of affairs are unified. But, Maurin argues, to get the requisite unity, we need a tie or relation, but that only gives us a new ensemble (x, F, and the relation/tie/nexus). That ensemble likewise needs to be unified, and so we are off on a familiar regress. Maurin goes on to consider ways of insuring the requisite unity while either avoiding the regress or rendering it harmless. The results, she argues, are not encouraging, so she concludes that if states of affairs are posited to show how particulars and universals can be unified, they do not serve the purpose very well.

CHAPTER I

An exercise in constituent ontology

Michael J. Loux

I

I want to do some comparative ontology. I want to examine a certain pattern of ontological explanation, to identify and compare various ways the pattern has been or could be deployed, and to argue that one instance of this pattern is, in a number of ways, superior to the others. The pattern concerns the phenomenon of character, that is, the fact that familiar concrete particulars have character or (as we might put it in non-philosophical or commonsense parlance) the fact that familiar particulars possess properties, fall under kinds, and enter into relations. Many (but not all) philosophers have believed that the individual facts making up this phenomenon are the sorts of facts that stand in need of explanation. As they see it, familiar particulars have their character derivatively; they derive their character from other things, things that have their own distinctive forms of character non-derivatively.

But these philosophers have not all agreed about how this derivation works itself out. Indeed, there are two opposed accounts of the way familiar particulars derive their character. Some philosophers hold that the underived sources of character are things that exist 'apart from' or 'in separation from' familiar particulars and that it is in virtue of standing in some relation to these privileged bearers of character that familiar particulars have the character they do. These philosophers tell us, for example, that familiar particulars exemplify transcendent universals or that sensible individuals participate in separated intelligible forms. Other philosophers, by contrast, tell us that the items underlying the character of familiar particulars are immanent in those particulars, immanent in the sense that they are something like their parts, components, or constituents. On this view, a kind of mereological structure underlies the character of familiar particulars. Particulars have their distinctive forms of character in virtue of having the appropriate underived sources of character as components.

So there are two different strategies for accounting for the pre-philosophical phenomenon of character. They have been called, respectively, the relational and constituent strategies.[1] I will stick with these labels.

The relational strategy is perennially important; it is also thoroughly familiar. It is, after all, the dominant strategy in contemporary discussions of character. But while the relational approach may dominate contemporary discussions, over the whole history of metaphysics, the constituent approach is arguably the dominant strategy. And it is the strategy I want to consider.

To one accustomed to recent ontological discussions, my interest in the constituent strategy might appear puzzling; for among defenders of the relational approach, the consensus is that the constituent strategy is, at bottom, incoherent: its central claim embodies a category mistake. The claim is that the items that have character non-derivatively are components or parts of familiar particulars. Those items, however, are abstract entities, whereas familiar particulars are concrete objects, and, we are told, no concrete object can be made out of abstract entities.

More than anything else, I think, this objection explains why contemporary metaphysicians have been so ready to endorse the relational approach. To endorse the opposing constituent approach, they have assumed, is to make the category mistake just set out; it is to endorse the incoherent idea that abstract entities can be parts or ingredients of concrete particulars. This is an important objection, one we need to address if we are to take the constituent approach seriously. After all, there can be little point in pursuing an ontological strategy that is doomed from the start.

Is it so doomed? I am not convinced it is. It is not clear that the distinction between abstract and concrete will bear the weight the objection assigns it. For the objection to work, we need some principled way of drawing the distinction so that the things philosophers want to call abstract turn out abstract and those they want to call concrete turn out concrete. We need, that is, criteria that give the right results; but, further, those criteria must be such that by reflecting on them we can see why a concrete entity cannot have abstract entities as components or constituents.

But what are the criteria here? We might suppose that an entity is concrete iff it has a spatial location and that it is abstract iff it is not concrete.[2] One difficulty is that this way of drawing the distinction either gives the wrong results or presupposes controversial philosophical claims that are independent of the issues at hand. Traditional dualists tell us

---

[1] Wolterstorff (1991).   [2] See Simons (1994) for this sort of criterion.

that minds are non-spatial beings; but, then, our criteria force us to hold either that individual minds are abstract entities or that materialism is true. One might try to repair things by saying that an object is concrete iff it either has a spatial location or is made up of temporal parts and abstract iff not concrete.[3] Minds have temporal parts, don't they? But do they all? Orthodox theists will certainly deny this; but, then, the revised criterion either gives the wrong result by holding that at least one person is an abstract entity, or it forces us to hold an independently controversial claim – atheism. And atheism isn't the only controversial claim associated with the revised criterion. The account works for finite mental substances only if they really do have temporal parts; but presentists, philosophers who insist that only what exists now or in the present is real, will deny that there are such things as temporal parts. So the account works only if some form of four-dimensionalism is true.

But there is a further difficulty, one that arises for both ways of drawing the distinction. Properties, we may assume, are abstract entities. Unfortunately, many constituent ontologists will insist that the properties constitutive of a familiar particular have a spatial location: they are where the particular is.[4] And these same constituent ontologists will typically go on and say that a single property can wholly and completely occupy more than one spatial location at a time – indeed, as many locations as the familiar particulars it goes to constitute. Of course, the relationists who want to accuse constituent theorists of a category mistake will deny that properties have spatial location; but if the issue of spatial location is one that, in general, divides constituent and relational ontologists, the assumption that properties have no spatial location can hardly play a role in an argument designed to adjudicate between the two approaches.

In any case, the contrast between abstract and concrete is problematic. Some philosophers respond to the problems by resorting to lists or inventories. The idea is that even if we cannot identify criteria for drawing it, the distinction gets vindicated by the fact that we tend to agree about which items fall under the respective headings.[5] Properties, propositions, and relations are all abstract; whereas, persons, plants, animals, and atoms are all concrete. I have considerable sympathy with this move. Although I do not have criteria of the desired sort for drawing the distinction, I believe that there is a distinction here. Nonetheless, I cannot resist pointing out

---

[3] See Lowe (1995) and Chapter 10 of Lowe (1998) for an account along these lines.
[4] See, for example, Donagan (1963).
[5] See van Inwagen (2006). See Strawson and Grice (1956) for the parallel claim about the analytic/synthetic distinction.

that there is less agreement about the classification than sanguine philosophers might have us believe. Trope theorists, for example, disagree about whether tropes are abstract or concrete; but most trope theorists want to deny that, in the final analysis, there is anything besides tropes.[6] Likewise, metaphysicians disagree about the status of events: some think they are concrete; others, abstract.[7] Still, there are ontologists who insist that events exhaust the inventory of what there is. Again, we are all familiar with the claim that states of affairs or facts are the ultimate realities; nonetheless, there is disagreement about whether such things are abstract or concrete.[8] Let us assume, however, that such disagreements can be resolved and that there is a genuine distinction here, one given by the traditional inventories. A difficulty remains. Once we acquiesce in this strategy, we are left without any account of just what makes a thing abstract or concrete; and in the absence of that sort of account, we lack the resources for showing why it should be problematic to think that concrete entities are composed of or constituted by abstract entities.

At this point, the objector will likely retrench and make one kind of concrete entity – material particulars – the focus of the objection. The parts of a material particular, the revised objection will go, are one and all material; but only at the risk of a category mistake can we suppose that things like properties are material objects. Constituent ontologists, however, want to claim that the properties of a material particular count as its components or constituents, so we once again get the conclusion that constituent ontologists are guilty of some sort of category mistake.

As we will see, it is not quite accurate to say that all constituent ontologists want to make the properties of a material particular its constituents; nonetheless, many do. But none of those who do will find the revised objection any better than the original. The difficulty, they will claim, is that the revised objection mistakenly identifies the constituents of a material particular with its commonsense parts. Constituent ontologists, however, are anxious to distinguish the two; and while conceding that the latter must be material, they will deny that this is true of the former. As early as Aristotle, we meet with this distinction. He distinguishes between 'the parts that measure a thing according to quantity' and 'the parts of which its substance is composed' (*Met.* VII.10, 1034$^{\rm b}$33–35). The former are

[6] Simons (1994) and Williams (1953) take opposing sides on the status of tropes.
[7] See, for example, Davidson (1970) and Chisholm (1976) for this opposition.
[8] Chisholm (1976) and Armstrong (1997b) hold opposed views on the status of states of affairs.

the commonsense parts of a thing; the latter, its constituents or what we might call its metaphysical parts. Now, parts of both sorts are less than, fall short of the wholes they compose; but Aristotle is telling us that the two sorts of parts fall short in different ways. Each of the commonsense parts of a thing is spatially less than the thing: the primary place each occupies is a proper part of the primary place occupied by the whole. Accordingly, the part can be used to provide a spatial measure of the whole, so that we can speak of the whole as being so many feet long, so many cubits wide, or so many hands high. Aristotle's talk about the substance of a thing, by contrast, is talk about its being what it is, its being the kind of thing it is. Hence, the idea at work in talk about the substantial or metaphysical parts of a thing is that each such part involves or induces a form of being that is less than or a component of the overall form of being displayed by the whole thing. While Aristotle would concede that the commonsense parts of a thing are one and all material, he would insist that its substantial or metaphysical parts can include an item that is not properly material at all.

Unlike Aristotle (who is a presentist), David Lewis uses a temporal parts framework as the backdrop for his characterization of what I am calling the constituent approach and speaks of non-spatiotemporal parts;[9] and while he thinks that the spatiotemporal parts of a material object are every bit as material as the object itself, he takes it to be a defining feature of the constituent approach that non-material things like properties can count as the non-spatiotemporal or metaphysical parts of a material object. Lewis, of course, does not himself favor a constituent approach to character. Indeed, he denies that we need to give a substantive account (whether of the relational or constituent variety) of the phenomenon;[10] but he recognizes that constituent ontology does not, from the very start of the project, harbor a category mistake.

The idea that there is a contrast between the commonsense material parts of a thing and its metaphysical parts or constituents is shared by every practitioner of the constituent strategy; nor is it any accident that this is so. Recall that the proponent of this strategy makes the constituents of a thing responsible for its overall character; but its commonsense mereological structure is just one aspect of that character. And not just the arrangement of a thing's commonsense parts is due to a thing's constituents. Constituent ontologists will say that the intrinsic nature of the parts themselves is due

---

[9] See D. Lewis (1983).   [10] Ibid.

to the constituents of the whole, or they will say that those parts have constituents of their own that account for their nature. In either case, we have
the result that, in the story the constituent ontologist tells, constituents
or metaphysical parts turn out to be prior to commonsense material
parts.

   We may concede that the distinction serves to answer the revised objection, but we will want to know more about constitution. As a start, we
can identify its formal properties. If we restrict ourselves to what might
be called the proper constituents of a thing, we can agree that the relation of constituent to whole is irreflexive, asymmetrical, and transitive.
Functionally, it is a relation of composition, so it might be tempting
to identify it with other more familiar composition relations, but the
temptation should be resisted. It is not the relation tying the members
of a set to the set: familiar particulars aren't sets. Nor is it the relation
tying properties to the conjunctive property whose conjuncts they are.
Many constituent ontologists refuse to restrict the constituents of familiar
particulars to their properties; and even those that do accept the restriction will typically deny that familiar particulars are themselves properties,
whether molecular or atomic.[11] More plausible is the suggestion that the
constituent/whole relation is a case of the relation of composition at work
in what is properly called mereology, the logic of parts and wholes; but
even this suggestion has its problems. The relation in question (called
summing or fusion) is just too generous; and in this respect it agrees with
both set theoretical composition and the composition involved in property conjunction. In all three cases, if it is possible for a given plurality of
objects to compose the relevant whole, then the plurality does compose
it. Not so in the case of the objects constituting a familiar particular. It is
possible for those objects to exist without constituting the particular: they
play their constitutional role only contingently, and constituent ontologists routinely take this fact to underlie the contingency of the constituted
particular.

   Now, some constituent ontologists will claim that we can supplement
the concept of fusion with restrictions which insure that the only composites are those we meet in the case of actually existing ordinary objects.[12]

---

[11] An exception may be Laurie Paul. See Paul (2002) and section VI of this chapter.
[12] The question of whether the constituent/whole relation can be understood by way of some restricted
form of fusion is one that divides constituent ontologists. Typically, bundle theorists (both those
who construe properties as universals and those who construe them as tropes) endorse a mereological
interpretation of the constituent/whole relation. Substratum theorists typically refuse to endorse a
mereological account. For a mereological reading, see Williams (1953) and Paul (2004). For non-
mereological accounts, see Bergmann (1967: 22) and Armstrong (1997b: 178–83).

But whether they endorse a thoroughly mereological interpretation of the constituent/whole relation, constituent ontologists will agree that if a plurality of objects, $a \ldots n$, constitutes a particular, x, then it does so only contingently. Nonetheless, they will also agree that the resulting whole, x, has necessarily the property of having all and only $a \ldots n$ as constituents. Call this claim Constituent Essentialism. It needs to be distinguished from what is called Mereological Essentialism, the claim that a thing has each of its commonsense parts necessarily. It is plausible to think that constituent ontologists are free to disagree about the latter claim; but constituent ontologists claim that what I have called Constituent Essentialism is something like a framework principle for their approach. They hold that familiar particulars are nothing but composites of their constituents; but, then, they argue, it is difficult to understand how it could be so much as possible for a particular to have constituents other than those it does. Given a different group of constituents, we would have the existence of a different composite and, therefore, a different familiar particular.

So constituent ontologists take it to be structural facts about their style of ontology, first, that the items constituting a given particular do so only contingently and, second, that the particular has the constituents it does necessarily. Constituent ontologists will typically add that it has those constituents uniquely, and they will claim that this, like the claim I have dubbed Constituent Essentialism, is a framework principle for this style of metaphysical explanation. On this view, all there is to a familiar particular is its constituents; but, then, it should be impossible for numerically diverse objects to be made up of identical constituents. I will call this claim the Principle of Constituent Identity and will formulate it as the claim that necessarily, for any objects, x and y, if x and y have all and only the same constituents, x and y are identical.

Towards characterizing the concept of constitution at work in immanentist theories, I have said that the relation of constituent to whole is a compositional relation that is irreflexive, asymmetrical, and transitive. Furthermore, I have said that while the constituents of a thing only contingently constitute it, the thing has its constituents necessarily and uniquely. This characterization is very general. We can envisage any number of concepts that satisfy the formal and functional constraints identified in the characterization. But that is how it should be. Although constituent ontologists will accept our general characterization of constitution, their accounts of the constitution of familiar particulars will differ radically. In what I have said so far, I have said about as much as one can say about the constituent strategy in general. To get clearer on the strategy, we need to examine particular examples of the strategy and to understand how they agree and differ. So let us look at examples.

II

We can begin our exploration of the constituent approach by focusing on the idea that what we are presented with in the case of any familiar particular is just a variety of forms of character. We are presented with a multiplicity of natures that together make up a kind of unity. Whether we are experiencing the particular or merely thinking of it, those natures or forms of character represent all that there is to grasp or apprehend about the particular. Apart from them, we want to say, the particular is nothing for us. Reflection on this piece of phenomenology can lead us to the idea that what the particular is just is those different natures or forms of character congealed into something like a unity. Now, the technical counterpart to the notion of character at work in the phenomenology is the concept of a first-order property or, more precisely, the notion of a first-order property that is fully determinate within its range. Accordingly, reflection on the phenomenological insights has its natural expression in the characteristic ontological claim of the traditional bundle theory – the claim that a familiar particular is nothing but a bundle of fully determinate first order properties, the fully determinate first-order properties commonsense associates with the particular.[13]

So where commonsense sees a geranium, a cat, or an apple, what we really have is just a cluster or bundle of fully determinate properties. The cluster is a kind of whole and the properties, something like its parts. They are not, to be sure, spatial or spatiotemporal parts of the whole. It is rather that each involves a form of being that is a component in the overall form of being associated with the relevant familiar particular. The properties, then, are what we have been calling constituents. They are, however, constituents in a single composite: together they make up a unity. Whence the unity? The answer of the traditional bundle theorist is straightforward: we have a unity – a single commonsense object – in virtue of the fact that all the different fully determinate properties are together, are compresent, are concurrent.

So we have our first version of constituent ontology in a rudimentary form of the traditional bundle theory. What I want to suggest is that we can get a good sense of the main options that the constituent strategy affords,

---

[13] Section VI of Part I, Book I of Hume (1739) for this sort of approach to the bundle theory.

a good idea of all the most interesting and important kinds of constituent theories, if we reflect on the sorts of problems that arise for this rudimentary attempt at doing ontology in the constituent style; for the various kinds of constituent theories can be viewed as attempts to deal with problems that arise for this sort of account. To show this, I will focus on four different problems that can be thought to arise for our rudimentary theory:

(1)   that the theory entails the truth of the Identity of Indiscernibles;
(2)   that the theory commits us to excessive essentialism (what I have called ultraessentialism);
(3)   that the theory cannot accommodate our pre-philosophical idea that things persist through change;
(4)   that the theory cannot explain the individuality or concreteness of familiar particulars.

III

Let's begin with (1). Its backdrop is the idea that it is possible for numerically different particulars to exhibit one and the same form of character coupled with the assumption that where this happens, numerically one and the same property is a constituent in numerically different composites. Given this backdrop, the formulation of the objection is straightforward.[14] Bundle theorists hold that the constituents of a familiar particular are exhausted by its properties; but as constituent ontologists, they are committed to the Principle of Constituent Identity (the claim, recall, that necessarily if a thing, x, and a thing, y, have all and only the same constituents, x and y are identical). But, then, bundle theorists are committed to the Identity of Indiscernibles, the claim that necessarily if a thing, x, and a thing, y, have all and only the same properties, then x is identical with y; and since bundle theorists seek to provide a reductive account of familiar particulars, the properties at work in the version of the Identity of Indiscernibles to which they are committed are those I call pure. Roughly put, pure properties are those whose content does not already involve the framework of existing particulars. More precisely, a property is pure just in case it is not impure, and a property, P, is impure just in case there is a contingent particular, y, and a relation, R, such that necessarily a thing, x, has P iff x enters into R with y. So the bundle theorist is committed to denying that it is possible for numerically different familiar particulars to have all and only the same

---

[14] For a detailed formulation of this objection, see Chapter 7 of Loux (1978) and Chapter 3 of Loux (2006b).

pure properties. But, the objection goes, this is possible. Kant's two gloves, Black's radially symmetrical universe, and David Lewis' Nietzschean world of recurrence all show this.[15] But, then, either the Principle of Constituent Identity or the characteristic claim of the bundle theory is false. The former, however, is a framework principle of the ontological enterprise itself, so it is the latter that is false.

This line of argument has often been taken to yield not just this negative conclusion, but a positive conclusion as well.[16] The reasoning is as follows: since the Principle of Constituent Identity is true, numerically distinct, but qualitatively indiscernible objects must each contain a constituent over and above its pure properties, a constituent idiosyncratic to its possessor; and since every familiar object is possibly such that it has a twin, every familiar object has such a constituent. The constituent has been called a bare particular, and what a bare particular does is provide for the possible diversification of a bundle of pure properties; but, we are told, it also serves as the subject or bearer of all the properties in the bundle. The claim is that what gives us the existence of the whole familiar object is just the fact that its bare particular exemplifies each of the properties constitutive of the individual; and we are told that it is a structural fact about this connection or tie that it holds merely contingently. So where the bundle theorist claims that the constituents of a familiar object are all of a single type and that the unity of the ordinary object derives from the fact that those constituents enter into the symmetrical relation, tie, or connection of compresence, what we can call the bare particular theorist tells us that those constituents are of two distinct categorial types and that the unity of the object derives from the fact that one of those constituents is connected to all the others by an asymmetrical tie or connection.

But philosophers have typically resisted the bare particular analysis. The central objection has been that the items it takes to be the ultimate subjects of predication turn out to be things that are not, in any plausible sense, identifiable objects of reference. The difficulty, of course, is their bareness. But there is more here than a difficulty in specifying how we would go about identifying a bare particular. That difficulty is real; but as I have argued elsewhere, there is the deeper difficulty that the very idea of a thoroughly bare entity is of dubious coherence.[17] Something is bare just in case it has no properties essentially. But isn't having no properties essentially a property that is essential to anything that has it? And what about the property of being a numerical diversifier? Isn't that essential to

[15] See Kant (1768: 381) and section 13 of Kant (1783), Black (1952), and D. Lewis (1986a: 157–58).

[16] See Allaire (1963) for the classic formulation of this reading of the objection.

[17] See Chapter 3 of Loux (2006b). For a response to this objection, see Sider (2006).

the diversifier? The problem, however, is that once we allow our diversifiers to have these sorts of properties essentially, then they no longer provide us with the final answer to questions about diversification; for all diversifying particulars have the same pure properties essentially, so the problem they were introduced to solve arises for them as well.

But if the bare particular analysis fails to explain the possibility of numerically diverse, but qualitatively indiscernible particulars, perhaps trope theory provides a version of the constituent approach that succeeds here. The trope theorist denies that when we speak of two individuals having the same form of character, what we say entails numerical identity of constituents.[18] The properties that correspond to our commonsense notion of character, they tell us, are particular; they are as particular as the wholes they compose. 'Trope' is, of course, the technical term for a property understood this way. On this view, where two numerically different individuals have, as we pre-philosophically put it, the same form of character, they include among their respective constituents similar tropes. The similarity in question comes in degrees, with exact similarity the upper limit. Exact similarity, however, is not identity. Accordingly, the possibility of completely indiscernible objects is non-problematic on this view. Diverse, but indiscernible objects would be composed of constituents that are exactly similar; but not a single constituent of the one object would be a constituent of the other. But, then, the trope theorist can agree that it is possible for numerically different objects to be qualitatively indiscernible without rejecting the Identity of Indiscernibles. So familiar particulars are wholes with tropes as constituents; and although some trope theorists add an underlying substratum as a constituent,[19] the standard versions of trope theory are bundle theoretic accounts.

Now, trope theorists like to speak freely and almost casually about this or that trope, but the fact is that it is not altogether clear what a trope is. The difficulty here is one of individuation. Take the color of the desk top on which I am writing. Presumably it is just one trope. But what happens when I cut the desk top in two? Do I thereby bring two color tropes into existence? If I do, then what was beforehand not a trope now is one; but how can what was not a trope become one? Well, perhaps we should say that the two color tropes were there beforehand. The difficulty, however, is that I could go on and divide each of the two new sections of the original desk top into two. But, then, were there four rather than two color tropes before the first division? It is not clear that any answer we give here will be

[18] See, for example, Williams (1953), Campbell (1990), and Simons (1994).
[19] See Martin (1980).

satisfactory. And, of course, analogous problems will arise for the size and the shape tropes of the original desk.

Early trope theorists like D. C. Williams do not seem to have been sensitive to these difficulties. A more recent defender of trope theory – Keith Campbell – has been quite straightforward in conceding the difficulties.[20] His response is to propose a version of trope theory that takes all of the spatiotemporal world to consist of just five superimposed fields, where each field is construed as a single cosmic trope that spreads itself across the totality of spacetime. The five fields are those of gravitation, electromagnetism, the weak nuclear force, the strong nuclear force, and matter or inertial mass. Now, Campbell denies that any of his five cosmic tropes can be divided into anything smaller, and he concludes that the problems about individuation simply do not arise for them. Nothing short of the whole cosmic sweep of a field counts as a trope, and since there are five qualitatively different such fields, there are exactly five tropes – no more, no fewer.

It is, however, not clear that Campbell's version of trope theory avoids the problems he identifies in more traditional versions of the theory. Campbell tells us that a trope is 'a single . . . particularized nature.'[21] If his cosmic trope theory is to avoid the problems about individuation, each of his five fields had better present us with a single unanalyzable form of character. But is this how things work out? I don't think so. If each of his fields were a single unanalyzable character or nature, the world would present itself as a thoroughgoing homogeneity. If we are to get the heterogeneity that characterizes our world, then the five fields must each distribute its proper quantity in varying intensities across spacetime. Such differential distribution is required to explain how one region of spacetime is qualitatively different from another; and Campbell seems to concede that the relevant quantities do vary in intensity across spacetime. The difficulty is that once we allow these sorts of differences in quantitative intensity, we have to deny that each of the five fields represents 'a single . . . particularized nature'; and we introduce the materials for generating precisely the sorts of problems of individuation that Campbell seeks to avoid.

IV

Let us return to the rudimentary bundle theory that provided our introduction to the constituent strategy. A second objection against that theory argues that it commits us to an excessive form of essentialism where every property associated with a familiar object turns out to be essential to it.

---

[20] See Chapter 6 of Campbell (1990).   [21] Campbell (1990: 20).

The objection points out that since constituent ontologists make what I have called Constituent Essentialism a framework principle and since the bundle theorist identifies the constituents of a familiar object with its fully determinate properties, the bundle theorist is committed to the view that every fully determinate property a familiar object has, it has necessarily: for no such property is it true that the object could have existed and lacked that property. However, not all the properties of a thing are essential to it; a thing has many of its properties contingently. But, then, either the bundle theory or the principle of Constituent Essentialism is false; the latter, however, is a framework principle, so it is the former that is false.

The obvious reply to this objection is to modify the rudimentary bundle theory by rejecting the idea that a familiar particular is identical with a bundle consisting of all the properties we say it possesses or has. We could hold instead that it is identical with a bundle consisting of a subset of those properties. The properties in that privileged subset, we could concede, are essential to the object; but while holding that the object has or possesses the remaining properties, we could insist that it has or possesses them merely contingently.

For this strategy to succeed, however, we need some principled way of distinguishing the properties essential to an object from those that are merely contingent to it. Now, some philosophers will have no problem drawing such a distinction. They will claim that the properties essential to an object are those that follow from *what* the object is, from the kind to which it belongs.[22] Unfortunately, this move is not an option for our modified bundle theorists. Like their ancestor, the rudimentary bundle theorist, our modified bundle theorists are constructivists about familiar concrete objects. The idea is that the proper constituents of an ordinary object are responsible for what we might call the global character of the object, for the character of the object taken as a whole. Proponents of the move we are considering are anything but constructivists about ordinary objects. They take the nature or character of the whole familiar particular as given and tell us that that global nature determines just which properties of a thing count as what bundle theorists want to call its constituents.

If they are to succeed in distinguishing, from among the properties a particular has, a subset of properties that can be said to be essential to the particular, our modified bundle theorists will need to rely on features of those properties that do not already presuppose the existence of the fully constituted particular. Peter Simons, a trope theorist, suggests a strategy

---

[22] I am thinking of philosophers within a broadly Aristotelian tradition. For further discussion of this idea, see section VIII.

here.[23] The idea is that among all the compresent tropes we associate with a thing, a proper subset includes tropes all of which are internally related to each other in a very exacting way: they are all such that if any trope in the subset ceases to exist, all the others do as well. The tropes in the subset make up what Simons calls the nucleus of the relevant thing and are essential to it; whereas, those tropes that are compresent with, but not a part of, the subset are merely contingent to the object.

Since it is a trope theoretic account, this version of the bundle theory (Simons calls it the nuclear theory) is subject to the difficulties about the individuation of tropes we discussed earlier, and one might have doubts that if there are such things as tropes, they display the kinds of internal dependency relations Simons needs if his account is to work. But even if these doubts are misplaced, it is not clear that the resulting view answers our second objection. The difficulty was presaged a couple of paragraphs back. Our second objection was that the bundle theory cannot accommodate our pre-philosophical essentialist intuitions. And our concern with the bundle theory was a concern with a theory of character of the constituent variety. The objection was that a constituent account of character that restricts the constituents of a familiar object to its properties cannot account for the contrast between what is necessary and what is contingent. But as we noted, a constituent approach to character makes the overall or global character of a familiar object a complex of the diverse forms of character associated with the constituents of that object, with the result that those forms of character are metaphysically prior to the character of the object taken as a whole. On Simons' theory, however, no one of the tropes in a theory's nucleus can exist apart from any of the others. But, then, do we not have the result that the character of the nucleus is itself a kind of indissoluble or unanalyzable whole, a single form of character that cannot be taken apart? And if we do, we do not have a *constituent* theory that enables us to draw a distinction between what is necessary and what is contingent.

A way to see the difficulty here is to note, that on Simons' view, each trope in the nucleus of a familiar particular is such that its existence entails not only the existence of all the other tropes in the nucleus but its compresence with all those tropes as well, and these entailments hold just in virtue of the trope's being the trope it is. But, then, each trope in the nucleus of a familiar object endows that object with precisely the same form of character; for necessarily, a familiar particular with any one of those tropes in its nucleus is such that it has the total form of character associated with the

----

[23] Simons (1994).

whole nucleus. So we do not have a panoply of discrete and separate forms of character, each induced by a distinct constituent. We have instead a single indissoluble form of character entailed indifferently by each and every trope in the nucleus; and that's to say that Simons' view is not a version of constituent ontology.

The difficulties confronting the formulation of a modified bundle theory may lead one to fall back on the original rudimentary bundle theory. The strategy with regard to our second objection will be to concede that, in a strict sense, the bundle theory is committed to some sort of ultraessentialism, but to insist that, nonetheless, bundle theorists can do justice to the pre-philosophical intuition that this or that ordinary object could have had properties different from those it actually does. How will one manage this? By appeal to counterpart theory.[24] The claim will be that while there is no possible world in which a given actual bundle of properties has different constituents, it is, nonetheless, true that the familiar object that is the relevant bundle has counterparts in other worlds, particulars that are like it in important respects, more like it than other objects in their respective worlds. It is, furthermore, true that the particular's counterparts will all share certain properties with the particular, but will differ from it with respect to other properties. This fact allows us to accommodate the pre-philosophical intuitions underlying standard essentialism. We can say that properties of the first sort are essential to our particular, whereas properties of the second sort are contingent to it.

Many philosophers, of course, reject counterpart theory out of hand; but even those who are willing to give the view a hearing will complain that our attributions of similarity are invariably relative to context. Accordingly, the selection of a thing's counterparts would seem likewise to be relative to the interests and purposes underlying that selection with the result that any distinction between the essential and the accidental that counterpart theory affords will lack the sort of objectivity our pre-philosophical essentialist intuitions require.

Laurie Paul makes this concern central in her formulation of the bundle theory.[25] She endorses a mereological reading of the constituent/whole relation, telling us that she is operating with a restricted notion of fusion. Although she never spells out the exact principles governing the restriction, she tells us that their effect is to limit the sums or fusions of properties to those clusters of properties that are actually found together. But while

---

[24] See Chapter 4 of D. Lewis (1986a) for a detailed defense of counterpart theory.
[25] Paul (2004).

restricted, her notion of fusion yields far more objects than commonsense wants to recognize. There, where commonsense sees a single object – a ceramic cup, say – Paul sees a host of overlapping, but distinct bundles of properties. Now, she wants to claim that among the constituents making up the relevant bundles are properties that bear on the modal status of other properties. Thus, corresponding to the property of being red, there is the property (call it Q) whose bearers are possibly such as to lack the color red. Suppose that the ceramic cup includes as its constituents both the color red and Q. Then, Paul tells us, we can say that the cup is merely contingently red. Suppose, however, that a bundle of properties includes red, but not Q. Then, according to Paul, we can say that the object corresponding to the bundle is essentially or necessarily red.

Paul is uncomfortable with irreducible or primitive *de re* modality, so she tells a reductive story about Q and its ilk. For our purposes, however, that story can be ignored; for what is central here is the attempt to have a bundle theory that respects an objective as opposed to a merely relative distinction between the *de re* modalities; and we get the desired objectivity by making the relevant modal properties constituents of the bundles of properties that are ordinary objects. But, then, attributions of *de re* modality are no longer inevitably relative to the context of attribution. When true, they are expressions of the actual constitution of objects themselves.

But is Paul's the sort of modal objectivity the traditional essentialist would want? I don't think so. Consider our red ceramic cup. It is a bundle including not just the color red and the modal property Q, but other properties – say, F, G, H, I, and J. So our cup is a bundle of properties, and it is only contingently red. But note: there, where our contingently red cup is, there is another bundle of properties including all the properties of our original ceramic cup except the modal property Q. Since it lacks Q, this new cup is essentially red. So there are spatiotemporally coincident bundles of properties, and despite their empirical indiscernibility, one is contingently red and the other, essentially red. More generally, wherever we have an object, x, and a property, P, such that x has P merely contingently, there is another spatiotemporally coincident object, indistinguishable from x in its non-modal properties, that has P essentially. Traditional essentialists will certainly object to this staggering proliferation of essence. But the objection won't merely be that essences come too cheaply on Paul's account. The essentialist will likewise object that they appear almost magically. If things indistinguishable in their non-modal properties can, in this way, differ in their *de re* modal properties, the tie between a thing's nature or character and its *de re* modal properties is severed. There is no explaining why a thing has the essential properties it does. We can, of course, say, in the case of any such property, that the thing in question lacks the property of possibly lacking that property; but what kind of explanation is that?

V

Our third objection is that the rudimentary bundle theory cannot accommodate our pre-philosophical intuition that familiar particulars persist through change. This objection is different from our second objection. The second objection bears on persistence and variation through what we might call the modal dimension; whereas, this objection involves persistence and variation through time. The earlier objection concerns the various ways a familiar particular could have been otherwise; for the formulation of that objection, it is not required that the particular realize the relevant possibilities by actually undergoing a change.

Nonetheless, the two objections are closely related. According to our third objection, a bundle theorist is committed to the view that composites are individuated by their constitutive properties. Change, however, always involves an alteration in the properties a thing has. Accordingly, if we are bundle theorists, we must say that where a thing undergoes a change, what exists before the change is one bundle of properties and what exists after is a bundle made up of different properties. But, then, the bundle theorist must deny that what enters a change is numerically identical with what emerges from the change. But without numerical identity, there can be no persistence. So we have our conclusion: the bundle theorist must reject the pre-philosophical intuition that familiar objects persist through change.

Almost all bundle theorists have responded to this objection in the same way. They have denied that persistence requires literal identity.[26] They have insisted instead that our pre-philosophical intuitions about persistence can be accommodated within a perdurantist framework, where a thing persists from one time to another by having numerically different temporal parts. They will concede that it is inaccurate to say that a familiar persisting object is a bundle of properties. What we should say instead is that a persisting object is a whole whose parts are the different phases we think of as making up its career. Those phases or their least parts are the real bundles of properties. So a familiar object is a whole made up of overlapping, but

---

[26] See, for example, Casullo (1988), which is a response to van Cleve (1985), where some of the objections discussed here are set out.

temporally distinct bundles of properties – a kind of temporal worm whose least parts are bundles of properties.

Notice that in responding to our third objection in this way, bundle theorists resurrect the sorts of problems associated with our second objection; for a temporal parts theorist seems committed to holding that the temporal boundaries of a thing are essential to it; and, of course, this holds for the temporal boundaries of the proper temporal parts of a thing no less than the whole thing itself.[27] But, then, much that we want to construe as contingent to a thing turns out to be essential to it; and it seems that the only available strategy for preserving the desired contingency here is that afforded by counterpart theory.[28]

Notice also that it is not just bundle theorists who want to endorse a temporal parts account of persistence. This is a strategy we meet in almost all recent constituent ontologists. Thus, David Armstrong and Gustav Bergmann, both bare particular theorists, tell us that familiar persisting things are temporally extended objects whose least parts are composites, each made up of a bare particular and the properties it exemplifies.[29] Of course, it is not surprising that these ontologists join bundle theorists in endorsing a perdurantist theory of persistence; for no less than bundle theorists, they make the properties that can be gained or lost in change constitutive of familiar particulars, so they too seem committed to denying that we have numerical identity through change.

The suggestion, then, is that a constituent ontologist is committed to a perdurantist theory of persistence. Any constituent theorist who wants to endorse endurantism (the view that a thing persists by existing wholly and completely at different times) will find this suggestion disconcerting. The claim will be that constituent ontologists need a different story about the persistence of familiar objects. Laurie Paul attempts to incorporate such a story into her version of the bundle theory.[30] In a way, her story is just the reverse of the temporal parts theory. The temporal parts theorist tells us that a thing persists by having its proper parts exist at different times. Paul, by contrast, tells us that a thing persists by itself being a proper part of temporally distinct objects. Her idea is that what persists is a kind of skeleton of an ordinary object: it is a bundle of those properties we take to be both salient to the object and stable across its career. Now, a bundle of this sort can be fused with temporal properties like that of existing at midnight on January 1, 2007. According to Paul, we have persistence through time

---

[27] For an argument for this claim, see van Inwagen (1981).   [28] See Heller (1990: 61–63).
[29] See Chapter 7 of Armstrong (1997b) and Bergmann (1967: 34).   [30] Paul (2002).

where a single skeleton bundle is a proper part of more comprehensive bundles including distinct temporal properties of this sort and where the more comprehensive bundles bear to each other the appropriate relations of causality, continuity, connectedness, and so on; and we have persistence through change where such temporally distinct bundles include different non-temporal properties, properties we pre-philosophically think of a thing as losing and gaining across its career.

Paul's account of temporal persistence is an endurantist theory: what persists does so by existing wholly and completely at different times. But while technically endurantist, Paul's is not an account of persistence that will satisfy many traditional endurantists. The difficulty is just that what persists on her view is not the thing traditional endurantists want to tell us persists. Paul's persisting object is not the fully fleshed out familiar particular we interact with. As we have said, it is rather a kind of skeleton of that object. She characterizes the persisting thing as a type – a universal that can be immanent in numerically different, fully fleshed out particulars. So we get genuine endurance on this account, but only by endorsing revisionism. Paul concedes that her account is revisionary; but she seems to think that since we have conflicting intuitions here, some form of revisionism is inevitable. And she would likely urge that given the plethora of different objects at a particular spatiotemporal location, our intuitions about which one does the persisting can hardly be firm. Of course, traditional endurantists will not find this consideration compelling. From their perspective, what is counterintuitive is the underlying idea that there, where we meet the familiar particular of commonsense, there are all the objects, whether universal or particular, to which Paul's theory commits us.

VI

The three objections we have been discussing have a long history. The final objection, however, is one that is seldom explicitly formulated. Bundle theorists, we have seen, tell us that familiar particulars are nothing but bundles of first-order properties. So we begin with first-order properties and we are supposed to end up with a thing that has those first-order properties. But how is it that this theory makes the transition from property to thing having the property? How is it that we go from ϕ-ness to the ϕ-er, from ϕ-ness to the thing that has ϕ-ness? Confronted with this question, bundle theorists will likely respond that we get individuals out of properties by way of agglomeration. We begin with one first-order property, add another first-order property, add still another. What ultimately emerges is an individual having all those first-order properties. But why should we suppose that agglomeration yields an individual? Why not suppose instead that what results from this agglomeration is just a conjunctive property whose conjuncts are the various first-order properties that have been agglomerated? Nor will it dispel the mystery here to introduce compresence. Let the properties φ-ness and ψ-ness be compresent. What is the result? Just the presence in a particular spatiotemporal region of the complex property of being both φ and ψ.

If we can be permitted the contrast between abstract and concrete, then we can put the objection by saying that the rudimentary bundle theorist gives no account of how we go from abstract properties to the concrete individual that has them. The bundle theorist tells us that familiar concrete particulars are composed of first-order properties. So there are these abstract entities, the properties, say, redness, triangularity, and the property of being two feet long; somehow these abstract entities get put together. But why suppose that their being put together results in a concrete individual that is red, triangular, and two feet long rather than a further abstract entity – the conjunctive property of being red, triangular, and two feet long? There is a gap here, a gap separating two ontological categories, that of a kind of abstract entity – properties – and that of a kind of concrete entity – the familiar particulars that have those properties. How is it that this categorial gap gets crossed?

One could, of course, bite the bullet here and hold that familiar objects really are nothing but properties, albeit very complex properties; and it may be that Laurie Paul is a bundle theorist who actually holds this.[31] But I think most ontologists would agree that any theory that construes familiar particulars as properties is guilty of some sort of category mistake. Bundle theorists who agree owe us a response to our fourth objection. Unfortunately, I know of only one bundle theorist who shows any sensitivity to the problem underlying the objection. That bundle theorist is Hector Castañeda.[32] Castañeda tells us that first-order properties form sets. Those sets are as abstract as the properties that are their members. How, then, do concrete particulars come on the scene? By way of a special operator, what

---

[31] See Paul (2002), where this is suggested. In conversation, Paul has confirmed the suggestion, saying that ordinary objects are nothing more than very complex properties.

[32] Castañeda's attention to this problem is embedded in an ambitious attempt to develop a version of the bundle theory that provides comprehensive answers to a whole range of problems in metaphysics, philosophical logic, and the philosophy of mind. The best and most detailed statement of the overall theory is found in Castañeda (1975).

Castañeda calls the concretizing or *c*-operator. We are not told as much about this operator as we might like. It is described as a Platonic form that operates on a set of first-order properties to yield the concrete individual whose constituents are the members of the set. Thus, the *c*-operator operates on the set whose only members are the properties of being a cat, being brown, and being frightened, and what results is the frightened brown cat, where this is a complex or bundle whose constituents are just the three properties in the set.

Pretty clearly, Castañeda is responding to the problem underlying our last objection. Does he actually solve the problem? Most of us, I suspect, will object that rather than solve it, Castañeda's appeal to the *c*-operator does nothing more than put a name on the problem. He gives us no account of how his operator is supposed to take us from abstract to concrete objects. He doesn't tell us what it means to say that the operator *applies* to sets of properties. He doesn't even tell us what it means to say that we have an *operator* here.

It might seem that the only recourse for a constituent ontologist is to appeal to the idea of a bare subject or possessor of properties. But, perhaps, there is another way out. Perhaps, one could make the idea of a possessor of properties a primitive feature of the world without endorsing the idea of a bare individual. How? By claiming that among the constituents of a familiar particular, there is one that while not a property, is, nonetheless, a universal, but a universal categorially suited to play the role of first-order property possessor. Late nineteenth- and early twentieth-century British idealists like F. H. Bradley spoke of 'concrete universals.'[33] The sort of constituent I have in mind is aptly described by that expression. It is, of course, notoriously unclear what Bradley and the others meant by the term, so we cannot expect to find in their work clear examples of the sort of view I have in mind. However, if we can trust Christophe Erismann, medieval realists like William of Champeaux and Odo of Cambrai held just such a view.[34] According to Erismann, these philosophers were immanentists who took what Aristotle called first substances – familiar particulars like the individual human being and the individual horse of *Categories* 5 – to be composites. Among an individual's constituents, one provides something like the core of its being. This constituent is a universal, the sort of universal Aristotle labeled a second substance; more exactly, it is a fully determinate second substance, a lowest level second substance or *infima species*. On this view, the species *man* is taken to be a single numerically identical

---

[33] Bradley (1927: 162).   [34] Erismann (2007).

constituent of all individual human beings. It is not, however, a property, but a kind – a sortal universal. By itself, the species does not give us the full-fledged particular human beings of everyday experience. The species is, after all, a universal. What gives the full-fledged particularity of an ordinary object is the bundle of accidents (quantities, qualities, etc.) associated with that object. These accidents are, we might say, added to the common species. How? By being predicated of it. This notion of predication is not our notion of predication as a kind of linguistic activity. It is rather the notion of a metaphysical or ontological relation/tie between non-linguistic objects, a relation that holds quite independently of our linguistic or conceptual activity. So the species is a subject for the metaphysical predication of a plurality of accidents, and the product of the predication is the familiar particular that is Socrates or Callias. Accordingly, the upshot of adding the property of courage to the species *man* is not the species plus a quality. Since we have a predicative relation at work, the product is a qualified individual, a courageous human being.

So in the work of these early medieval immanentists, we have a theory that builds the role of first-order property possessor into certain universals. On this score, it differs from what I have been calling the rudimentary bundle theory. But while denying that familiar particulars are bundles of properties, it agrees with the rudimentary bundle theory in construing familiar particulars as wholes whose only constituents are universals. Accordingly, it is committed to something like the Identity of Indiscernibles; it is committed to the closely related claim that it is impossible for numerically different particulars to agree in all their pure universals. That is obviously a problem; but the theory has other defects as well. It tells us, for example, that a single entity – the substance-species *man* – is the subject for the predication of the various bundles of accidents that together with it yield the different concrete members of that species. But different members of the species will have different and incompatible accidents. I am tan; you are pale. Socrates is wise; Callias, foolish. In both cases, we have a pair of accidents, each of which is predicated of the single kind that is found in you and me as well as in Socrates and Callias. But, then, how can that kind avoid being at once tan and pale as well as both wise and foolish? Abelard, I am told, raised similar difficulties for the view; and surely he was right to do so.

The constituent ontologist who wants to defend what we might call primitive concreteness might try to escape this second difficulty by insisting that not just the kind but all the constituents of a familiar particular are sortal universals. On this view, there would be universals like *wise thing, pale thing, triangular thing, six foot tall thing,* and *cold thing.* The view would dispense with properties altogether and make universals like these the underived sources of character for familiar particulars. A familiar particular would be a composite of such universals, and the principle of unity for the particular would be the mere fact that the relevant universals are compresent. Would the defender of this sort of view actually succeed in escaping our second difficulty? It is not clear. On this view, it would be false that the species *man* has both the property of being tan and the property of being pale as well as both the property of being foolish and the property of being wise. Nonetheless, it would be true that the sortal *man* is compresent with both the universal *tan thing* and the universal *pale thing* as well as both the universal *wise thing* and the universal *foolish thing.* Is this a problem? It is difficult to say, but this much is clear: the view in question, no less than the medieval view from which it derives, would be committed to the claim that it is impossible for distinct familiar particulars to exhibit all and only the same universals.

To avoid the familiar problems about the possibility of indiscernible, but numerically different particulars, one might propose a nominalistic ontology that has as its metaphysical atoms what we might call 'tropers.' Whereas tropes are particular properties – things like this redness, this triangularity, and this pallor, tropers are qualitatively thin individuals – things like *this individual red thing, this individual triangular thing,* and *this individual pale thing.*[35] The claim would be that familiar objects are bundles of compresent tropers. So the view would again dispense with properties and would insist that the ultimate constituents of familiar particulars are intrinsically characterized or natured, but would construe those constituents as particulars rather than universals. Such intrinsically characterized particulars would be the ultimate or underived sources of character: a familiar particular would be, say, pale because it has a pale troper as a constituent. Since the relevant constituents would be particular rather than universal, it would be

---

[35] Peter Forrest disagrees. He takes trope theorists to be postulating what I am calling tropers. I think he is wrong on the interpretation of the theory, but he does an excellent job of describing what I am calling tropers:

> As I understand it, tropes are not so much properties that familiar objects have as rather mini-substances that would ordinarily be thought of as having a location and one other property. However, on the Trope Theory, these tropes are not analyzed as things with a location and a property, or even as a location having a property, but are treated as that out of which both objects (as mereological sums of co-located tropes) and repeatable properties (as classes of exactly similar tropes) are composed. (Forrest 1993: 47)

I am indebted to Robert Garcia who directed me to the Forrest comment. For a detailed discussion of the trope/troper distinction, see Garcia's contribution to this volume.

impossible for numerically different familiar objects to have numerically one and the same troper as a constituent. Accordingly, there would not be numerically one thing that is both tan and pale or wise and foolish, nor even one thing compresent with both an intrinsically tan and an intrinsically pale thing or with both an intrinsically wise and an intrinsically foolish thing. Furthermore, since a troper would be idiosyncratic to the bundle to which it belongs, the possibility of qualitatively indiscernible particulars would not be in conflict with the Principle of Constituent Identity and so would present no problem for this brand of constituent ontology. But while the possibility of qualitative twins presents no problem for this view, the view would initially appear to give rise to problems analogous to those we meet in traditional trope theory – problems about the individuation of what I am calling tropers.

VII

With all of this, we have a good sense of the overall landscape of recent work in constituent ontology. We have as well a good sense of the difficulties confronting anyone pursuing this style of ontological explanation. What I now want to do is to look back to the origin of the constituent tradition in the work of the first really self-conscious constituent theorist – Aristotle. I want to lay out his view, to display it as a genuine version of the constituent approach, to compare and contrast it with the various modern theories we have looked at, and to suggest that, in a number of important ways, his account is superior to those theories. In particular, I will argue that he is more successful than more modern constituent theorists in dealing with the phenomena that underlie our four objections.

Given our purposes, we can be brief here. Aristotle thinks that there are two kinds of composites. In each case, the composite has two constituents, and those constituents are related predicatively: one constituent in the composite is predicated of the other (*Met.*, VII.3, 1029^{a}22–26), where, again, the notion of predication is that of a metaphysical or ontological relation/tie between non-linguistic entities. In the core case, a substantial form is predicated of something (typically, some parcel of stuff) that is proximate matter for that form, and the product of the predication is an individual member of a substance-kind, the substance-kind corresponding to the predicated form. The substantial form is an irreducibly basic universal, and the product of its predication is something like the individual human being or the individual horse of *Categories* 5. But the composites that result from the predication of substantial forms are things that can be subjects for the predication of items from the various accidental categories; and where an accident is predicated of an individual substance, the product is a composite of the sort Aristotle labels a *coincidental*, something like a sunburnt hyena, an overweight dolphin, or a musical man.

So we have a multi-layered complexity. If we begin with a coincidental like the musical man of *Physics* I.7 (190ᵃ1), then we have a composite whose constituting subject is itself a composite involving the appropriate matter and the appropriate substantial form; and, of course, the composition can reach lower since the matter constitutive of a substance can itself be a composite of some lower level matter and some lower level form; and the composition can reach lower still. At some point, Aristotle insists, the composition comes to a halt: we have a subject that is not a further composite. Aristotle himself believed that the relevant subject is the matter for the four elements, and he seems to have taken that matter to be something that satisfies the dark saying of *Metaphysics* Z.3: it is 'of itself neither a particular thing, nor of a particular quantity, nor otherwise positively characterized' (1029ᵃ25). It may be that defenders of an Aristotelian account are not compelled to endorse the traditional conception of a bare first matter; but even if they do not, defenders of a genuinely Aristotelian approach will concede that we confront a multi-layered complexity as we move downwards in the ontological analysis of a coincidental.

If they follow Aristotle, however, they will deny that we can move in the opposite direction, beginning with a coincidental and finding a composite that has the coincidental as subject and some accident as predicative constituent. Aristotle denies that there is, for example, any composite that has as its constituents the musical man and the accident of being six feet tall: there is no such thing as the six foot musical man. Accidents can be predicated exclusively of substances; that, Aristotle thinks, is a categorial fact about them (*Met.*, IV.4, 1007ᵇ2–5). But while he denies that there is a composite answering to the expression 'the six foot musical man,' Aristotle can agree that the sentence

(1) The musical man is six feet tall

expresses a truth. What he will deny is that (1) expresses a predication in which the musical man is subject and the quantitative accident of being six feet tall is the predicated entity. He will claim instead that it expresses a case of what he calls accidental unity. He will say that it expresses the fact that the coincidental *the musical man* is accidentally one with the substance (the man) of which the relevant quantitative accident is predicated.

The account we have been summarizing conforms to the overall pattern we have identified in our characterization of the constituent strategy. What delivers a compound is the predication of a form/accident, and Aristotle insists that in both cases the predication is accidental (*Met.*, VII.3, 1029ᵃ22– 23). We do not have essential or what Aristotle calls *kath hauto* predication. His notion of *kath hauto* predication is not quite the same as our notion of necessary predication. For Aristotle, *kath hauto* predication is what- predication: the predicated universal marks out its subject as *what* it is. Such predications are all *de re* necessary; but for Aristotle, the modality is derivative. What makes a given case of *kath hauto* predication *de re* necessary is that it is a predication underlying the essence of its subject. *Kath hauto* predication is contrasted with *kata sumbebekos* predication, where this is how-predication rather than what-predication. Here, the predicated universal merely modifies or characterizes a subject that is antecedently marked out as what it is by some other universal; and predications of this sort are, in general, *de re* contingent. Now, Aristotle tells us that both cases of primitive predication represent cases of merely *kata sumbebekos* predication. Whether a form is predicated of its matter or an accident is predicated of an individual substance, the subject is something whose 'to be is different from that of the thing predicated' (*Met.*, VII.3, 1029a22–23); and in both cases the predication is *de re* contingent: it is possible for the subject-entity to exist outside the relevant predicative configuration.

But while he thinks that the predication of a substantial form or an acci- dent is contingent, Aristotle endorses the doctrine I have called Constituent Essentialism. He thinks that a composite (whether individual substance or coincidental) has its constituents necessarily. He tells us that we have a case of coming to be/passing away just in case we have variation in con- stituents (*On gen.*, 1.3, 317ᵃ24–25). Aristotle rejects the doctrine known as Mereological Essentialism, the view that a thing has its commonsense parts necessarily. Accordingly, he is committed to holding that a thing can lose a commonsense part – a limb, say – without undergoing a change in its constituents. More precisely, he is committed to holding that a variation in a thing's commonsense parts does not entail a numerically different matter; and Aristotle recognizes this commitment. He insists that when a thing loses a limb, grows a nail, or loses/gains weight, the thing's matter remains numerically the same. The matter does not undergo a substantial change; it undergoes a merely accidental change: what happens is that it gets bigger or smaller (*On gen.*, 1.5, 321ᵃ22–25).

So while he thinks that the constituents of a composite only contingently go together to compose it, Aristotle endorses the doctrine of Constituent

Essentialism; and like other constituent ontologists, he holds as well what I have called the Principle of Constituent Identity. He denies that it is possible for non-identical objects to have all and only the same constituents. His commitment to this principle is evident from a famous passage at the end of *Metaphysics* Z.8, where he tells us that two individuals from the same *infima species* – Callias and Socrates – share a single form, but differ in their matter (1034^a5–8). The idea is that where we have numerically different composites with a single constituting universal – the shared substantial form – those composites must differ in their other constituent. Pretty clearly, the Principle of Constituent Identity is the implicit premise: necessarily, composites with all and only the same constituents are identical.

So Aristotle takes the existence of a familiar particular to rest on a contingent relation/tie between its constituents; and he endorses both Constituent Essentialism and the Principle of Constituent Identity. On these points, he joins company with other constituent ontologists. He thinks that universals (both substantial forms and accidents) are constituents of ordinary objects. As we have seen, not all constituent ontologists agree with him on this point. However, almost all those who make universals constituents endorse some version of what might be called the Principle of Instantiation, the claim that necessarily every universal is instantiated. Aristotle is no exception (*Cat.*, 11, 14^a7–10). He thinks, at least, that for the case of irreducibly fundamental universals, the principle holds; and, since he endorses a presentist theory of time, he takes the principle to involve the claim that necessarily every irreducibly fundamental universal is now or currently instantiated (*Cat.*, 6, 5^a26–29 and *Phys.*, IV.10, 218^a1–8).

So Aristotle's theory of the structure of familiar particulars is a good example of the constituent strategy. It is, of course, somewhat misleading to speak of Aristotle's theory as just another example of the constituent approach. His account is the fountainhead of the constituent tradition. It is the paradigm of the constituent strategy, laying out for all subsequent practitioners of the strategy the core principles structuring constituent ontology. But I want to suggest that our interest in Aristotle's theory should not be merely historical. I want to suggest that as a piece of philosophy the theory is superior to subsequent exercises in constituent ontology. Let me begin by showing that Aristotle is more successful than his successors in accommodating the phenomena at issue in our four objections. For reasons that will become clear, I will not follow the precise order in which I originally set out the objections. Instead, I will begin with the issue of essentialism.

It should be clear that Aristotle's theory does not commit him to ultra-essentialism. He holds that the two fundamental forms of predication are accidental. The case where a form is predicated of its matter is a case of predication *kata sumbebekos*; nonetheless, that predication has as its product a composite falling under a substance-kind, and the predication of a kind of its members is a case of essential (or what Aristotle calls *kath hauto*) predication: it is a case of what-predication and it is *de re* necessary. Individual members of substance-kinds can, however, serve as subjects for the predication of items from the dependent categories; and the predication here is, in general, accidental: it is how-predication rather than what-predication, and it is *de re* contingent. So although all core predications hold accidentally, we get the desired result that familiar particulars have, as we say, some of their features essentially and others, accidentally. The distinction that defines the doctrine of essentialism is thus preserved on this view.

Some will object, however, that Aristotle avoids ultraessentialism only at the cost of commitment to its polar opposite, antiessentialism. For at least one case, the objection would go, Aristotle's theory is committed to the sort of antiessentialism we meet in the bare particular theory. The argument goes as follows: Aristotle insists that a form is predicated of its matter *kata sumbebekos*; and he holds that if the matter for a given form is essentially this or that kind of thing/stuff, its being that hinges on a prior predication in which a lower level form is predicated of a lower level matter; but since he denies the possibility of an infinite regress in material causation, Aristotle is committed to a first matter that satisfies the dark saying of Z.3; he is committed to prime matter as traditionally understood – as something with no essence at all.

This is a large issue, and I do not have the space here to do full justice to the problem, but let me make a few comments. First, the antiessentialism of the bare particular theory is far more pervasive than anything one can claim to find in Aristotle's theory. Bare particulars are supposed to be the subjects for all predications; but if bare substrate makes any appearance at all in Aristotle's account, it is only in one context – that presented by the four elements, where it plays the role of subject for the predication of pairs of the elementary contraries (hot/cold and wet/dry).[36] Second, there is good reason to think that, despite the dark saying of Z.3, Aristotle wants to endow the matter for the elements with something like an essence; for

---

[36] See *De Generatione et Corruptione* II.1 (329^a25–329^b3). The literature on this topic is enormous. See Chapters 3 and 7 of Loux (1991) for a discussion of this literature.

he tells us that the proximate matter for a form has *kath hauto* or essentially the potentiality for that form (*Met.*, IX.4, 1070^{b}12); but, then, the matter for the elements has essentially the properties of being potentially hot and wet, being potentially hot and dry, and so on. That is more essence than any we meet in the case of David Armstrong's thin particulars or Gustav Bergmann's bare particulars. Finally, Aristotle himself entertains the suggestion that the first matter (the matter that has no matter) is something that is intrinsically or essentially characterized or natured (1049^{a}25–27). That he is willing to entertain such a suggestion is not surprising since his commitment to the matter of the dark saying rests on the purely empirical 'finding' that there is elemental transformation; and, of course, we cannot forget that Aristotle was just wrong about the elements. Accordingly, I hold out the hope that an Aristotelian can consistently construe the ultimate subjects of substantial predication as things that are non-composite, yet intrinsically characterized.

So Aristotle accommodates our pre-philosophical intuitions about essence and accident. He accommodates as well our intuitions about persistence through change. Although he is a constituent ontologist, his commitment on that score does not yield the unsatisfactory result that change in properties is impossible. Aristotle distinguishes the properties predicated of individual substances from those that are constitutive of them. The latter include substantial forms; the former, items from the accidental categories. Aristotle's constituent essentialism entails that a substance cannot survive the loss of its substantial form; but since the accidents associated with a familiar substantial individual are not among its constituents, an individual substance can survive a change in its accidents. But while a substance can survive a change in accident, the corresponding coincidental cannot survive that change. The man who was musical can cease to be musical. The musical man, by contrast, cannot survive that change; and Aristotle's constituent essentialism tells us why.

One might, however, think that there is a problem lurking here. Call the change in which the man ceases to be musical *C*. Then, the man has the property of possibly existing after *C*; the musical man, however, does not have that property. But the musical man and the man are one and the same thing. Do we not, then, have a violation of the Indiscernibility of Identicals (the principle that necessarily, if a thing, *x*, and a thing, *y*, are identical, then every property of *x* is a property of *y* and vice versa)? Aristotle would deny that we do. He concedes that the man and the musical man are one, but he denies that they are identical. He distinguishes between two kinds of unity: unity in being and accidental unity; and he holds that only the former kind of unity displays the full range of formal properties (including that of being governed by the Indiscernibility of Identicals) that we associate with numerical identity.[37] Nor is it obvious that there is anything untoward here. This is not a case of collocated material objects. We take it that so long as he is musical, there is just one material object there where the man is. We don't give the man and the musical man two votes, and anything you do to the one you do to the other. Nonetheless, we do not have identity here. The man is a proper constituent of the coincidental that is the musical man, and clearly a composite cannot be identical with any of its proper constituents. So while not identical, the man and the musical man are one. They are, however, one only in virtue of a contingent fact – the fact that the man is musical. As Aristotle puts it, the man and the musical man are accidentally one.

Third, Aristotle has no difficulty explaining how it is that there are concrete individuals, things that are human, courageous, and six feet tall. The concreteness of familiar particulars does not present a special problem for two category ontologies that distinguish a subject constituent from a predicative constituent; and Aristotle's is just such an ontology. As he puts it, his composites (whether substantial individuals or coincidentals) are this suches (*Met.*, VII.10, 1033^{b}20–24). Each is a whole whose constituents include not merely a properly predicative entity – a such, but also something categorially suited to play the role of subject of predication – a this; and what results is a this such, an individual with some distinctive form of character. And here it is important to see that Aristotle understands his basic universals in a way quite different from the traditional bundle theorist. Neither substantial forms nor accidents are self-standing entities. They are suches; that is, they are *ways* self-standing thises are. They are *how* those thises are. The idea is that the core universals are essentially predicative entities; they are things that are, so to speak, adjectival and, hence, dependent on their subjects. So the idea of something that is a concrete property possessor, a subject for predication is not something we need to construct. It is there in the materials out of which ordinary objects are constituted.

That leaves us with our first objection. The rudimentary bundle theory, we have said, is committed to an unacceptably strong version of the Identity of Indiscernibles. Now, it is anachronistic in the extreme to suggest that Aristotle has a view on Kant's two gloves, Max Black's radially symmetrical universe, or David Lewis' recurring history. But this much is certain: he

---

[37] See 1015^{b}16–34 with *Topics* I.7 (103^{a}6–38) and *Physics* III.3 (202^{b}15–16). For an important discussion of this contrast, see F. Lewis (1982).

is fully aware of the implications of what I have called the Principle of Constituent Identity for his own theory. We have already made reference to the crucial Z.8 text on Callias and Socrates. The idea there is that since different members of a species share a constituent – their substantial form – they must differ in their matter. Accordingly, we get the result that numerically different parcels of matter serve as subjects for the predication of that single form.

There is, however, a problem here, one that is too often overlooked in discussions of this issue. Individuals from the same species have as their constituting matter parcels of the same kind of stuff; but, then, the problem the material constituents were supposed to solve arises for the material constituents themselves. They are one in species and so have the same form. Whence, then, their numerical diversity? There is an impending regress here. Where is the regress to be halted? Not, I would suggest, at the level of prime matter as traditionally understood, that is, at the level of a matter characterized by the dark saying of Z.3. If Aristotle does endorse a matter so characterized, he is committed to denying that it is the sort of thing that can be cut up, divided, or partitioned to give us numerical diversity. If we stick with Aristotle's picture of the cosmos, then we must hold that any halt to our regress has to occur at the level of the four elements – fire, earth, air, and water. What we need is some principle that will distinguish one portion of water from another; one portion of air from another; and so on. Intuitively, it is easy to say how one chunk of earth, say, differs from another: they differ in their places. Place, it would seem, is the ultimate principle of numerical diversity. Two portions of the gunk that is one of the four elements differ in their primary places.

Two comments are in order here. First, this claim is a tensed claim, a claim in the present tense. Second, the suggestion that it is their places that diversify parcels of stuff might be resisted on the grounds that since places are items from an accidental category, material substances are prior to them.[38] But notice: it is only if we suppose that this priority has to be spelled out by way of a picture that presents us with an ontological 'moment' in which we have masses of stuff (fire, earth, air, and water) in search, so to speak, of places to occupy. That is a picture of the priority Aristotle would almost certainly reject. He would think instead that given the totality of elementary stuff, we are thereby given a rudimentary framework of places; and hopefully that framework provides the resources for the diversification we are after.

---

[38] For Aristotle's treatment of place, see *Physics* IV.1–5.

So Aristotle has the resources for handling the phenomena underlying our four objections. There remains, however, a problem with Aristotle's theory that has no easy solution, at least not if we follow Aristotle to the letter. The problem bears on his commitment to the Principle of Instantiation. Aristotle thinks that every basic universal is instantiated, and he understands this claim in presentist terms. In endorsing a version of the Principle, Aristotle joins company with most recent constituent ontologists. However, his presentist reading of the principle results in a version of the principle that diverges from what we meet in the likes of David Armstrong, David Mellor, and Gustav Bergmann, all of whom would insist on formulating the principle in eternalist terms.[39] They insist only that every basic universal is instantiated at some time or other, whereas Aristotle has every basic universal instantiated now.

The difficulty is that for many universals, it seems to be a contingent matter whether they are actually instantiated; and this holds whether we understand the instantiation in eternalist or presentist fashion. But, then, if we accept the Principle of Instantiation, we seem committed to the view that there are universals that are merely contingent beings; and that, of course, is the view of almost all modern defenders of the constituent strategy.[40] There is, however, a problem with this view. The fact is that, for every universal, there are necessary truths that appear to take the universal as their subject-entity. But if a proposition is genuinely of the subject-predicate form, the proposition can be necessarily true only if its subject-entity exists necessarily. Accordingly, unless we can show that, for the propositions in question, the appearance of subject-predicate form is illusory, we are committed to holding that the relevant universals are all necessary beings; and the fact is that the results of attempts to show the appearance illusory have been singularly unimpressive. Aristotle, of course, endorsed the line of reasoning just laid out and so concluded that since the Principle of Instantiation is true, it is not just true, but necessarily true that every basic universal is now instantiated ($1039^{b}20–1040^{a}7$). The result is the notorious doctrine of the necessary eternality of the species, a doctrine that in the face of contemporary evolutionary biology most will find impossible to maintain.

Is there a way out of these difficulties? I think so. I do not think that a constituent ontologist needs to accept the Principle of Instantiation whether in its eternalist or presentist form. If one thinks otherwise, one may be confusing the existence and the instantiation of a universal. A constituent ontologist is committed to holding that for a first-order universal to be

[39] See Chapter 3 of Armstrong (1997b), Mellor (1991: 170–82) and Bergmann (1967: 34).
[40] See, for example, Chapter 3 of Armstrong (1997b).

instantiated is for it to be a constituent in some familiar particular; but that commitment does not preclude uninstantiated universals. Or one may be supposing that to accept the existence of uninstantiated universals is to endorse a relational framework with transcendent universals existing in splendid isolation from the spatiotemporal world. But it is not endorsing uninstantiated universals that makes one a relationist; it is rather supposing that for a thing to instantiate a universal is for it to stand in some *sui generis* non-mereological relation or tie to a universal. One can endorse the existence of uninstantiated universals without entertaining that supposition. Finally, one might be supposing that while the Principle of Instantiation may not be a requirement on a constituent theory, it is a requirement on any theory that makes universals suches or ways things are. It is true that the two ideas tend to go hand in hand; but it is not as though we can find the foundation for the Principle of Instantiation in the idea that universals have a predicative categorial structure. We could hold on to that idea while holding that they are ways things *could be* rather than ways things *are*, that they are *predicable* rather than *predicated* entities. The point is that the Principle of Instantiation doesn't derive from the idea that universals are how some subject *is*; that idea already incorporates the principle. What I would recommend, then, is that anyone wanting to provide a contemporary version of the Aristotelian theory reject the Principle of Instantiation. What one should do is to concede that the fundamental first-order universals are necessary beings, hold that the instantiation of a basic first-order universal is a matter of immanence in some contingent composite, and conclude that the Principle of Instantiation is false.

VIII

If we make this modification in the Aristotelian theory, then, we get a theory that is more successful than more recent versions of constituent ontology at handling the phenomena central to our four objections. Nonetheless, there remains much in the Aristotelian theory that contemporary philosophers are not likely to find attractive. For starters, Aristotle's account is rooted in his peculiar brand of essentialism. Central in this view is the contrast between what- and how-universals, the contrast between universals that mark out a familiar particular – an individual living being – as what it is and those that merely modify or characterize a particular antecedently marked out as what it is by some other universal.[41] Although he thinks that

---

[41] We meet this contrast as early as the *Categories* in its distinction between *being said of a subject* and *being in a subject* (1^a20–1^b9). From *Posterior Analytics* 1.4 onwards, we meet the distinction under the titles '*kath hauto*' and '*kath sumbebekos*' (73^b10–16).

this contrast marches in tandem with the modal contrast between what is *de re* necessary and what is *de re* contingent to a particular, Aristotle takes the modal distinction to be derivative from the prior what/how contrast; and the idea is that this contrast is genuinely ontological. It is not a distinction in how we happen to think or talk about objects; it is reflective of the very being of objects. Accordingly, it is an absolute distinction, one that is not relative to context. The contrast is supposed to be there in advance of any conceptual or linguistic frameworks that happen to structure our inquiry; and it is supposed to be the job of those frameworks to get the application of the contrast right.

It is, of course, the kinds to which they belong that mark out Aristotle's primary substances as what they are; and among those kinds, it is their lowest level biological kinds – their *infimae* species – that provide the most complete articulation of what the primary substances are. We get the best, the most determinate answer to the 'What is it?' question by identifying a thing's species. And, again, this is not a merely linguistic or conceptual point. An *infima* species gives the conditions of existence for its members: for an individual substance, to be is to be a member of its lowest level kind.

And Aristotle wants to claim that a familiar particular's membership in its *infima* species is rooted in the substantial form correlated with the species. It is because that form is a constituent in the particular that it falls under the appropriate kind and the substantial form is construed as an irreducibly fundamental causal principle.[42] While it is necessarily such that it is a constituent in all and only the members of the associated kind, it is a thing that has no constituents of its own. Accordingly, it induces an autonomous or irreducibly primitive type of being or character, a form of being that while *sui generis* to the kind, is not reducible to types of being/character which can be found in structurally and functionally more elementary kinds of things.

So Aristotle's theory commits us to a doctrine of essentialism that makes the what/how distinction a genuinely ontological distinction; and underlying that contrast is a doctrine of substantial forms, where they are irreducibly fundamental sources of the types of character peculiar to the various biological kinds. Neither doctrine is likely to be attractive to contemporary philosophers. Contemporary theorists will either deny that they can make sense of a contrast between the what and the how or will insist that any contrast that exists here is relative to our purposes and interests in inquiry

---

[42] For a detailed discussion of this feature of Aristotle's account, see section VI of Loux (2006a). Perhaps, the clearest formulation of this idea is found in Aristotle's account of form as nature in *Physics* II.I.

and so of no interest to the ontologist.[43] And they will object to the doctrine of substantial forms. In so doing, they will be joining a train of critics going back to the origins of modern philosophy, where the doctrine was claimed to be bankrupt – at best, a vacuous pseudo-theory; at worst, something akin to superstition.

If we begin with the second set of concerns, we can concede that as directed against some late medieval and renaissance appeals to form, the criticisms are likely on target. As Aristotle himself presents it, however, the theory of forms is neither vacuous nor superstitious. It allows for a rich and detailed account of the structure and behavior distinctive of the various biological kinds; and it makes room for the appeal to those lower level structures and mechanisms that subserve the causal role of form. Indeed, it demands that appeal.[44] What it precludes is a thoroughgoing reductionism that claims to provide a complete account of the nature and behavior of the members of a biological kind by reference exclusively to such lower level structures and mechanisms. Of course, many contemporary meta-physicians will find even that objectionable. They identify a successful theoretical account with the sort of reductive analysis just described. If, however, one is skeptical of the requirement that we provide reductive accounts of all the phenomena distinctive of the various biological kinds, our own included, then the Aristotelian conception of form should not be rejected out of hand; for, at bottom, Aristotelian talk of form is just the constituent ontologist's way of expressing the idea that for the under-standing of a given biological kind, an austerely reductive analysis will not suffice.

Of course, the assumption here is that we can make sense of Aristotle's essentialist conception of a kind; and that, in turn, brings us back to the other difficulty, that of understanding the contrast between the what and the how. The difficulty, recall, is supposed to be that if there is any contrast here at all, it is one that can be drawn only relative to our shift-ing theoretical interests as these get reflected in the varying descriptions we employ in our characterization of the things we seek to understand. The conclusion is precisely the one Quine drew in his famous attack on Aristotelian essentialism.[45] The best the Aristotelian can get is a purely linguistic distinction; there is no non-relative ontological distinction to be found here.

[43] For an exception, see Almog (1991).
[44] See the discussion of *Physics* II.9, where Aristotle argues for the hypothetical necessity of matter (199^b33–200^a14).
[45] See Quine (1960: 195–208).

Now, Quine may have been comfortable with this conclusion, but I doubt that many of the rest of us will be. Unlike Quine, most of us want to endorse a genuinely objective (i.e. non-relative) distinction between what is *de re* necessary and what is *de re* contingent. Now, it is easy enough to draw the distinction provided we have no difficulty with the appeal to modal discourse. We can say that a universal is predicated necessarily of a thing just in case the universal is predicated of that thing and it is impossible for the thing to exist without instantiating the universal and that a universal is contingently predicated of a thing just in case it is predicated of the thing, but not necessarily predicated of it; or we can appeal to the language of possible worlds and give the possible worlds equivalents of these definitions. Quine, of course, would not find these formulations satisfactory; but for those of us who do not reject modal language out of hand, the formulations do tolerably well as accounts of *de re* modality. Indeed, the problem with *de re* modality is not a problem of definition. The problem is rather one of explaining just why the particular facts of *de re* modality should obtain. The difficulty is one of explaining why, for example, a given universal should be *de re* necessary to a particular object. In some cases, of course, there is no difficulty: the universal is trivially necessary in the way that the property of being self-identical or the property of being red or not red is trivially necessary. The problem arises rather in the case of a universal that is non-trivially necessary to a thing. The Aristotelian essentialist has no difficulty explaining why the universal is *de re* necessary to the thing: the universal is *de re* necessary because of what the thing is. Either the universal marks the thing out as what it is, or in some sense it follows from what the thing is. Doubtless, there are all sorts of bells and whistles the Aristotelian needs to sound here to make the account precise, but the core idea should be clear. Suppose, however, that we refuse to see the what/how contrast as an objective contrast; suppose we concede only a linguistic contrast that is relative to our aims and purposes in inquiry; then, if we want to preserve a genuinely objective contrast between the *de re* modalities, we have little option but to take the fact that a given universal is *de re* necessary or *de re* contingent to a given object to be a primitive fact, the sort of fact that has no explanation. And there will be many, many such facts that we will need to take as primitive; for each object, as many as the properties non-trivially predicated of that object. And the difficulty is not just that we are forced to take innumerably many such facts as primitive. There is the further difficulty that, in so doing, we fly in the face of our intuitions. It seems as true as anything can be that the non-trivial facts of *de re* modality have their roots in what things are. Why is it that John is necessarily rational?

Because of what John is – a human being. Why is it that the organism out back is necessarily deciduous? Because of what it is – a maple tree rather than, say, a fir.

So there is a real cost to rejecting the core insight of Aristotelian essentialism – at least for the philosopher who endorses a genuinely ontological distinction between the *de re* modalities. That philosopher has to take each of the innumerable facts of *de re* modality as unexplained primitives and in so doing runs counter to our deepest modal intuitions. All of this suggests that there may be more to the what/how contrast than the contemporary skeptic would have us believe; and if that contrast represents a genuinely ontological distinction, then an Aristotelian theory of kinds becomes a serious option in philosophy. Now, if we are constituent ontologists who couple a realism about natural kinds with a skepticism about the demand for reductive accounts of all the various kinds of living beings, then Aristotle's overall theory ceases to look like an esoteric chapter in the history of philosophy, and his talk about substantial forms as irreducibly basic principles of essential character begins to look like serious philosophy.

So there is a convergence of philosophical commitments, commitments a contemporary metaphysician might reasonably have, that makes Aristotle's version of constituent ontology look attractive. These include (1) the belief that facts about character stand in need of explanation, (2) the belief that the constituent approach gives us that explanation, (3) the belief that it is facts about the essences of familiar particulars (that is, facts about what they are, facts about the kinds of things they are) that underlie non-trivial facts of *de re* modality, and (4) an antireductivism about at least some of the essences or kinds to which familiar particulars belong. And Aristotle's theory has the further virtue of accommodating the phenomena associated with our four objections. Taken together, these considerations may fall short of an ironclad argument for Aristotle's theory, but they do go some distance toward making the idea that a contemporary metaphysician might want to endorse something like Aristotle's constituent ontology seem a little less implausible.

CHAPTER 2

Against ontological structure

Peter van Inwagen

Let us use the term 'individual' for the common objects of everyday perception and thought and reference and also for any things sufficiently like
them that those things count as, well, let us say, 'the same sort of thing for
metaphysical purposes.' I use the word without regard for any philosophical associations it may have (e.g. it may be hard for some philosophers
to hear or read the word 'individual' without supposing that one of its
functions is to stand in opposition to some other word, such as 'universal' or 'attribute'). So: we human beings are individuals, tables and chairs
are individuals, pebbles and boulders are individuals, protons and variable
stars are individuals, elves and goblins are individuals, gods and demons are
individuals, reflections in a mirror and shadows and holes and surfaces are
individuals . . . That is to say, the items in this list are individuals provided
(i) that they exist, and (ii) that they really are 'the same sort of thing for
metaphysical purposes' as the common objects of everyday perception and
thought and reference. (As to the point of the second qualification, consider the case of protons. Suppose that 'a proton is a *thing* – like a *rock*!,' a
statement I once heard a Nobel laureate in physics make. That statement,
if it were taken as a serious contribution to metaphysics, would seem to
imply that 'protons' are indeed sufficiently like pebbles and boulders to
count as the same sort of thing for metaphysical purposes. But it has been
said that – owing to the very non-everyday properties ascribed to protons
by quantum-field theories like the Standard Model – to take that statement
and other such offhand statements by physicists at metaphysical face-value[1]

---

[1] Many such statements could be quoted. Here's another, also by a Nobel laureate (it's about atoms,
not protons, I concede – but it's the protons in the nuclei of atoms that are responsible for the
'repelling' it touches on):

> If in some cataclysm all scientific knowledge were to be destroyed and only one sentence
> passed on to the next generation of creatures, what statement would contain the most
> information in the fewest words? I believe it is the atomic hypothesis (or atomic fact, or
> whatever you wish to call it) that all things are made of atoms – little particles that move

is to embrace 'the philosophy of "A" level chemistry,' a statement that is pretty obviously intended to imply that protons are very far indeed from being sufficiently like pebbles and boulders to count as the same sort of thing for metaphysical purposes. The point of this example is that whether one counts so-and-sos as 'individuals' in the present sense will depend to a very great extent on what features one ascribes to so-and-sos.)

'Nominalists,' let us say, are metaphysicians who hold that everything that exists is an individual.[2] 'Realists,' let us say, are metaphysicians, who hold that there are 'attributes' or 'qualities' or 'properties' or 'features' or 'characteristics.' (As I use them, these five terms are synonyms. I generally prefer 'property'; when, on occasion, I use 'attribute,' it is simply because I have grown tired of writing 'property' and have decided to use another, synonymous word for a while.) There are, however, disagreements among realists about the nature of these 'properties.' One important disagreement concerns the question whether properties are particulars[3] – 'tropes' or 'individual accidents or 'property instances' – or universals. (And, of course, some realists hold that some properties are particulars and that others are universals.) A second important disagreement among realists about the nature of properties, and one that is less commonly remarked on, is between those who believe that some or all properties have causal powers and those

---

around in perpetual motion, attracting each other when they are a little distance apart, but repelling upon being squeezed into one another. In that one sentence, you will see there is an enormous amount of information about the world, if just a little imagination and thinking are applied. (Feynman et al. 1963–65: vol. 1, 2)

[2] But what about the possibility, just now conceded in the text, that, e.g., protons may not be individuals? Does this definition imply that nominalists are in danger of finding themselves committed to denying the existence of protons? (One does not have to turn to physics to find entities that raise this question or raise questions that are essentially the same as this question. It is easy to imagine a metaphysician who holds that reflections and shadows and holes and surfaces are real things that are not sufficiently like human beings and tables to count as the same sort of thing for metaphysical purposes. Does this position commit its adherents to the thesis that nominalists, *qua* nominalists, must deny the existence of shadows?) And isn't that apparent implication of what I have said a problem – a problem either for my definition of 'individual' or my definition of 'nominalism'? There is a problem, I suppose, but it is a verbal, not a substantive problem, and requires only a verbal solution. It is a merely verbal problem owing to the fact that, if a proton is insufficiently like such paradigmatic individuals as chairs and stars to count as the *same* sort of thing for metaphysical purposes, it is at any rate vastly more like them, metaphysically speaking, than is a trope or a universal (supposing those things to exist). And it is tropes and universals that nominalists mean to deny the existence of. In my view, these reflections imply that the problem is merely verbal. And here is its merely verbal solution. Let us say that sub-atomic particles are, if not individuals, then *semi-individuals* – or quasi-individuals or honorary individuals or whatever. (And let shadows and reflections and the rest also be semi-individuals.) And let us say that nominalism is the thesis that everything that exists is either an individual or a semi-individual. Let this (merely verbal) refinement of the concept of 'nominalism' be implicit in every statement about 'nominalism' and 'nominalistic ontologies' and 'individuals' in the remainder of this essay.

[3] I use 'particular' to mean 'non-universal.' Individuals and tropes – if tropes exist – are both particulars.

who deny this. Consider, for example, the following passage from Jonathan Lowe's *The Four-Category Ontology*:

> Perception . . . involves a causal relationship between the perceiver and the object perceived and we perceive an object by perceiving at least some of its properties. We perceive, for instance, a flower's colour and smell.[4]

This passage occurs in the course of an argument for the conclusion that some properties must be tropes or individual accidents (or whatever one chooses to call them; Lowe's term is 'modes') – for, in Lowe's view, universals cannot enter into causal relations and therefore cannot be perceived. Other realists – L. A. Paul, for example– think that some universals can be perceived.[5] But Lowe and Paul agree that some *properties* can be perceived and therefore can enter into causal relations. With scant regard for the historical appropriateness of these terms, I will call realists who hold that properties have causal powers aristotelian realists or aristotelians, and I will call those realists who deny that properties have causal powers platonic realists or platonists. (The lower-case spellings are intended to dissociate my use of these two terms from the philosophies of their eponyms.)

I will call any metaphysical theory whose primary concern is with individuals and properties and the relations between them an ontology.[6] I propose a taxonomy of ontologies that groups them into three broad classes:

> *Nominalistic* ontologies: ontologies according to which there are individuals and only individuals (and are therefore no properties).[7]
> *Platonic* ontologies: ontologies according to which there are both individuals and properties, and properties are without causal powers (or: 'properties do not enter into causal relations').

---

[4] Lowe (2006). The quoted passage occurs on p. 15.
[5] And, I would suppose, everyone who holds that individuals are 'bundles of universals' must believe that universals can be perceived: the whole purpose of the 'bundle theory' is to provide an account of individuals according to which they do not contain an unperceivable ontological constituent.
[6] In this essay alone. In other essays I have used the count-noun 'ontology' in other senses.
[7] By a nominalistic ontology, I therefore mean what Michael Loux would call an *austere* nominalistic ontology. A *non*-austere or *luxuriant* nominalistic ontology – a luxuriant nominalism, for short – would be an ontology that denied the existence of universals but affirmed the existence of tropes (or whatever one chooses to call them): the referents of phrases like 'the wisdom of Solomon,' 'the rectangularity of central park,' and 'the aridity of Arizona' – phrases that denote properties of Solomon, Central Park, and Arizona, respectively, and which do *not* denote properties of the Twin Earth counterparts of those objects. In my taxonomy of ontologies, a luxuriant nominalism is an aristotelian ontology. (Luxuriant nominalisms, of course, lay claim to the title 'nominalism' on the ground that they entail that everything is a particular.) It may be that there is only one nominalistic ontology: nominalism *tout court*, nominalism *simpliciter*, the ontology whose central thesis is that there are individuals and only individuals. If there are distinct nominalistic ontologies, they are individuated by their different and incompatible accounts of what it is for something to be an individual.

Aristotelian ontologies: ontologies according to which there are properties and properties have causal powers and enter into causal relations.

Aristotelian ontologies may be divided into those that are monocategorial and those that are polycategorial.[8] (Of course nominalistic ontologies are also monocategorial ontologies, and all platonic ontologies are polycategorial ontologies.) I know of only two examples of monocategorial aristotelian ontologies:

- The 'New Bundle Theory,' invented by – but by no means endorsed by – James Van Cleve: there exist only properties (and these properties have no fusions or mereological sums; individuals – including adherents of the New Bundle Theory – do not exist).[9]
- The ontology that is being worked out by L. A. Paul: there exist only properties (but the members of any non-empty set of properties have a fusion; the fusion of any set of properties is itself a property; among the various fusions of properties are individuals – like L. A. Paul; thus certain objects that traditional ontologies would place in other categories than 'property' do exist, but, whatever else they may be, they are one and all members of the only ontological category there is,[10] the category 'property').[11]

My primary concern in this essay is not with these monocategorial aristotelian ontologies but with polycategorial aristotelian ontologies, and with the contrast between those ontologies and polycategorial ontologies of the other kind, namely the platonic ontologies.

Polycategorial aristotelian ontologies are the most important of the ontologies that Wolterstorff and Loux have called *constituent* ontologies.[12]

---

[8] These terms seem to imply that things fall into various 'ontological categories' – a category that comprises individuals, it may be, or a category that comprises properties. I endorse the implication. (I note that, although almost all metaphysicians who accept the existence of both individuals and properties would take it for granted that nothing is both an individual and a property, this seemingly obvious thesis is not universally accepted: L. A. Paul's ontology represents individuals – what *I* am calling individuals – as certain very complex properties.) A monocategorial ontology, then, is an ontology that recognizes only one *primary* ontological category: only one ontological category that is not a proper subcategory of some other ontological category; and a polycategorial ontology is an ontology that recognizes more than one primary ontological category. (Note that the concept of a primary ontological category does not rule out overlapping primary categories.) In the present essay, I will not attempt to define 'ontological category.' For a proposed definition, see van Inwagen (2012), reprinted in van Inwagen (2014: 183–201).

[9] Van Cleve (1985).

[10] At any rate, the only 'primary' ontological category there is (see note 8): if there are other ontological categories, they are subcategories of 'property.'

[11] The earliest statement of Paul's ontology was in Paul (2002) (reprinted in Rea 2008). More recent statements of the ontology can be found in Paul (2012a) and (forthcoming). There are useful summaries of the ontology in Paul (2006a) and (2006b).

[12] See Wolterstorff (1970a) and Loux (2006a).

And platonic ontologies (polycategorial, one and all) are just exactly those that Wolterstorff and Loux have called *relational* ontologies. The concepts 'constituent ontology' and 'relational ontology' are best explained in terms of the concept of ontological structure (which, by an odd coincidence, is the central topic of this chapter).

Let us say that a relation is *broadly mereological* if it is either the part–whole relation or is in some vague sense 'analogous to' or 'comparable to' the part–whole relation. And let us say that a *constituent* of an individual (in the sense of 'individual' set out above) is either one of its parts or an object that is not, in the strict sense, one of its parts, but nevertheless stands in some broadly mereological or part-*like* relation to it.

Let us say that to specify the *mereological structure* of an individual (in the sense of 'individual' set out above) is to specify the other individuals, if any, that are its parts in the strict and mereological sense – to specify all the individuals bear the part–whole relation to it – and perhaps to say something about how those other individuals stand to one another in respect of certain relations thought to be 'structure relevant' (spatial relations, it may be, or causal relations). And let us say that to specify the *ontological structure* of an individual is to specify the non-individuals that bear some broadly mereological relation to it.[13]

A relational ontology is a polycategorial ontology (one of whose primary categories is 'individual' or something in the ontological neighborhood, something to very much the same ontological purpose: 'substance,' perhaps, or 'particular' or 'concrete object') that implies that individuals have no ontological structure – that implies that individuals are, in Armstrong's terminology, blobs. (This is a feature that relational ontologies share with nominalistic ontologies – for, of course, if there are only individuals, then any part or constituent of an individual is an individual.) According to any relational ontology, the only structure individuals have is good, old-fashioned everyday structure: *mereological* structure.[14]

A constituent ontology, like a relational ontology, includes 'individual' in its inventory of ontological categories. But, unlike relational ontologies, constituent ontologies imply that individuals have an ontological structure: they have constituents (perhaps parts in the strict sense, perhaps not) that do not belong to the category 'individual.'

---

[13] I stipulate that to say, e.g., 'No non-individual bears any broadly mereological relation to Catherine the Great' is not to 'specify the non-individuals that bear some broadly mereological relation to Catherine the Great.'

[14] Unless, perchance, the 'relationist' thinks that some individuals are 'extended simples'; someone who holds this view may want to say that extended individuals have no mereological structure but do have a spatial or spatiotemporal structure.

The so-called bundle theory (*sc.* of the nature of individuals) can serve as a paradigm of a constituent ontology – provided that we suppose the bundle theory to imply that there really *are* bundles of properties (that is, bundles of universals) and that something is a bundle of properties if and only if it is an individual. And provided, too, that we suppose that the bundle theory assigns bundles of properties (on the one hand) and properties *tout court* (on the other) to distinct and non-overlapping ontological categories. That is, only those versions of the bundle theory that do not treat apparent singular reference to and singular quantification over 'bundles of properties' as a disguised form of plural reference to and plural quantification over properties are examples of a constituent ontology. And only those versions of the bundle theory that do not treat bundles of properties as themselves properties are examples of a constituent ontology. By 'the bundle theory' I thus mean what might be called the standard-or-garden-variety bundle theory, the *classical* bundle theory, and not Van Cleve's New Bundle Theory or Paul's ontology. The classical bundle theory is a constituent ontology for the simple reason that it implies that individuals have constituents – properties or universals – that do not belong to the category 'individual.' And, obviously, if an ontology implies that individuals have 'bare particulars' as constituents, that ontology too will be a constituent ontology. But almost all constituent ontologies imply that among the ontological constituents of individuals are properties (although those properties may be tropes rather than universals). And, of course, any ontology according to which individuals have properties as constituents will identify the important relation that is variously called 'having' or 'exemplifying' or 'instantiating' – the most salient of the relations that Solomon bears to wisdom, Central Park to rectangularity, and Arizona to aridity – with constituency.[15] That is, any such theory will imply that the properties that an individual *has* (or exemplifies or instantiates) are exactly those that are its constituents: 'the individual *x* has the property F' is equivalent to 'the property F is a constituent of the individual *x*.'

My own favored ontology can serve as an example of a relational ontology.[16] According to this ontology, members of the primary category that can be variously called 'substance,' 'concrete object,' 'individual,' and

---

[15] More exactly, any such theory will identify an *individual's* having a property with that property's being a constituent of that individual. But, if individuals have properties, it is hard to see how it could be that properties do not have properties. If properties indeed have properties, then constituent ontologies face the problem of explaining the relation between the use of the phrase 'has the property' in the statement 'This apple has the property redness' and its use in statements like 'Redness has the property instantiation' and 'Redness has the property "being a spectral-color property".' I do not mean to imply that this problem is insoluble – or even particularly difficult.

[16] My 'favored ontology' is not the ontology of material things that was set out in my book *Material Beings*. It is, rather, the much more abstract and general ontology I described in van Inwagen 2006

'particular' are without ontological structure. Such structure as a dog (for example) has is the structure that supervenes on its parts (cells, electrons) and their spatial and causal relations to one another; and every part of a dog or any other individual is itself an individual, a member of the primary ontological category 'individual.' This must be, for (the Favored Ontology contends) everything that is not an individual is a member of the primary ontological category 'relation' (this category comprises propositions or 0-adic relations, properties or monadic relations, and proper relations: dyadic relations, triadic relations, . . . , and variably polyadic relations[17]). And relations are *abstract objects*: necessarily existent, non-physical, and non-spatial things. Being necessarily existent, non-physical, and non-spatial, abstract objects cannot enter into causal relations: an abstract object can be neither agent nor patient.

Now if properties, like propositions and proper relations, are abstract objects, there is no possible sense of 'constituent' in which a property can be a constituent of an individual like a boulder or a dog. Consider, for example, my dachshund Jack and the property xenophobia – that is, aggressive hostility toward any living thing that one has not been properly introduced to. Xenophobia is certainly one of Jack's properties (and it is certainly a universal, since he shares it with his little life-partner, my other dachshund, Sonia), but it is in no possible sense one of his constituents. For the proponent of the Favored Ontology, the dyadic relation 'having' that Jack and Sonia each bear to the property xenophobia is as abstract and 'external' as the variably polyadic relation 'being numbered by' that they enter into with the number 2.

According to the Favored Ontology, a property or attribute is something that one ascribes to an object by saying something about it; xenophobia, for example, is what one ascribes to something by saying that it's a xenophobe. The attribute xenophobia – the thing I say about Jack or Hitler when I say of either of them that he's a xenophobe – is, according to the Favored Ontology, an unsaturated assertible,[18] to be contrasted with a saturated assertible or proposition (the proposition that there are xenophobes, for

---

(reprinted in van Inwagen 2014: 153–82). I concede that in that essay I did not explicitly state that properties (or, more generally, relations) constitute an ontological category, for my primary concern was with the question whether there *were* properties and relations. But the idea that 'substance' and 'relation' were the two primary ontological categories is certainly tacitly present throughout 'A Theory of Properties.'

[17] That is, relations that be entered into by m things *and* by n things, where m and n are distinct numbers. Such relations are expressed by open sentences containing plural variables – 'the xs are fellows of the same college,' for example, or 'x numbers the ys.'

[18] My use of this term (in the essay cited in note 16) has caused some confusion. Observing, correctly, that I have borrowed it from Frege (the German word is *ungesättigt*), some of the readers of that

example). An attribute may be said to stand to a sentence in which one variable is free as a proposition stands to a closed sentence. Saturated and unsaturated assertibles – propositions on the one hand, and attributes and proper relations on the other – are much alike in many respects. Both are necessarily existent things to which spatial, temporal, and causal concepts – and the concept 'constituent of an individual,' as well – have no application. (And what does 'has no application' mean in this context? Well, here's an example that may serve as a model for what I am trying to express by using this phrase. Johnny's algebra teacher asks him to 'extract' a cube root; he requests a forceps to use in this operation. His request, you will probably concede, is ill informed: the extraction of a cube root is an operation to which the concept of a physical extracting tool has no application. It ought to be as evident that there is no sense of 'constituent' in which unsaturated assertibles are constituents of individuals as it is that there is no sense of 'extraction' in which a physical tool can be of use in the extraction of a cube root.)

A second example of a relational ontology is provided by David Lewis's ontology of properties (what he calls 'properties,' and not what he calls 'universals').[19] According to Lewis, a property is a set of possible objects. (Something is a property if and only if it is a set all of whose members are possible objects.) The property of being a pig or porcinity, Lewis says, is simply the set of all possible pigs – a set far larger than the set of actual pigs. Consider an actual pig, Freddy. Freddy of course has porcinity. And what is this relation 'having' that holds between the pig and the property? Why, simply set-membership. And the relation that a set of possibilia bears to its individual members is certainly not constituency. Freddy is no doubt

---

essay have inferred, incorrectly, that my use of the term implies that I accept something resembling Frege's concept/object distinction: a property/object distinction modeled on the concept/object distinction. Far from it, however, for I do not understand the concept/object distinction. The objects I call properties are just that: objects. More exactly, they are objects in the very general sense that this word has in logic and mathematics: a property can be the referent of a noun or a noun-phrase ('wisdom'; 'Solomon's most famous property'; 'the property of being an x such that x is wise') and properties can be 'quantified over' ('Some properties are uninstantiated'; 'An impossible property entails every property'); and when we quantify over properties we use the same logical machinery that we use when we quantify over shoes and ships and bits of sealing wax and cabbages and kings. (If one maintains that we do not use the same logical machinery in both cases, one must tell some 'story' that accounts for the obvious logical validity of many arguments that involve an intimate mixture of quantification over individuals and quantification over properties – arguments like: 'Every living organism has some properties that are properties of all inanimate objects; There is a property that is a property of some living organisms; *hence*, If no inanimate object is a living organism, there is a property that is a property of every inanimate object and of some things that are not inanimate objects.' I am happy not to have to tell such a story.)

[19] See D. Lewis (1986a: 50–69).

in some sense a constituent of the set of all possible pigs – 'constituent' is a very flexible word, and it is probably flexible enough to permit that application – but there is no conceivable sense in which the set of all possible pigs is a constituent of Freddy.

Let this suffice for an account of 'constituent ontology' and 'relational ontology.'[20]

I will now give some reasons for preferring a relational to a constituent ontology – reasons for repudiating the idea of ontological structure. The nominalists, of course, will want to remind me that relational ontologies are not the only ontologies that deny the reality of ontological structure. A nominalist might remind me of this fact by a making a speech along these lines: 'The picture we nominalists have of individuals is identical with your picture of individuals: we, like you, see them as what Armstrong calls blobs.' And this reminder would be perfectly correct. But in this essay, my topic is constituent ontologies, not nominalism.[21] I could rephrase my description of my project this way: to put forward reasons for repudiating the idea of ontological structure *given that there are properties or attributes*.

My principal reason for repudiating the idea of ontological structure is a reason *I* have for repudiating this idea, but it is not one that I can expect anyone else to share. This reason is a very straightforward one: I do not understand the idea of ontological structure or, indeed, any of the ideas with which one finds it entwined in the various constituent ontologies. I do not understand the words and phrases that are the typical items of the core vocabulary of any given constituent ontology. 'Immanent universal,' 'trope,' 'exist wholly in,' 'wholly present wherever it is instantiated,' 'constituent of' (said of a property and an individual in that order): these are all mysteries to me. Perhaps the greatest of all these mysteries – the one most opaque to my understanding – is the kind of language that is used when quantities with numerical measures are said to be among the constituents

---

[20] Consider the thesis ('existential uninstantiationism') that properties can exist uninstantiated, and the thesis ('existential instantiationism') that properties cannot exist uninstantiated. Advocates of relational ontologies tend to be existential uninstantiationists, and advocates of constituent ontologies tend to be existential instantiationists. But it is at least possible consistently to accept both a relational ontology and existential instantiationism, and it may even be possible consistently to accept both a constituent ontology and existential uninstantiationism. For that reason, I decline to regard existential instantiationism as essential to the idea of a constituent ontology, and I decline to regard existential uninstantiationism as essential to the idea of a relational ontology. Similar remarks apply to the question whether properties are 'sparse' or 'abundant.' Advocates of relational ontologies tend to hold that most open sentences (all of them but a few Russellian monsters) express properties, and advocates of constituent ontologies tend to hold that very few open sentences express properties. But I think that these tendencies are only tendencies, and that both can be resisted without contradiction.

[21] For my reasons for rejecting nominalism, see van Inwagen (2006).

of individuals. The following passage from *On the Plurality of Worlds* is a good example of such language. (In this passage Lewis is expounding a theory that, although he stops short of endorsing it, is for him a living option. He certainly does not think that the words in which he expounds that theory are meaningless. Note that the 'universals' referred to in this passage are not 'Ludovician properties': they are immanent universals, not sets of possible objects.)

> [C]onsider two particles each having unit positive charge. Each one contains a non-spatiotemporal part corresponding to charge. [It is a universal] and the same universal for both particles. One and the same universal recurs; it is multiply located; it is wholly present in both particles, a shared common part whereby the two particles overlap. Being alike by sharing a universal is 'having something in common' in an absolutely literal sense. (D. Lewis 1986a: 64)

Such talk bewilders me to a degree I find it hard to covey. Perhaps I can 'evoke the appropriate sense of bewilderment' by quoting a passage from a referee's report I wrote a few years ago. (I should say that I was not recommending that the editor reject the paper under review because I thought that core vocabulary of the author's ontology was meaningless; I was rather trying to convince the editor that the ideal referee for the paper was not someone who, like me, thought that that vocabulary was meaningless.)

> The author contends that the "features" of an electron (the electron's mass, charge, and spin are the examples of its features the author cites) are "constituents" of the electron. I don't care who says this – not even if it's David Lewis – it just doesn't make any *sense*. Consider the case of mass. Let Amber be a particular electron. Amber's (rest) mass is $9.11 \times 10 \exp - 31$ kg. (I've rounded the figure off to two decimal places; pretend I've written out the exact figure.) If '$9.11 \times 10 \exp - 31$ kg' is a name of something (if the 'is' of the previous sentence is the 'is' of *identity*), it's a name of an abstract object. (And if '$9.11 \times 10 \exp - 31$ kg' *isn't* a name of anything – if it is, as Quine liked to say, a syncategorematic phrase – or if it is a name of something but is not a name of Amber's mass, why would anyone suppose that 'Amber's mass' is a name of anything? It looks to me as if either 'Amber's mass' and '$9.11 \times 10 \exp - 31$ kg' are two names for one thing, or 'Amber's mass' isn't a name for anything: there just isn't anything for 'Amber's mass' *to* name other than $9.11 \times 10 \exp - 31$ kg.[22]) You can perform *arithmetical operations* on this object, for goodness' sake. You can divide it by a number, for example

---

[22] This parenthesis is one illustration among many possible illustrations of a very general point about the semantics of physical-quantity terms. Consider, for example, what is perhaps the simplest case of a physical quantity: distance (or length or displacement). The two putative denoting phrases 'the

(if you divide it by 6, the result is $1.518 \times 10 \exp - 31$ kg), and you can multiply it by another physical quantity (if you multiply it by 10 m/sec/sec, which is the magnitude of an acceleration, the result is $9.11 \times 10 \exp - 30$ kg-m/sec/sec). These "results" have other names. Other names for the first result are 'one-sixth the rest mass of an electron' and 'the amount Amber's mass would increase by if Amber were accelerated to half the speed of light from rest.' Another name for the second result (if Amber is near the surface of the earth) is 'the magnitude of the gravitational force (in the direction of the center of the earth) that the earth is exerting on Amber' – since 10 m/sec/sec is the magnitude of the acceleration toward the center of the earth of a body (near the surface of the earth and in free fall) that is due to the earth's gravity.

Performing calculations like the ones I performed to get those results is what solving the problems in physics textbooks largely consists in: applying arithmetical operations like multiplication and division to items like masses, charges, and spins.[23] I can attach no sense to the idea that something one can apply arithmetical operations to is a "constituent" of a physical thing.

And, I contend, what goes for 'quantitative' immanent universals like mass and charge goes for 'non-quantitative' immanent universals like color universals and shape universals. Since these universals are non-quantitative, I cannot, in trying to describe the bewilderment I experience when I try to understand what their proponents have said about them, complain that they are objects that one can apply arithmetical operations to. The bewilderment I experience arises when I try to form some conception of what immanent universals could *be*. I can see that they are not what I call properties – not things that stand to one-place open sentences as propositions stand to closed sentences. Not things that are like propositions in that the concepts 'truth' and 'falsity' apply to them, and unlike propositions in that they are not true or false *simpliciter* but are rather true of false *of* things – true, perhaps, of this thing and not of that thing. I can see that they can't be properties (what I call properties) because, if for no other reason, they are supposed to have some sort of presence in the physical world: they can be constituents of physical things and can be located in space (albeit their spatial features are strikingly different from those of individuals, the paradigmatic space-occupiers). But if not properties, *what?* The features

equatorial diameter of the earth' and '$1.276 \times 10 \exp 7$ m' are either both real denoting phrases and denote the same thing *or* are both syncategorematic.

[23] Or one might want to say that applying arithmetical operations like multiplication and division to items like masses, charges, and spins is the typical *final stage* of finding the solution to a physics problem. (In the earlier stages, one generally has to engage in some mathematical reasoning that involves techniques rather more 'advanced' than multiplication and division; the purpose of this reasoning is to reach the point at which one can find the answer to the problem by applying simple arithmetical operations to the particular physical quantities that were specified in the statement of the problem.)

attributed to immanent universals by those who believe in them seem to me be an impossible amalgam of the features of individuals and the features of attributes. I must make it clear that when I say these things, I do not pretend to be presenting an argument. What I am presenting is rather a confession. Just as a confession of faith – someone's recitation of the Nicene Creed, for example – is not a presentation of an argument for the thesis that anyone other than the speaker should accept the propositions the confession comprises, a confession of bewilderment is not a presentation of an argument for the thesis that anyone else should be bewildered by whatever it is that the speaker finds bewildering.

What goes for immanent universals goes for tropes. I don't understand what people can be talking about when they talk about those alleged items. I will attempt, once more, to evoke the appropriate sense of bewilderment.

Consider two tennis balls that are perfect duplicates of each other. Among their other features, each is 6.7 centimeters in diameter, and the color of each is a certain rather distressing greenish yellow called 'optical yellow.' Apparently, some people understand what it means to say that each of the balls has its own color – albeit the color of one is a perfect duplicate of the color of the other. I wonder whether anyone would understand me if I said that each ball had its own diameter – albeit the diameter of one was a perfect duplicate of the diameter of the other. I doubt it. But one statement makes about as much sense to me as the other – for just as the diameter of one of the balls *is* the diameter of the other (6.7 centimeters), the color of one of the balls *is* the color of the other (optical yellow).

On that point, the friends of immanent universals – those who are not also friends of tropes – will agree with me. Setting to one side the fact that it is difficult to suppose that they and I mean the same thing by 'property,' they and I agree that one property, such as 'optical yellowness' or the color optical yellow (as far as I can see, 'optical yellowness' and 'the color optical yellow' are two names for one thing), may be a property of two individuals, such as two tennis balls; they and I disagree about what it is for a property to be a property *of* a given individual. The friends of immanent universals spell this out in terms of constituency, and I don't spell it out at all – nor do I have any sense of what it would be to *spell out* what it is for a given property to belong to a given object or objects. Those of you who are familiar with a controversy I had with David Lewis a long time ago will see that we have wandered into the vicinity of what I once called 'the Lewis–Heidegger problem.'[24] The Lewis–Heidegger problem may be framed as a question: 'How does a certain concrete object, a certain individual (an optical yellow

---

[24] In van Inwagen (1986: 204ff.).

tennis ball, for example) reach out and take hold of a certain abstract object, a certain proposition (the proposition that at least one individual is optical yellow in color, for example), and make it *true*?' The question, 'How does a concrete object (like an optical yellow tennis ball) reach out and take hold of a property (like the color optical yellow), an abstract object, and make it *had* or *exemplified* or *instantiated*?' is at least a very similar question. (It could be regarded as a generalization of the former question – a generalization based on the fact that propositions are true or false *simpliciter* and properties are true or false *of* things.) In my opinion, these questions have no answers: no meaningful statement among all possible meaningful statements counts as an answer to either of them. And if that is so, the questions are meaningless: 'The *riddle* does not exist. If a question can be put at all, then it *can* also be answered.'

I am experienced enough to know that there are philosophers who take offense when you tell them that what they are saying is meaningless or that they are proposing answers to questions that have no answers. I'll say what I have said many times: in philosophy, and particularly in metaphysics, the charge 'What you are saying is meaningless' should be no more offensive than the charge 'What you are saying is wrong.' Meaninglessness is what we *risk* in metaphysics. It's a rare metaphysical sentence that does manage to express a proposition and expresses a false one – and on those rare occasions on which a metaphysical sentence does do that ('The physical world has always existed' might be an example), that is generally because a metaphysician has encroached on someone else's territory. If my metaphysical writings contain meaningless sentences, and no doubt they contain a good many of them, that is simply because I'm doing my job – trying to work out a metaphysical position. If I weren't willing to risk saying and writing things that were, in Wolfgang Pauli's immortal phrase, *not even wrong*, I'd take up the history of philosophy.

Enough about my *principal* reason for rejecting constituent ontology in all its forms. I'll now say something about one of my ancillary reasons, a reason that is epistemological or methodological or something in that area. Bas van Fraassen, as many of you will know, is rather down on what he calls analytic metaphysics.[25] Most of the barbs he directs at 'analytic metaphysics' miss because they are based on misapprehensions or bad reasoning.[26] But one of them hits the mark squarely: I heartily applaud all

[25] See van Fraassen (2002: 1–30).
[26] So *I* say, at any rate. See van Inwagen (2007a) and my APA Central Division Presidential Address in van Inwagen (2009). The latter is reprinted in van Inwagen (2014: 31–49).

that van Fraassen says against those metaphysicians who ape the practice of scientists – or what they take to be the practice of scientists – by appealing to 'the method of inference to the best explanation.' If I had ever thought that there was a method called 'inference to the best explanation' that could be used as an instrument of metaphysical discovery (or which could be used to validate a metaphysical theory however it had been discovered), van Fraassen would have convinced me otherwise. But thank God I never have! I suspect, however, that use of this 'method' is widespread among those who construct constituent ontologies, and I suspect that at least some 'relationists' besides myself will find it as foreign to their way of thinking as I find it to mine. Let me try to flesh these intuitions of mine out – these intuitions about what has motivated the work that has led to the construction of constituent ontologies – by giving an example. The example is fictional, but, like many fictions, it has got some important bits of reality embedded in it.

A certain philosopher, Alice, sees, or thinks she sees, a certain metaphysical problem. She calls it, perhaps, the Problem of One over Many: How can *two or more* objects be in a perfectly good sense *one*, or in a perfectly good sense *the same* (one in color or of the same color, for example)? This Granny Smith apple and this copy of *A Theory of Justice* are both green. It follows that, in spite of the fact that they are two distinct things, they are one in color. How can we account for such facts? What metaphysical picture of the nature of individuals like apples and books can explain how individuals that are not the same *simpliciter* can nevertheless be the same *in a certain respect*? Obviously (Alice announces), the way to proceed is to explain this phenomenon in terms of individuals' having certain *structures*, and in postulating some common item in the structures of numerically distinct individuals that are the same 'in a certain respect.' Now the kind of structure that Alice proposes to appeal to in giving an explanation of this sort obviously can't be what I have called mereological structure, for in most cases in which an individual *x* and an individual *y* are the same in some respect, no individual – no atom, no neutron, no quark – is a part of both *x* and *y*. The kind of structure that will do the explanatory job that Alice wants done must therefore involve individuals' having constituents that belong to some ontological category other than 'individual.' Alice therefore (let us suppose) makes a proposal regarding a common constituent of – to revert to our illustrative example – the apple and the book. She proposes, let us say, that both the apple and the book have among their constituents a certain *immanent universal*: an object that is wholly present wherever any of the individuals of which it is a constituent is present. She proposes, that

is, that the common *feature* of the book and the apple – what is ordinarily
called greenness or the color green – is a common *constituent* of the book
and the apple. And why should one believe in such a thing? Well (Alice
contends), the theory that explains best describes best: if the postulation of
such a common constituent is both a prima facie successful explanation of
the sameness of color of numerically distinct individuals and superior to
all other prima facie successful explanations of that *explanandum* (if there
indeed are other prima facie successful explanations), that will be sufficient
to warrant our believing that that constituent really exists. (Cf. the kind of
warrant enjoyed by an early twentieth-century geneticist's belief in genes or
by Einstein's belief in the effect of the presence of mass on the local metric
of space-time.)

So Alice proceeds. Before we take leave of her, let us allow her to
summarize what she claims to have achieved by proceeding in this way:
'I have solved a metaphysical problem – I have explained how individuals
that are not the same (that are numerically distinct) can nevertheless be the
same in a certain respect – and, in doing so, I have made a contribution
to ontology: I have provided a good reason for supposing that a certain
ontological category exists (that is, has members, is non-empty). I have,
moreover, demonstrated an important truth about the way in which the
members of this category – "immanent universal" – are related to the
members of another category, "individual."'

I am happy to concede that the story of Alice – which was put forward
as a parabolic representation of the philosophical method that gives rise
to constituent ontologies – is not only fictional but a caricature. I could
hardly present anything other than a caricature of a philosophical method
in such a brief compass. But I do think it is a caricature that is not utterly
divorced from the actual practice of many metaphysicians. I don't suppose
that I shall succeed in convincing anyone who is not already inclined to
agree with me that Alice's use of 'inference to the best explanation' is a
bad method for metaphysics. In my judgment, it can lead only to quasi-
scientific theories that (supposing that the words in which they are framed
mean anything at all) fail to explain what they were supposed to explain.
(I distinguish quasi-science from pseudo-science. A pseudo-scientific theory like astrology makes empirical predictions; a quasi-scientific theory
does not.) When I say that Alice's theory fails to explain what it is supposed to explain, I do not mean that someone else may eventually devise
a theory that explains what her theory has failed to explain. I mean rather
that there's nothing there to be explained, that no set of statements among
all possible sets of statements counts as an explanation of what it is for
an individual to have a property or for two individuals to have the same

property.[27] (I am, you see, what Armstrong would call an ostrich nominalist – or would be but for the fact that I am not a nominalist. Perhaps
I am an ostrich platonist.) And I would say more or less the same thing
about any metaphysical theory that presents itself as an explanation of
some phenomenon: assuming that that phenomenon exists at all,[28] it will
not be a thing that it makes any sense to speak of explaining.[29]

And what does the Favored Ontology have to say about the common
properties of individuals? I'll answer this question by setting out what I
have to say about the common properties of individuals, for I am the only
proponent of the Favored Ontology I am aware of.

I do believe that there is an object I call 'the color green.'[30] And, of
course, I think that the color green or the property greenness is exactly
what all green individuals have in common, and I of course think that they
share this thing that they have in common with no non-green individual.
But I should never want to say that the fact that greenness was a property
of both the apple and the book explained the fact that they were both green
or the fact that they were both of the same color. In my view that would be
as absurd as saying that the fact that the proposition that the book and the
apple are both green is *true* explained the fact that the book and the apple
were both green. ('Daddy, why is the sky blue?' 'Well, sweetheart, that's
because the proposition that the sky is blue is true.' 'Oh, Daddy, how wise
you are!') I do think that there are such things as propositions, and I do think
that they have the properties truth and falsity, and I do think that ascribing
these properties to propositions plays an important and indispensable role

---

[27] That is, no possible set of statements is an explanation of these things that is of the kind that
constituent ontologies claim to provide. But the fact that the book and the apple are both green
could have other kinds of explanation. It is no doubt possible to construct a causal narrative that
explains how the book got to be green and no doubt possible to construct a causal narrative that
explains how the apple got to be green. And those two narratives, taken together, would, in one
sense, explain the common greenness of the book and the apple. Again, it may well be possible to
identify certain physical features of the surfaces of objects of a certain sort, a 'sort' that contains
things like apples and books, such that for a thing of that sort to be green *is* for it have a surface
with those features – and possible to identify a corresponding set of surface-features of objects of
the book-apple sort for each color. If those things were accomplished, one could, in one sense, give
an account what it is for distinct objects of that sort to be of the same color.

[28] The phenomenon that Alice set out to explain is uncontroversially real; at any rate, it is uncontroversially true that there are green individuals that have no individual as a common part. (Which
is not to say that *no* philosopher has denied its reality: 'One cannot conceive anything so strange
and so implausible that it has not already been said by one philosopher or another.') But the reality
of many of the alleged phenomena for which metaphysicians have proposed explanations is more
controversial: synthetic propositions known *a priori*, uncaused free choices, temporal passage . . .

[29] For an able defense of the contradictory of this thesis, see Paul (2012b).

[30] At any rate I think that there are attributes or properties, and I'm willing to suppose for the sake of
the present example that greenness or the color green is one of them; but the physics and physiology
of color are subtle and difficult, and the metaphysics of color must take account of the subtleties
and difficulties that the special sciences have discovered.

in our discourse. (For example: 'No false proposition is logically deducible from a set of true propositions' and 'If q is logically deducible from a set of statements that includes p and all of whose members other than p are true, then the conditional whose antecedent is p and whose consequent is q is true' are fairly important logical principles.) But the concept of the truth of a proposition can play only a 'logical' role in an explanation of why some state of affairs obtains: the concept of truth can figure in an explanation only in the way in which concepts like logical deducibility and universal instantiation and transitivity can figure in an explanation. And the same point holds, *mutatis mutandis*, for the concept of the instantiation of a property.

'Well, then,' the interlocutor asks, 'what method *do* you recommend in ontology, if not the method of constructing theories to explain observed phenomena? And what has this method you would recommend got to do with your adherence to a relational ontology?'

The answer to the first part of this question is complex, but fortunately I have presented it elsewhere – and in some detail (see, for example, van Inwagen 2006). Stripped to the bare bones, the method is this:

> Look at all the things that you who are attempting to construct an ontology believe 'outside' ontology – the beliefs that, as it were, you *bring to* ontology. Subject them to quantificational analysis à la Quine. This will provide you with a large number of one-place open sentences that you believe are satisfied. Try to give a coherent account of the 'satisfiers' of those sentences, a project that will, in some cases, involve fitting them into a system of onto-logical categories. See whether the resulting system of categories satisfies you intellectually. Subject it to all the dialectical pressures you can muster – and attend to the dialectical pressures those who disagree with you bring against it. As you are carrying out these tasks, keep the following methodological rules of thumb in mind (and remember that they are only rules of thumb, not infallible guides to the truth):
>
> • Suppose you contend that certain objects (which you have somehow specified) form or make up or constitute an ontological category – call it 'category X'; remember that every object has, for every property, either that property or its complement: everything has a complete and consis-tent set of properties; and that obvious truth must apply to the members of X; if what you have said about X leaves it an open question whether certain specifiable members of X have the (intrinsic and metaphysically significant[31]) property F, you have probably not said enough about X.

---

[31] A hard qualification to make precise. Obviously I am not telling the advocates of the existence of tropes that there is a serious lacuna in their theory of tropes if it does not include or imply an answer to the question, 'Are tropes the same objects as the *formae accidentales* of Duns Scotus?' A similar point applies to 'the two putative denoting phrases A and B' in the rule that follows.

- Suppose you contend that certain objects (which you have somehow specified) constitute an ontological category – call it 'category X'; suppose that what you have said about X implies that each of the two putative denoting phrases A and B denotes a member of X; ask yourself whether A and B denote the *same* member of X; if what you have said about X leaves this an open question, you have probably not said enough about X.
- Do not multiply categories beyond dire necessity.
- Try to tie all your terms of art to ordinary language by some sort of thread that can be followed; for a good guide in this matter, look at any reputable introductory physics text, and learn from the way in which, starting with ordinary language, the author introduces technical terms like 'mass' and 'force' and 'energy' and 'momentum.'

And, finally, don't be seduced by anything like 'the Quine–Putnam indispensability argument.' (This imperative doesn't get a bullet point because it's not a rule of thumb. This imperative is an *injunction*.) If, for example, your analysis of scientific discourse convinces you that quantification over – say – the real numbers is an indispensable component of the practice of scientists, don't go on to maintain that the undoubted fact that science has been 'successful' is *best explained* by postulating the existence of the real numbers. Stay *out* of the explanation business. Here endeth the lesson.

As to the second part of the interlocutor's question ('What has the method you recommend got to do with your adherence to a relational ontology?'), I have no good answer. I can do no more than record my conviction that if you follow the method I recommend, you will end up with neither a monocategorial ontology (a nominalistic ontology or a 'properties only' ontology like the New Bundle Theory or the 'Pauline' ontology) nor a constituent ontology. I think you will end up with a relational ontology (if you end up with anything at all; perhaps you will confess failure). But I should not regard it as a tragedy if someone were to demonstrate that this conviction was wrong. If some philosopher showed me how to eliminate quantification over properties (and, more generally, over abstract objects) from our discourse – an achievement that would in my view make the world safe for nominalism – I'd be delighted, for I'd really *like* to be a nominalist. And if a philosopher adopted my proposed method and ended up with a constituent ontology or an aristotelian ontology of some other kind – well, if I didn't find that outcome delightful, I'm sure I should find it instructive: I should almost certainly learn something valuable by retracing the intellectual steps that had led that philosopher to that result. In any case, whatever you end up with, it won't be an explanatory theory. Explanatory theories belong to everyday empirical investigation (the investigations of police detectives, for example) and to the empirical sciences. What you can *hope* to end up with is an ontology that it is plausible to suppose is the ontology that we tacitly appeal to in our everyday and our scientific discourse.[32]

---

[32] This chapter is a deep revision of my earlier paper 'Relational *vs.* Constituent Ontologies,' which appeared in John Hawthorne and Jason Turner (eds.), *Philosophical Perspectives*, vol. 25: *Metaphysics* (Malden, MA: Wiley-Blackwell, 2011), pp. 389–45. Although there is much new material in the present chapter, a significant proportion of the material in the two versions is the same – although much of the 'old' material has been extensively revised and rewritten. The structure of the present chapter is different from the structure of its predecessor. I believe that the way the present chapter is structured makes better logical sense. This restructuring has resulted in some differences between the technical terminology of the two essays.

CHAPTER 3

In defense of substantial universals

E. J. Lowe

The Aristotelian tradition in metaphysics inspires two different conceptions of the ontology of substances and universals. One is the 'hylemorphic'
conception of Aristotle's *Metaphysics*, which is built around the distinction
between *matter and form*, while the other is the 'fourfold' conception of
Aristotle's *Categories*. In this chapter, the latter conception will be advo-
cated. According to it, there are four fundamental ontological categories:
in the terminology I prefer, those of *individual substance, substantial kind,
attribute*, and *mode*. This fourfold scheme is generated by two mutually
orthogonal distinctions: that between *particular and universal*, and that
between *substance and property*. Crucial to this scheme, then, is the distinction between two types of universal: *substantial universals* and *property
universals* (substantial kinds and attributes). The present chapter is devoted
to defending this distinction and will do so by developing three different
arguments in favor of it: the argument from *individuation*, the argument
from *instantiation*, and the argument from *laws*.

1. Hylemorphism

In Aristotle's mature ontological system, as presented in the *Metaphysics*,
individual substances are taken to be combinations of *matter* and *form*,
with each such substance being constituted by a certain parcel of matter
embodying, or organized by, a certain form – the form normally being
understood as being a *universal*, whereas the matter is conceived as being
irreducibly *particular* in character and, indeed, as being that which confers
particularity upon the individual substance whose matter it is. For example,
an individual house may be said to have as its immediate matter some bricks,
mortar, and timber, which are organized in a certain distinctive way fit to
serve the functions of a human dwelling. Similarly, an individual horse
may be said to have as its immediate matter some flesh, blood, and bones,
which are organized in a certain distinctive way fit to sustain a certain

kind of life, that of a herbivorous quadruped. In each case, the 'matter' in question is not, or not purely, 'prime' matter, but is already 'informed' in certain distinctive ways which makes it suitable to receive the form of a house or a horse. Thus, bricks, mortar, and timber would not be matter suitable to receive the form of a horse, but at best that of something like a *statue* of a horse. According to this view, the matter and form of an individual substance are each 'incomplete' entities, completed *by each other* in their union in that substance. But its form is *essential* to the substance, unlike its matter, in the following sense: an individual house, say, cannot lose the form of house without thereby ceasing to be, whereas – while it must always *have* matter of an appropriate kind so long as it continues to be – it need not always have the *same* matter of that kind. Individual bricks and timbers in a house may be replaced without destroying the house – indeed, this may be the only way to *preserve* a certain house – but once its bricks and timbers cease to be organized in the form of a house, the house necessarily ceases to be.

Clearly, according to this *hylemorphist* scheme, an individual substance is a 'combination' of matter and form in a sense which rules out our thinking of its matter and form as being *parts* of the substance, at least in the normal sense of 'part.' Here it might be objected that, for example, a *brick* in a house is a part of it in this familiar sense, and yet belongs to the 'matter' of the house: so can't we at least say that the *matter* of a house is a 'part' of it in this sense? Not easily: for even if we were to concede that a *brick* is literally a part of the house, *all* the matter of the house, considered collectively, can hardly be so regarded. For the house *coincides* with its matter as a whole and hence, it appears, that matter could not qualify as a *proper* part of the house, as the brick might. Nor, however, can the matter qualify as an *improper* part of the house, in the standard sense, since that would make it *identical* with the house: and yet the house is clearly not identical with its matter, not least because its matter can *change* while it *persists*. Equally, on the hylemorphist view, the house's *form* cannot be regarded as a part, either proper or improper, of the house, in the standard sense of 'part.' Nothing forbids the hylemorphist from saying that, in some *other* sense of the term, the matter and form of an individual substance are 'parts' of it, but saying this would at least not be very helpful, since it would invite confusion. It is better just to say that the matter and form are *constituents*, but not parts, of the substance. The key point is that, on this view, individual substances exhibit 'internal' ontological complexity, being *combinations* of 'incomplete' entities that are completed by each other in the substance that they constitute.

So far, I have spoken a good deal about substantial *forms*, but not much about the *features* of substances, and how they might be accommodated by the approach now under discussion. Very roughly, I think that the answer should run somewhat as follows. The *form* of a substance constitutes its *essence* – *what it is*, its 'quiddity' – whereas its features, or 'qualities,' are *how it is*. A *horse* is *what* Dobbin is, for example. If Dobbin is *white*, however, that is partly *how* he is – a *way* that he is. I say 'partly' only to acknowledge that there are many other ways Dobbin is besides being white – such as being heavy – and by no means intend to imply that Dobbin's whiteness is a *part* of Dobbin. However, Dobbin's whiteness might nonetheless be thought to be a *constituent* of Dobbin, on this view, distinct from his *form*, which is equinity. But how, then, are a substance's features related to its form? Some of its features, it seems, are *necessitated* by its form – such as warm-bloodedness in the case of Dobbin – and these may be called, in the strictest sense of the term, the substance's *properties*. Other of its features, however, are 'accidental,' such as Dobbin's whiteness, which may therefore be denominated one of his *accidents*. Even so, although Dobbin's whiteness is accidental, that Dobbin has *some* color is necessitated by his form and is thus essential to him. So we arrive at the following picture: an individual substance possesses a certain *form*, which constitutes its *essence*, from which 'flow' by necessity certain features of the substance, which are its *properties* in the strictest sense of the term. Some of these properties are 'determinables' rather than 'determinates,' such as *color* in the case of Dobbin, and then it is necessary that the substance should possess *some* determinate feature falling under the relevant determinable, but contingent which feature this is. Such contingent determinate features are the substance's *accidents*, which can obviously change over time compatibly with the continued existence of the substance. The overall picture, even in this relatively simplified version of it, is quite complex, with an individual substance portrayed as having a rich and in some respects temporally inconstant constituent structure of *form, matter, properties*, and *accidents*, with form and properties remaining constant while matter and accidents are subject to change.

2. Problems with hylemorphism

Hylemorphism certainly has many attractive features. But its core difficulty lies in its central doctrine – that every concrete individual substance is a 'combination' of matter and form. For what, really, are we to *understand* by 'combination' in this sense? Clearly, we are not supposed to think that combination in this sense just is, or is the result of, a 'putting together' of two mutually independent things, since matter and form are supposed to be 'incomplete' items which *complete each other* in the substance that combines them. Now, certainly, when some concrete things – such as some bricks, timbers, and quantities of mortar – are put together to make a new concrete object, such as a house, those things have to be put together *in the right sort of way*, not just haphazardly. But does this entitle us to suppose that the completed house is some sort of 'combination' of *the things that have been put together* and *the way in which they have been put together*? The challenge that the hylemorphist presents us with is to explain why, if we don't say something like this, we are entitled to suppose that a *new* individual substance is brought into being. One presumption behind that challenge would seem to be that a substance can't simply be a so-called *mereological sum* of other substances – and with this I can agree, at least if by a 'mereological sum' we mean an entity whose identity is determined solely by the identities of its 'summands,' rather as the identity of a set is determined solely by the identities of its members. I agree that only when other substances have been put together *in the right sort of way* does a new substance of a certain kind come into being, the *way* in question depending on the *kind* in question. Moreover, I have no objection to the reification of 'ways,' understood as features or forms, provided that we don't treat ways as *substances* – so here too I am in agreement with the hylemorphist. Reification is not the same as *hypostatization*, but is merely the acknowledgment of some putative entity's *real existence*. What I *don't* understand is what it means to say that the completed house's *form* – the way in which its 'matter' is organized – is an 'incomplete' constituent of the house which 'combines' together with that equally 'incomplete' matter to constitute the house, a complete substance. The words that particularly mystify me in this sort of account are 'incomplete,' 'combine' and 'constitute.' It's not that I don't understand these words perfectly well as they are commonly used in other contexts, just that I don't understand their technical use in the hylemorphic theory and, equally importantly, why a *need* should be felt for this use of such terms.

If I could understand the supposed *need* to say something like this, then I would make every possible effort to grasp the technical terminology. So let us remind ourselves why, allegedly, there is indeed such a need. As was just mentioned, the need supposedly arises in order to meet the challenge of explaining how *a new substance* is brought into existence. The suggestion seems to be that, unless we can see the new substance as being a combination of items neither of which can exist independently of the other in just such a combination, rather than as merely being composed of other independently existing things each possessing their own features, we shall be unable to justify the judgment that a new concrete object – an 'addition of being' – really has been brought into existence, rather than some previously existing things merely being rearranged.[1] Put in this way, the supposed problem is one that is familiar from recent debates in metaphysics.[2] Here, though, I would urge that some types of 'rearrangement' are ontologically more weighty than others. When a free proton and a free electron are 'rearranged' by increasing the distance between them from one mile to two miles, there is no reason at all to suppose that a new concrete object is brought into existence. But when they are 'rearranged' so that the electron is captured by the proton and occupies an orbital around it, then indeed we have a new concrete object of a very different kind: a hydrogen atom. This object has certain features, notably certain *powers*, which are quite different from those of protons and electrons and quite different, too, from those of a mereological sum of a free proton and a free electron. In the newly created hydrogen atom, the proton remains exactly what it was before, just *a proton*, and the electron remains just *an electron*. A new *form* is instantiated – one that is possessed neither by the proton nor by the electron – namely, the form of *a hydrogen atom*. This form is the form of the newly created object, *the atom*, not that of the proton or the electron, nor even of the *pair* of them. The form does not, in any sense that I can understand, 'combine' with the proton and the electron so as to constitute, together with them, the atom. The only things that do any 'combining' are *the proton and the electron*, when the former captures the latter and the latter occupies an orbital around the former. And the only things that *constitute* the atom are, again, the proton and the electron, which are its *parts*, in the perfectly familiar sense of 'part.' So, as can be seen, I am perfectly happy to describe the case of the newly created hydrogen atom in terms of 'combination' and 'constitution,' and indeed in terms of 'form.' It's just that I don't need, and don't understand, the 'logical grammar' of the hylemorphist who uses these terms in his own distinctively technical fashion. Furthermore, I have no serious need for the hylemorphist's category of *matter*. I might be prepared to say that the 'matter' of the hydrogen atom is or consists of *its proton and electron*, but just in the sense that these are its *parts* and serve to *compose* it. But the atom's 'matter' in this sense is not, as the hylemorphist takes it to be, some 'incomplete' constituent of the atom that is completed by the atom's 'form.' In fact, I would prefer to abandon the term 'matter' altogether,

[1] I borrow the phrase 'addition of being' from David Armstrong: see, for instance, Armstrong (2004).
[2] See, for example, Merricks (2001).

as modern physics has done, at least as a fundamental theoretical term. Thus, although modern scientists talk, for instance, of 'condensed matter physics,' fundamental particle physicists don't nowadays speak of protons and electrons as having, or being composed of, *matter* – although they might happily speak of them as being 'packets of energy' and certainly as possessing *mass*.

3.   The four-category ontology

The hylemorphist ontology described above is inspired by Aristotle, as modified perhaps by later thinkers such as Aquinas. But the basis of another kind of ontology can also be traced to Aristotle, this time to the Aristotle of his presumed early work, the *Categories*.[3] The kind of ontology that I now have in mind is one whose key notions are briefly sketched in the opening passages of that work, before the classificatory divisions commonly known as the Aristotelian 'categories' are set out later in the treatise. In those open-ing passages, Aristotle articulates a fourfold ontological scheme in terms of the two technical notions of 'being *said of* a subject' and 'being *in* a sub-ject.' *Primary* substances – what we have hitherto been calling 'individual' substances – are described as being *neither said of* a subject *nor in* a subject. *Secondary* substances – the *species* and *genera* to which primary substances belong – are described as being *said of* a subject but *not in* a subject. That leaves two other classes of items: those that are *both said of* a subject *and in* a subject, and those that are *not said of* a subject but are *in* a subject. Since these two classes receive no official names and have been variously denomi-nated over the centuries, I propose to call them, respectively, *attributes* and *modes*. It seems that secondary substances and attributes are conceived to be different types of *universal*, while primary substances and modes are con-ceived to be different types of *particular*. Since the Aristotelian terminology of 'being said of' and 'being in' is perhaps less than fully perspicuous, with the former suggesting a linguistic relation and the latter seemingly having only a metaphorical sense, I prefer to use a different terminology: that of *instantiation* and *characterization*. Thus, I say that attributes and modes are *characterizing* entities, whereas primary and secondary substances are *characterizable* entities. And I say that secondary substances and attributes are *instantiable* entities, whereas primary substances and modes are *instan-tiating* entities. These terminological niceties, which though necessary are apt to prove confusing, are most conveniently laid out in diagrammatic

---

[3] For Aristotle's *Categories* see Ackrill (1963).

form, using the familiar device known as *the ontological square*. In my own version of the ontological square, I prefer to use the terms 'individual substance' and 'substantial kind' in place of the potentially confusing 'primary substance' and 'secondary substance.' I also include a 'diagonal' relationship between individual substances and attributes, which is distinct from both instantiation and characterization, calling this, as seems appropriate, *exemplification*. Here is my version:[4]

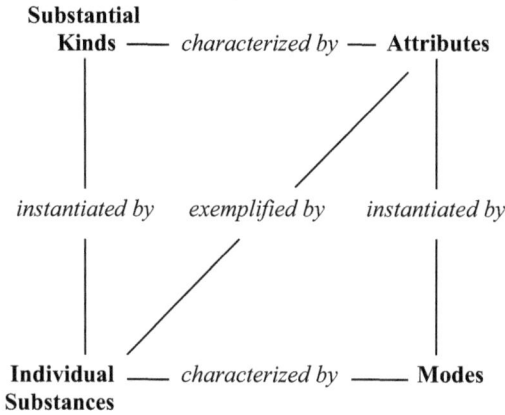

Substantial Kinds —— *characterized by* —— **Attributes**

instantiated by   *exemplified by*   *instantiated by*

Individual Substances —— *characterized by* —— **Modes**

I call the four classes of entities depicted here *ontological categories*, albeit with a cautionary note that these are not to be confused with, even though they are not unrelated to, Aristotle's own list of 'categories' later in his treatise. More precisely, I regard these four as the *fundamental* ontological categories, allowing that within each there may be various *sub*-categories, *sub-sub*-categories, and so on.

How, exactly, are the two 'Aristotelian' systems of ontology related to one another? Unsurprisingly, they overlap in many respects, but one key respect in which they obviously differ is that the *four-category ontology*, as I call it, unlike the hylemorphic ontology, does not include the category of *matter*. It might be thought that it also lacks the category of *form*, but that is not in fact so. For I believe that form, conceived as a type of universal, and more perspicuously termed *substantial* form, is really nothing other than *secondary substance* or substantial *kind*. We may refer to such universal forms either by using certain *abstract* nouns, such as 'humanity' and 'equinity,' or else by using certain *substantival* nouns –

---

[4] See Lowe 2006.

what Locke called 'sortal' terms – such as 'man' and 'horse.' I believe that this is a grammatical distinction which fails to reflect any real ontological difference. However, if that is so, then there is a very important ontological consequence. This is that primary or individual substances 'have' forms only and precisely in the sense that they are particular *instances* of forms. Thus Dobbin is a particular instance of the substantial kind or form *horse*, whereas Dobbin's *whiteness* is a particular instance of the color universal or attribute *whiteness*. By this account, it makes no sense at all to say that Dobbin is a 'combination' of the form *horse* and some 'matter.' He is, to repeat, just a particular *instance* of that form, other such instances being the various other particular horses that exist or have existed. Being an instance of this form, Dobbin must certainly have *material parts*, such as a head and limbs, but in no sense is he a 'combination' of anything material and the universal form in question. What I am saying, then, is that individual or primary substances are nothing other than *particular forms*, or *form-particulars* – particular instances of universal forms, in precisely the same sense in which modes (or 'tropes,' as they are now often called) are particular instances of attributes.

4. The argument from individuation

As I mentioned at the outset of this chapter, my primary aim here is to defend the distinction between substantial universals (substantial kinds) and property universals (attributes), which constitute two of the four fundamental ontological categories of the four-category ontology. An obvious question that may be leveled at adherents of this ontology is indeed this: why is it necessary to invoke two fundamentally different *types* of universal? For present purposes, I am not addressing the more basic question of why we need to invoke universals *at all* and should not want to endorse a thoroughgoing *particularist* ontology, whether that be a two-category ontology of individual substances and modes (or tropes), a one-category ontology of individual substances, or a one-category ontology of tropes. I assume, also, that if we are going to include universals in our ontology at all, then we need to include *property* universals or 'attributes,' as I call them. We might well need to debate over precisely *which* attributes to include and on *what basis* we should include them. We might not, for instance, deem it necessary to include *color* attributes such as *whiteness* and *redness*, perhaps on the grounds that these have no serious role to play in fundamental physics. But I take it that we shall need to include certain attributes, such as *mass* and *charge*, which do seem to play an indispensable role in physics.

However, since I don't want to commit myself here to any kind of physicalist reductionism, I shall not confine myself to austere examples drawn from fundamental physics in order to frame my arguments in favor of substantial universals, although I do believe that these arguments can be adapted, if need be, to make use only of such austere examples. Instead, I shall conduct the arguments using more familiar examples drawn from the domain of macroscopic concrete objects and their empirically detectable features.

My first argument, then, is *the argument from individuation*. It proceeds as follows. *Individual substances* – everyday examples of which would include such things as *Dobbin*, a particular horse – are, as this very nomenclature implies, above all *individual* things and *property-bearers*. But what confers their 'individuality' upon them? In virtue of what is Dobbin *one* thing, distinct and differentiable from all other individual things? What is it that provides Dobbin with his *identity conditions*? It cannot be the *property* universals that he exemplifies that do so, for such universals determine *no* specific identity conditions for the things that exemplify them. Consider, for instance, the property universals or attributes *whiteness* and *heaviness*, both of which, we may suppose, are exemplified by Dobbin. And consider an arbitrarily chosen individual substance, *S*, which likewise exemplifies these attributes. The mere fact that Dobbin and *S both* exemplify whiteness and heaviness imposes no constraint whatever upon a correct answer to the following question: *is it, or is it not the case, that S is identical with Dobbin?* By contrast, suppose that we can also say truly of both *S* and Dobbin that each of them is a *horse*. Then we *do* immediately have an important constraint imposed upon our identity question. This is because the predicate 'is a horse,' unlike the predicates 'is white' and 'is heavy,' carries with it not only a criterion of *application*, but also a criterion of *identity*.[5] A criterion of application tells us what determines the *extension* of a predicate – the set of entities to which it applies – whereas a criterion of identity tells us what determines whether or not one entity to which it applies *is identical with* 'another' entity to which it applies. In other words – switching from the formal to the material mode, or from talk of *predicates* to talk of *predicables* – it is only *substantial* universals, not property universals, that can determine the identity conditions of the individual substances that fall under them.

Of course, this claim might be challenged. One way to challenge it would be to say that the only 'criterion of identity' that we need ever

---

[5] See further Lowe (2009: Ch. 2).

have recourse to is *Leibniz's law*, which tells us that any 'two' individual substances x and y are identical only if *x and y share all their predicables*. (I am using the term 'predicable' here so as to remain neutral, for the purpose of this challenge, about the need to distinguish between two different *types* of predicable – substantial universals and property universals. As for my choice of the term 'predicable,' I use this to reflect Aristotle's 'said of' locution: a predicable is something that may be *predicated*, or *said of*, a subject – and, according to Aristotle, as I read him, all such things must be *universals*.) However, in the first place, a genuine *criterion* of identity needs to be expressible as a *biconditional*, not just a conditional, principle, since it needs to state a logically necessary *and sufficient* condition for the identity of any items to which it is supposed to apply. If we do this in the present case, by appealing not merely to 'Leibniz's law' as understood above but rather to the principle of the *identity of indiscernibles*, then we get something much more contentious: namely, that any 'two' individual substances x and y are identical *if* only if x and y share all their predicables. However, for very familiar reasons, it is highly questionable to say that no two distinct individual substances can share all their universal features, as Max Black's famous example of the symmetrical two-sphere world shows.[6] Furthermore, it is a deficiency in the principle of the identity of indiscernibles, conceived as a putative all-purpose criterion of identity, that it is incapable of revealing *category mistakes* where questions of identity are concerned. Why, for instance – to use a famous example borrowed from Frege – is it just *absurd* to inquire whether or not Julius Caesar is identical with a certain *number*, such as the number 7? We don't need to consider the *attributes* of Julius Caesar and the number 7, respectively, in order to rule out their identity – on the grounds, say, that Caesar was born and died, whereas the number 7 wasn't and didn't, or that Caesar was so-and-so many centimeters tall but the number 7 is not. We know that Caesar *can't* be identical with *any* number, because Caesar has the identity conditions of a *human being* and these are fundamentally different from those of a *number*. In fact, a properly stated criterion of identity will always make clear its *sortal-relative* character, giving it the following canonical form:

(Cϕ) If x and y are ϕs, then x is identical with y if and only if $R_\phi(x, y)$.

Here, 'ϕ' is a *sortal* or *substantival* general term, such as 'horse,' 'human being,' or 'number,' denoting a certain *substantial universal* that x and y are hypothesized as falling under, while 'R_ϕ' denotes a certain equivalence

---

[6] See Black (1952).

relation that is well-defined over the φs. Lacking this form, the principle of the identity of indiscernibles cannot be said to constitute a *bona fide* criterion of identity.

Another way to challenge the argument from individuation would be to contend that, while sortal or substantival general terms are indeed important on account of the role they play in the formulation of criteria of identity, all such terms are ultimately wholly analyzable by means of logical operations on *attributive* or *adjectival* general terms, of which 'white' and 'heavy' are examples. Thus, for instance, it might be alleged that the sortal term 'horse' is analyzable in terms of a conjunction of adjectival terms or, rather more sophisticatedly, in terms of a conjunction or disjunction of conjunctions or disjunctions of adjectival terms. But it is very hard indeed to see how such a program of analysis could in fact be successfully carried out. Aristotle himself, of course, believed that any *species* could be 'defined' *per genus et differentiam*. Thus, notoriously, he 'defines' *man* (or human being, as we would now say) as *rational animal*. But, evidently, only one of the terms in this *definiens* is adjectival – 'rational' – whereas the other, 'animal,' is again a *sortal* term. I have nothing to say in favor of definition *per genus et differentiam* myself, but I do at least commend Aristotle's insight that there is no prospect of defining a species – that is, a substantial universal – solely in terms of a set of *attributes*. Of course, we must be on our guard against sleight of hand where such definitions are attempted. For instance, it might be alleged that 'horse' can first be defined, in quasi-Aristotelian fashion, as something like 'herbivorous, quadrupedal, . . . *animal*' – where the ellipsis is filled by further adjectives – and then 'animal' is further analyzed as something like '*living thing* capable of self-movement.' The trouble with this, however, is that 'thing' is a so-called *dummy* sortal, conveying no specific identity conditions whatever. It might conceivably be the case that 'animal' is adequately analyzed as, say, '*organism* capable of self-movement,' but it certainly cannot be correct to suppose that 'organism' is synonymous with 'living thing.' After all, 'living thing' applies to *anything* to which the property of *being alive* may be attributed and this includes not just organisms but, for example, various *parts* of organisms, such as egg cells and nerve cells, which are certainly not themselves organisms and *a fortiori* not *animals*. Another, although rather more transparent, type of sleight of hand to guard against when dealing with attempted 'definitions' of sortal terms by means of adjectival terms involves the use of adjectives which are simply *derived* from sortal terms and consequently have no semantic priority over them. For example, it would be fatuous to attempt to define 'horse' as '*equine* living thing,' not only because it would apply to a living *nerve cell* of a horse quite as well as to an entire *horse*, but even more fundamentally because 'equine' derives its meaning from 'horse,' rather than vice versa, meaning as it does something like 'of or related to *horses.*'

5. The argument from instantiation

My second argument in favor of the distinction between substantial universals and property universals arises from the following question: what, fundamentally, is an *individual substance*? It is all very well to give examples of individual substances, such as Dobbin the horse. But what is it that entitles to categorize such an entity as *being* an individual substance, as opposed to an entity of any other ontological category? Why shouldn't we say, for instance, that Dobbin is an *attribute*, like whiteness or heaviness? Part of the answer, no doubt, is that Dobbin is a *particular*, not a *universal*. But that simply pushes our inquiry one stage further back. What, at bottom, does the distinction between particulars and universals *consist in*? Of course, there have been many answers to this question that have been offered over the centuries.[7] Some philosophers say that what is distinctive of particulars is that they *exist in space and time*, whereas universals do not. But that presupposes a 'transcendent' conception of universals – whereas, according to many 'immanent' realists, universals, like particulars, do indeed exist in space and time: although they may contend that universals are unlike particulars in that they are capable of being 'multiply located,' that is, of being 'wholly present' in more than one place at the same time. Another problem with the foregoing answer is that many philosophers think that some *particulars* don't exist in space and time, namely, *abstract* ones, such as numbers, sets, and propositions. As a putative alternative to that answer, some philosophers say that what is distinctive of universals is that they are 'repeatable' entities, whereas particulars are not. However, as it stands, this characterization of the distinction seems merely metaphorical. In what sense, precisely, is a universal supposed to be capable of being 'repeated,' in a way that is impossible for a particular? It may be that this is just another way of saying that universals are, whereas particulars are not, capable of 'multiple location.' But the notion of multiple location is by no means completely transparent and problem free, nor is it perfectly clear that particulars are not capable of it – indeed, some situations described in modern quantum physics, involving 'entangled particles,' are strongly suggestive of precisely this. Yet other philosophers suggest that what is distinctive of

---

[7] For an overview, see Lowe (2002a: Ch. 19).

particulars is that they are not subject to the principle of the identity of indiscernibles, whereas universals are – in other words, that there can in principle be two numerically distinct but exactly resembling *particulars*, but no two such *universals*. But, again, whatever the merits of this proposal might be with regard to particulars that exist in space and time, it is far from clear that it applies to *abstract* particulars, such as numbers: could there, for instance, be another number which *exactly resembled* the number 7, that is, which shared all and only the properties of the number 7, apart from the property of being *identical* with that number? Surely not. Of course, it might be contended that the number 7 is in fact a *universal* rather than a particular – and for my own part I would not be averse to saying this, but it would be wrong to say it simply in order to save the proposed way of distinguishing universals from particulars.

My own view is that the only satisfactory way to draw the distinction between universals and particulars, without committing oneself in a partisan way to a specific *theory* of universals, is to do so in terms of the formal ontological relation of *instantiation* – a relation which is irreflexive, asymmetrical, and intransitive. The proposal is that any particular must instantiate some universal and any universal must at least be *capable* of being instantiated by some particular – I say only 'be capable' so as to accommodate the transcendent realist who countenances the existence of uninstantiated universals. Particulars, then, just *are* 'instances' of universals, and universals just *are* entities that have, or at least *can* have, 'instances.'[8] Indeed, I take it that this way of distinguishing universals and particulars implies that the distinction is not only *mutually exclusive* but also *exhaustive*. Every entity is *either* a particular *or else* a universal – never *neither* and never *both*. Of course, there are some philosophers – apart from those denying the very existence of universals altogether – who could not accept this proposal, given their other commitments. For instance, I take it that an advocate of so-called *bare* particulars could not accept that every particular must instantiate some universal (unless, perhaps, 'bareness' could be supposed to denote a universal). But I regard it as a virtue of the proposal that it excludes bare particulars, since I find the notion of such particulars scarcely intelligible anyway. Equally, some philosophers may want to countenance the existence of universals which *couldn't* be instantiated, such as, perhaps, the property of being both round and square. But, again, I don't find it at all embarrassing that my proposal excludes the possibility of such universals. We should not confuse the fact that the *predicate* 'is

---

[8] Compare Lowe (2006: 77) and (2009: 38).

both round and square' is meaningful with the contention that it denotes
a real property.

Now we are in a position to consider the argument from instantiation
for the existence of substantial universals. The argument runs as follows.
Take an individual substance, such as Dobbin. Dobbin is a *particular* and
hence, according to the foregoing proposal, *an instance of a universal.* But
of *what* universal is Dobbin an instance? Suppose that we were to restrict
ourselves solely to *property* universals, such as *whiteness* and *heaviness.* And
suppose, as before, that Dobbin is both white and heavy. Can we then
say that Dobbin is an instance of *whiteness?* If we do, then we must
assuredly also say, by parity of reasoning, that he is an instance of *heaviness.*
That implies that one and the same particular may be an instance of two
distinct property universals. That is to say, two *property-instances,* of two
different property universals, may be *numerically identical.* Indeed, the
implication is that all of the property universals characterizing Dobbin
are *co-instantiated* by Dobbin himself, so that *he* is a numerically identical
instance of each and every one of them. But here is the difficulty. We have
a canonical way of referring to property-instances, which is this. If S is an
individual substance which is F, where 'F' denotes some property universal,
Fness, then we refer to the corresponding *instance* of Fness as 'S's Fness,'
or 'the Fness of S.' So, for example, we may refer to *Dobbin's whiteness*
and *Dobbin's heaviness* as being, in Dobbin's case, the relevant *instances*
of the universals *whiteness* and *heaviness* that characterize Dobbin. But,
according the suggestion now under examination, it is just *Dobbin himself*
that is the relevant instance of *both* of these universals. And that implies
that Dobbin's whiteness is *identical* with Dobbin's heaviness, both of them
simply being identical with *Dobbin.* But this seems absurd. After all, there is
surely no necessary connection between Dobbin's whiteness and Dobbin's
heaviness, since Dobbin could cease to be white without ceasing to be heavy,
and vice versa. However, if Dobbin's whiteness just *is* Dobbin, then when
Dobbin's whiteness ceases to exist, so does *Dobbin,* and therewith Dobbin's
heaviness.

Something, then, is fundamentally confused about the foregoing proposal. And what it is appears to be this. It is incoherent to suppose that
an individual substance, such as Dobbin, is literally an *instance* of any of
the property universals that characterizes that individual substance. The
relevant *instances* of those properties are, rather, items in the category of
mode, otherwise called 'tropes' or 'individual accidents' – not items like
Dobbin, which belong to the category of individual *substance.* Nonetheless,
Dobbin is a *particular* and, as such, an instance of *some* universal. But, for

the foregoing reasons, this universal cannot be any *property* universal that characterizes Dobbin. Consequently, it must be a universal of an altogether different type: a *substance* universal. What Dobbin *is*, fundamentally, is an instance of the substantial kind *horse* – just as I contended at the end of section 3 above. This then requires us to distinguish between two different formal ontological relations in which individual substances can stand to universals. The first is *instantiation* – and Dobbin stands in this relation to the substantial universal or kind *horse* – and the second is *exemplification*, in which Dobbin stands to the various property universals that may be 'said of' him. Exemplification, however, is not a *fundamental* formal ontological relation, in the way that instantiation is. This is because it obtains between Dobbin and, say, the property universal *whiteness* in virtue of the fact that Dobbin is *characterized* by an *instance* of that universal, namely, *Dobbin's whiteness*. Or, in an older terminology, Dobbin *is white* because a particular instance of whiteness 'inheres' in Dobbin. But it is not the case that Dobbin *is a horse* for any such reason. Rather, Dobbin is a horse because *he himself* is an instance of the substantial universal *horse*.

6. The argument from laws

The third and final argument to be developed here for the existence of substantial universals is the argument from *laws*, by which I mean, more specifically, *natural laws* or *laws of nature*. For present purposes I shall assume without argument that laws do indeed *involve* universals, aligning myself thereby with philosophers such as David Armstrong, Fred Dretske, and Michael Tooley, although I do not accept, for reasons that will become plain, the so-called Armstrong–Dretske–Tooley account of laws.[9] And here I should emphasize that, like Armstrong, I do not consider laws to be *propositions* or *statements*, but rather to be those states of affairs that are the *truthmakers* of law-statements – although, unlike Armstrong, I don't take states of affairs to be *ontologically basic* and, accordingly, don't take them to be the *basic* truthmakers of law-statements. In fact, I take *substantial universals* to be these basic truthmakers, as we shall see in due course.

In endorsing a universals-based account of laws, I am setting myself against neo-Humean 'regularity' accounts, which conceive of law-statements as expressing universal generalizations quantifying solely over particulars and having as their logical form, in the simplest sort of case,

---

[9] See, especially, Armstrong (1983).

'$\forall x(Fx \rightarrow Gx)$,' where '$F$' and '$G$' express or denote certain property universals. Armstrong has proposed, in opposition to this sort of account, one according to which the logical form of a law-statement, in the simplest sort of case, is '$N(F, G)$,' where 'N' expresses or denotes a second-order universal of *natural necessitation*, relating the first-order universals denoted by 'F' and 'G.' So, by this account, such a law-statement expresses the state of affairs of *F*ness's necessitating *G*ness. This kind of necessity is supposed by Armstrong to be different from *metaphysical* necessity, in that it is, supposedly, metaphysically possible for *F*ness to necessitate *G*ness in some possible worlds and yet not in others in which those same universals exist. At least, this is what he supposed when he first developed the account. However, it would be open to a philosopher to reject this particular aspect of Armstrong's original account while accepting the rest. Now, my own account of laws differs crucially from Armstrong's in that it invokes both *substantial* universals and *property* universals, but no second-order relation between universals. By my account, the logical form of a law-statement, in the simplest sort of case, is 'ϕF' – or, in plain English, 'ϕs (are) *F*.'[10] A simple example of a far from basic law will give the flavor of the difference between the two accounts: Kepler's first law of planetary motion. This, in plain English, states that *planets orbit elliptically* – that is, *move in elliptical orbits*. This indeed has the form 'ϕs *F*,' with 'ϕ' being replaced by the sortal term 'planet' and '*F*' by the predicate 'orbit elliptically,' which expresses a property universal. By contrast, on Armstrong's account, the canonical way to express this law would have to be something like 'Being a planet necessitates orbiting elliptically,' while on a neo-Humean regularity account it would be something like 'Anything that is a planet is a thing that orbits elliptically.' This very example, I suggest, already illustrates the naturalness of my preferred account in comparison with either of the others. The fact is that laws of nature – outside the philosophical literature on the subject, at least – very commonly *are* expressed by means of what linguists call *generic* sentences, in which the plural form of a sortal term features as the subject of a predicate expressive of a *disposition* or *habitude*. The four-category ontology has a very clear way to explain the truth-conditions of such sentences, when they are used to express laws, namely: 'ϕF' is true if and only if the attribute *F*ness characterizes the substantial kind ϕ. Here is another simple example to illustrate this point: it is a law of nature that *electrons are negatively charged* – and what this amounts to, according to

---

[10] See Lowe (2006: Ch. 8) and (2009: Ch. 9).

the four-category ontology, is simply that the attribute of *being negatively charged* characterizes the substantial kind *electron*.

This is not the place for me to present and defend in full my preferred account of laws. All I wish to do here is to explain why, in my view, a universals-based account of laws is best served by an ontology which distinguishes between substantial universals and property universals. But first I must answer a charge that is likely to be raised against my account, namely, that some very well-known natural laws do not appear to have the form that I propose. A case in point might be taken to be Newton's law of gravitation, which is typically represented by the following mathematical formula: $F = GM_1M_2/R^2$, where 'F' represents force, 'M' mass, and 'R' distance, while 'G' denotes the universal constant of gravitation. The objection is that this formula invokes only *property* universals, not any *substantial* universal. However, this objection is superficial, being based merely on a choice of mathematical notation. If we consider how Newton himself expressed his famous law, we see that he did so in some such terms as these, when he was expressing himself in plain English (or indeed plain Latin): *Bodies attract one another with a force that is directly proportional to the product of their masses and inversely proportional to the square of the distance between their centers of mass.*[11] Newton clearly thought that his law was a law governing the behavior of *bodies*, by which he meant – in common with other philosophers and scientists of his time, such as Locke and Boyle – *parcels of matter*. And 'body' or 'parcel of matter' is certainly a *sortal* term, not an *adjectival* term. It denotes a certain *kind* of thing, with certain determinate *identity conditions*. In the mathematical formula, this reference to *body* as the substantial kind to which the law applies is indeed suppressed, but only because it plays no role for computational purposes in working out the *numerical value* of the force acting between two bodies with specified masses and a specified distance apart. And this purely technical feature of the formula has no bearing whatever on the *ontological* involvements of the law that it serves to symbolize mathematically. So long as it is conceded that mass is a property that can only be possessed by *bodies* and that 'body' is a sortal term in good standing, the example of Newton's law of gravitation can present no challenge to the account of laws that I am now defending. Of course, I did remark earlier, in section 2, that the concept of *matter* is no longer fundamental to physical theory – and hence, to that extent, we should probably no longer think of bodies

---

[11] This is not an exact quotation, of course, but is close in form to various of Newton's own statements concerning gravity in the *Principia*, in which context he regularly deploys the term 'body' (or, rather, its Latin equivalent). See Newton (1729).

as being 'parcels of matter,' in the sense of Newton and Locke. But this is not to say that the notion of *body* has been superseded, only that a certain philosophical theory concerning the *constitution* of bodies has. Physical particles, such as protons and electrons, certainly fall squarely within the class of *bodies* for the purposes of Newton's law. Nor, of course, is it relevant for our present concerns that Newton's law is now, after Einstein, regarded as a mere *approximation* to the truth, since I was using it only for illustrative purposes. (Incidentally, similar points to those made above can, I believe, be made with regard to the *conservation laws* of physics.)

Now I need to say why a universals-based account of laws which invokes substantial universals is superior to one which invokes only property universals. Here I shall focus on just one reason for thinking this to be the case. The reason is that the former sort of account can be more *parsimonious* than the latter, with regard to the *simplicity* and *number* of laws that it recognizes, and also possesses greater *explanatory potential*. I shall illustrate these points by means of 'toy' examples. Suppose that physicists were to discover a new *kind* of fundamental particle – call them φ-particles or φs, for short. And suppose they discover that φs have the following combination of characteristics: *F*ness, *G*ness, and *H*ness. In reality, these characteristics might be, say, a certain *rest mass*, *charge*, and *spin*. According to my preferred account of laws, this situation can be described in the following very simple and intuitively natural terms: φs are *F*, φs are *G*, and φs are *H* – in short, φs are *F*, *G*, and *H*. But what can be said by a universals-based account of laws which does *not* countenance substantial universals, such as φ? It will not do for it to cheat by invoking a *pseudo-property* of φness, for reasons discussed earlier. In fact, it seems that it will have little option but to try to *analyze* what it is for something to be a φ-particle in terms of the properties that have been found to characterize those particles, namely, *F*ness, *G*ness, and *H*ness. In short, it will have to say that 'is a φ-particle' is analyzable as 'is a particle which is *F*, *G*, and *H*.' But now there is immediately a problem, because if we substitute this proposed *analysans* for 'φ' in the law-statements given above, we just get a set of *analytic trivialities*: 'Particles which are *F*, *G*, and *H* are *F*,' 'Particles which are *F*, *G*, and *H* are *G*,' and 'Particles which are *F*, *G*, and *H* are *H*' – or, in Armstrong's preferred way of representing laws, '$N[(F\&G\&H), F]$,' '$N[(F\&G\&H), G]$,' and '$N[(F\&G\&H), H]$.' Clearly, then, the advocate of a universals-based approach to laws who rejects substantial universals must have recourse to another strategy, and the only one that appears to be available is to try to formulate the relevant laws in terms of *non*-analytic statements connecting the property universals *F*ness, *G*ness, and *H*ness.

Consider, for instance, the following trio of laws, represented Armstrong-style: '$N[(F\&G), H]$,' '$N[(F\&H), G]$,' and '$N[(G\&H), F]$.' None of these is an analytic triviality. Unfortunately, however, none of them need be *true* in the situation being envisaged. Recall, this is a situation in which scientists have discovered that ϕs are F, G, and H. But, while this may be taken to imply that being a ϕ necessitates being F, G, and H, it doesn't imply, for instance, that being F and G necessitates being H. To make the example more concrete, suppose again that Fness, Gness, and Hness are, respectively, a certain *rest mass*, *charge*, and *spin*. It may be true that ϕ-particles have all of these characteristics *necessarily*, without this implying that any particle having the same rest mass and charge as a ϕ-particle necessarily also has the same *spin* as a ϕ-particle. I leave it to advocates of the view in question to solve this problem, if they can, in the most economic way possible. But it doesn't look likely that they will be able to represent the required laws as simply and parsimoniously as can be done by appeal to the substantial universal ϕ.

I also claimed that my approach to laws accords them *greater explanatory potential* than the rival universals-based view does. This can also be illustrated by a 'toy' example from particle physics. Suppose we ask why it is that only *certain combinations* of fundamental properties are found to be exemplified by the particles in our physical universe. For instance, the following two combinations are found: (1) the rest mass of an electron, unit negative charge, and spin one half, (2) the rest mass of an electron, unit positive charge, and spin one half. Combination (1) is exemplified by any particular *electron*, while combination (2) is exemplified by any particular *positron*. But, it appears, not *every* specific rest mass, charge, and spin, each of which is found to be *separately* exemplified by some particular particle or other, are always found to be exemplified *together* by some *single* particle. Thus, suppose that particle a is F, particle b is G, and particle c is H. It doesn't follow that there is any particle that is F, G, and H. Why not, though? My preferred account of laws has a simple enough answer, namely, that there is no particle *kind*, ϕ, such that ϕs are F, G, and H. That is why we find no *particular* particle that exemplifies the combination of Fness, Gness, and Hness. For, on my view, any particular particle must instantiate *some* particle kind, the laws concerning which determine what properties that particle can exemplify. But what can the rival universals-based view say about this matter? Presumably, it must just say that, as a matter of basic or brute nomological fact, the combination of Fness, Gness, and Hness is ruled out, because these three properties somehow *jointly exclude* their combination. That is, in Armstrongian notation, something like the following three laws must presumably obtain: $N[(F\&G), \sim H]$, $N[(F\&H), \sim G]$, and $N[(G\&H), \sim F]$. This proposal has at least two disadvantages relative to my own. The first is that it invokes *negative* universals. The second is that, although each law apparently entails the other two, there is nothing to indicate which if any of them has nomological priority over the others. Of course, it might be suggested that we can also represent the situation by a *single* law, provided that we allow laws in which the necessitation 'relation' applies to just a *single* universal – $N[\sim(F\&G\&H)]$ – although this still commits us to negative universals and still doesn't solve the priority problem.

There is one final point that I want to mention. As I remarked at the outset of this section, I consider that substantial universals are the *basic* truthmakers of law-statements. I do not believe that *laws* as such – conceived in Armstrongian fashion as a species of states of affairs – exist at a fundamental ontological level. Thus, on my account, it is the substantial kind *electron* that is the basic truthmaker of the law-statement that electrons are unit-negatively charged. This is because I take unit negative charge to be an *essential* property of electrons, with the consequence that in every possible world in which electrons exist, it is true that electrons are unit-negatively charged. Assuming that an entity x is truthmaker for a proposition p if p is true in every possible world in which x exists – in other words, if the existence of x metaphysically necessitates the truth of p – it follows that the substantial kind *electron* is indeed a truthmaker of the law-statement that electrons are negatively charged.[12] That it is a *basic* truthmaker of that law-statement follows from my assumption – defended in this paper – that the category of substantial kind, or substantial universal, is one of the *fundamental* ontological categories.

---

[12] I present my views on truthmaking in Lowe (2006: Ch. 12).

CHAPTER 4

A kind farewell to Platonism
For an Aristotelian understanding of kinds and properties

Gabriele Galluzzo

1. Introduction

Realism, the view that there are universals, comes in rather different forms. Although sharing a common belief in the existence of universals, realists are at variance on a number of crucial issues, including for instance the ontological status we should accord to universals as well as which universals there are. We are all familiar with some common sources of disagreement. Some realists, for instance, take universals to be entities of a radically different sort from the particulars of our ordinary perceptual experience or of scientific observation. For these philosophers, universals are transcendent, that is, they exist apart from particulars, and abstract, that is, they exist neither in space nor in time. Accordingly, particulars have the characters they do because they bear some special non-mereological relation (be it called 'instantiation,' 'exemplification,' or 'participation') to abstract entities. Philosophers of this ilk are often labeled 'Platonists'.[1] Other realists, by contrast, provide a rather different account of how universals should be conceived of. They maintain, more particularly, that universals are not transcendent but immanent, that is, they do not exist apart from their particular instances, but in them. Particulars, therefore, have the characters they do not because they bear some special relation to some abstract entities, but rather because they share some common constituents. Philosophers in this second group are often called 'Aristotelians.'[2] Although Aristotelians are not always clear on this particular point, they usually take the existence of universals to be bound up with space and time. It is certainly true that it is particulars that exist primarily in space and time; but – Aristotelians

---

[1] For some considerations about the relationship between contemporary Platonism and the historical Plato see Ademollo (2013).

[2] For Aristotle's views on universals and their relationship to the contemporary metaphysical debate see Galluzzo and Mariani (2007); Loux (2009); Galluzzo (2013); and Mariani (2013). The majority of contemporary scholars take Aristotle to be a realist about universals. For a nominalist interpretation see Frede (1987a) and (1987b); Frede and Patzig (1988).

insist – there is a perfectly reasonable sense in which also the metaphysical constituents of sensible objects can be said to exist in space and time, or at least not outside space and time. Universals, it is often said, are wherever and whenever their particular instances are. Besides disagreeing on the ontological status of universals, Platonists and Aristotelians part company also concerning the so-called Principle of Instantiation and hence concerning which universals there are. Typically, Platonists reject the principle and so admit of uninstantiated universals, while Aristotelians accept it and so do not countenance uninstantiated universals. Although it has been convincingly argued that immanence is logically independent of the acceptance of the principle just as much as transcendence is logically independent of its denial, immanence and acceptance of the principle as well as transcendence and its denial are theoretical options that usually go hand in hand.[3]

Recent works on universals may sometimes mislead people into thinking that the contrast between Platonists and Aristotelians in the senses specified exhausts disputes among realists. But things are not quite so. In this chapter, I wish to discuss a different source of disagreement, namely the question as to whether we should distinguish between two irreducibly different categories of universals, i.e. kinds and properties. At a very first approximation, the distinction is the one between universals, the kinds, that express the essence or nature of their particular instances by telling us *what* they are and universals, the properties, that do not express the essence or nature of their particular instances and hence tell us not what but only *how* they are. Since all realists accept properties, the problem at issue can also be phrased as whether or not we need and should introduce kinds in addition to properties. Of course, in a very broad sense, also kinds can be called 'properties'; *being a human being*, a kind-generated feature, can be reasonably thought of as an essential property of mine and contrasted with *being pale*, which is, instead, a feature that does not express my nature or essence. However, since on the view that I shall explore kinds and properties are thought to be universals of irreducibly different categories, it is better to reserve the term 'properties' for the properties that are not kind-generated. I shall use, instead, 'features' or 'characteristics' when I wish to refer to both kinds-generated properties and properties in the strict sense of the term.

In some sense, the contrast between those who are prepared to distinguish between properties and kinds and those who are not is a contrast between an Aristotelian and a non-Aristotelian brand of thought, for it

---

[3] Cf. Loux (2007b).

is especially within the Aristotelian tradition that the distinction between kinds and properties has been accorded particular importance. However, at the first level of the analysis, I wish to reserve the label 'Aristotelian' for the theory of immanent universals and so present the acceptance of kinds as neutral between Platonic and Aristotelian realism. As in the case of properties, in other words, one is free to construe kinds as transcendent abstract entities or as entities existing in particular objects. Depending on which view one takes, there may be differences as to the number of kinds one is more inclined to accept; hence, there may be good reasons to favor one account or the other. However, nothing in the very notion of a kind commits us to being Platonist or Aristotelian about universals. The notion of kind is neutral also with respect to the issues bearing on the level of analysis, that is, with respect to issues concerning ontological reduction. A robust reductionist might think that the only genuine kinds are those that have as their instances the microstructural particles studied by contemporary physics, the assumption being, presumably, that middle-size ordinary objects can be somehow constructed out of such basic particles. A less revisionary philosopher, by contrast, can countenance kinds for both basic physical particles and middle-size objects. Finally, more convinced anti-reductionists may insist that, although there are kinds for both microstructural particles and middle-size objects, the kinds of the latter are in some sense explanatorily prior to the kinds of the former. In this case as well, however, nothing in the notion of a kind, it seems to me, should incline one towards one view or another. Additional argument must be provided to show that some seemingly uncontroversial instances of objects can in fact be reduced to others. Neither does accepting the distinction between kinds and properties depend much in itself on one's reductionist or anti-reductionist tastes. Admittedly, some scientific realists, the philosophers more sensitive to the ontological implications of modern sciences, actually deny that we should introduce kinds in addition to properties.[4] But it is strange that one's willingness to accept the distinction between kinds and properties should depend on just which objects one is prepared to take as basic or fundamental. And it is far from clear that modern physics compels us to dispense with kinds more than it invites us to introduce them. Thus, it is better to preserve the neutral character of the kind–property distinction and try to assess its costs and benefits independently of further decisions about where the distinction should be applied if accepted.

---

[4] Cf. Armstrong (1997b).

There are mainly four issues I want to deal with in connection with the distinction between kinds and properties. (i) One is the very nature of the distinction and how it should be conceived of. My focus will be in particular on the notion of property and on the relationship it bears to that of kind. In section 2, I shall suggest that some light can be shed on the nature of properties if we make use of a distinction which Aristotle draws in his logical works between two senses of the words 'accident' and 'accidental'. (ii) In section 3, I shall move to the reasons why kinds are not dispensable. I shall examine in particular one argument to the effect that kinds can be reduced to, and possibly eliminated in favor of, collections of properties and argue that it is not conclusive. All things considered, kinds seem to hold explanatory priority over properties. (iii) In section 4, I shall address the issue of how many kinds we should posit and argue for the view that, if kinds are introduced to explain certain fundamental facts about particulars, we do not need to posit higher-order kinds but only first-order ones. (iv) In section 5, I shall finally go back to the dispute between Aristotelians and Platonists. My main contention will be that Platonism about universals invites, if not compels, us to posit more kinds than we really need. Accordingly, for reasons of ontological economy and explanatory simplicity, we should rather favor the idea that kinds are immanent in their particular instances.

2.   Two senses of 'accident' and the notion of property

I have described the contrast between kinds and properties as one between universals that express the essence of particular objects and so tell us *what* they are and universals that do not express the essence of particular objects and so tell us not what they are but *how* they are. So, membership in a kind is essential to an object, while properties are non-essential features of an object. Does this mean that properties are contingent features of particular objects or, to put it in more Aristotelian terms, attributes a thing can indifferently have and not have while remaining what it is? Not necessarily. To see this point, it may be useful to appeal to a distinction between two senses of 'accident' or 'accidental,' which Aristotle develops in his logical works and especially in the *Topics* and the *Posterior Analytics*. In the strict sense, the accidental features of an object are those that the object can indifferently have or not have while remaining what it is.[5] In this sense, 'accidents' are contingent features of an object: *being seated* or *being bent*

---

[5]   Cf. Aristotle, *Topics*, I, 5, 102b4–7; *An. Post.*, I, 4, 73b4–5.

(as a result of being seated) are standard examples of accidents of a human being in the strict sense of the term, for they are features which a human being can indifferently have or not have while remaining what he or she is. In a broader sense, however, the accidental characteristics of an object are those that fall outside its essence.[6] Clearly, properties that are accidental in the strict sense are also accidental in the broad sense, for they certainly fall outside the essence of an object. But the class of accidents in the broad sense includes also characteristics that, while falling outside the essence of an object, are not contingent, but rather necessary. According to Aristotle and his medieval followers, for instance, *being capable of learning grammar* is an accident of a human being in the broad sense of the term (but not in the strict sense): although the capacity of learning grammar belongs necessarily to human beings, it is not among the essential features of a human being, that is, among the features one would point to in response to the question as to what a human being is. Thus, the essential features of an object, such as *being a human being*, are also necessary, but not all the necessary features of an object are also essential, as the case of *being capable of learning grammar* shows. My suggestion, in brief, is that we take properties as opposed to kinds as accidents in the broad sense so as to include both properties that are simply contingent and properties that are necessary but non-essential. Let me flesh out this general idea by illustrating two natural consequences of Aristotle's intuition.

On Aristotle's account membership in a kind is essential to a particular object, while some properties, i.e. the non-contingent ones, are necessary but not essential to the object that has them. How do we distinguish between features of an object that are simply necessary and those that, in addition to being necessary, are also essential? Clearly, not on purely extensional grounds, because, for Aristotle, *being a human being* and *being capable of learning grammar* are not only coextensive, but necessarily coextensive. Thus, some extra criterion must be introduced to distinguish kinds or kind-generated features from necessary properties. It seems that Aristotle's favorite criterion is centered on the notion of *explanation*.[7] It is membership in a kind that explains why objects have a set of necessary properties and not the other way round. It is not because an object is capable of learning grammar that it is a human being, but it is rather because

---

[6] Cf. Aristotle, *Topics*, I, 5, 102a18–20; *An. Post.*, I, 6, 75a18–22.

[7] On this see Kung (1977) and also Brody (1972) and (1973). For a contemporary endorsement of this approach see Koslicki (2012). On Aristotle's notion of essence in general see: Cohen (1978); Kung (1977); F. Lewis (1984); Code (1986); Wedin (1984); Matthews (1990); Charles (2000).

it is a human being that it is also capable of learning grammar.[8] In the *Posterior Analytics* Aristotle seems to be prepared to extend this account to mathematical objects as well. $2R$ (the property of having the sum of the internal angles equal to two right angles) is a necessary property of triangles. However, triangles are not triangles because they have the property $2R$. It is rather the case, according to Aristotle, that triangles have the property $2R$ because they are triangles, that is, because they belong to the kind *triangle*. Thus, the general idea is that membership in a kind explains why an object possesses a set of necessary properties and not the other way round.[9] One way in which Aristotle makes this point is by saying that necessary properties somehow 'flow from' the essence of the kind, by which I guess Aristotle means that they are *implied* by the essence of the kind: by reasoning about the kind to which an individual belongs, by reasoning for instance about the full definition of the kind an individual belongs to, we could in principle deduce the necessary properties that follow upon the kind in question. It is important to stress that the notion of explanation that is at stake here should be taken as an ontological notion giving content to the relationships between different universal entities and not as a merely epistemic one. We are not interested here in understanding whether our apprehension of a certain kind is prior or posterior to our apprehension of certain properties, but rather in the relation of ontological priority and dependence between

---

[8] I think my intuition here about explanation is close to the one defended in Brody (1972) with the only difference that I wish to extend the model of explanation Brody presents so as to include not only scientific but also metaphysical explanation.

[9] Someone may be worried by the fact that, on this account, *being a human being* and *being capable of learning grammar* (or *being a triangle* and having the property $2R$) turn out to be modally equivalent *de re* features of a human being (of a triangle) in terms of possible worlds, in that they both belong to human beings (to triangles) in all possible worlds. *Being a human being* and *being capable of learning grammar* (as much as *being a triangle* and having the property $2R$) are not only coextensional but necessary coextensional features. I do not take this fact alone to provide good reasons either for rejecting the distinction between kinds and necessary properties or for thinking that the possible worlds framework is inadequate to capture our intuition about ascription of properties. This alternative would be forced upon those who take the possible worlds framework (whether in the realist or in the ersatzist version) to be in some sense prior to the things' possession of the *de re* properties and hence to provide an explanation of or some kind of foundation for our modal discourse. On the contrary, I take the possible worlds framework to furnish only a partial clarification of our main intuitions about property ascriptions and so not to be prior to the things' possession of *de re* properties. On this view, it is not surprising that the difference between essential and necessary features of an object be not captured by the possible worlds framework, as the framework only records which properties are had in which worlds and is not sensitive to why such properties are had. Neither should it worry too much that the framework may be in need of some integrative criteria to capture distinctions that cannot be formulated from within the framework. For a different view, according to which the possible worlds framework should be taken to ground the *de re* properties of things, and a criticism of Aristotelian essentialism, see Paul (2006b). For some interesting observations about the limit of the modal approach to essentialism see Fine (1994a). See also Fine (1989), (1994b), (1995); Chapter 1 of Oderberg (2007).

different types of universals. Nothing prevents us from saying that, at an epistemic level, knowledge of certain properties may help us to identify a kind and fix its extension. The fact remains, however, that kinds remain ontologically prior to the properties that follow upon them.

Another, related feature of Aristotle's account is that certain properties are associated with certain kinds or, to put things differently, a certain kind brings along with it a certain group of properties. Since there are some (secondary) aspects of this idea which I wish to drop, it may be better to spell out in some detail what it consists in. In the logical works and especially in the *Categories*, Aristotle believes that, besides belonging to a fully determinate specific kind, an object, i.e. a substance, also belongs to many higher-order, generic kinds which are structured in some sort of ascending order of generality.[10] A human being, for instance, besides belonging to the specific kind *human being*, also belongs to a series of hierarchically ordered generic kinds, such as *animal, living being, bodily substance*, and so on up to the highest kind *substance*. Each of the kinds in the hierarchy has associated with it a set or group of necessary properties. Thus, there will be properties that a human being will possess in virtue of being a human being, others that he or she will possess in virtue of being an animal and so on and so forth. A certain group of properties, in other words, is characteristic of or necessarily characterizes a certain kind.[11] Aristotle is of the opinion that the properties that characterize a certain kind in the hierarchy get transmitted to all the kinds occupying a lower level in the hierarchy: if the property *being capable of motion* is necessarily associated with or characterizes the kind *animal* it will also be a necessary property of all the lower-order kinds as well as of the members of such kinds, e.g. human beings, horses, mice, etc. However, it would be wrong to say that the properties in question characterize the lower-order kinds in the same way as they characterize a certain higher-order kind. Aristotle standardly illustrates this point by means of a geometrical example.[12] The example is in itself problematic but it helps at least to give us an intuitive idea of what Aristotle may have in mind. The property *2R* belongs necessarily to all kinds of triangle, for instance to equilateral triangles as well as to isosceles triangles. However, it is not in virtue of being an isosceles triangle or an equilateral triangle, but simply in virtue of being a triangle, that something

---

[10] This is a view which Aristotle came to abandon in the *Metaphysics*.

[11] For the use of 'characterization' to indicate the relation between kinds and universal properties see Lowe (2006). For a discussion of the relationship between kinds and properties see Lowe (2006: Ch. 4).

[12] Cf. *Aristotle, Post. Anal.*, i, 4, 73b38–74a3.

has the property $2R$. Thus, even if the property $2R$ is a necessary property of all triangles, it characterizes only the kind *triangle* and not the sub-kinds *isosceles triangle* and *equilateral triangle* (if the relation between *triangle* and *isosceles triangle* or *equilateral triangle* can indeed be understood in terms of kind and sub-kinds). Aristotle says that $2R$ belongs *primarily* to the kind *triangle* and only secondarily or derivatively to the sub-kinds *isosceles triangle* and *equilateral triangle* – which is, I suggest, some analogue of my talk of a property's being characteristic of or characterizing a certain kind.

Whether we accept or not Aristotle's complex hierarchy of both kinds and properties, we may still be willing to retain the general idea that some properties are necessarily associated with or characterize certain kinds. But what does it mean, exactly, to be associated with or to characterize? There are at least two different readings of such relationships. Both readings agree in maintaining, to use Lowe's terminology, that the kinds and the properties that characterize them are mutually dependent for their existence. A certain kind could not be instantiated by an object unless the properties associated with it were also instantiated by that object; nor could the properties be instantiated by an object unless the kind were instantiated as well. The two readings, however, part company with respect to the relation of identity dependence between kinds and properties. According to one view, kinds depend for their identity on the properties that characterize them. On this reading, which kind we are talking about depends on which properties are necessarily associated with it.[13] Although this may well be a reasonable view to take, it is certainly not the only possible view, and certainly not the one that Aristotle takes. For him to make the identity of a certain kind depend on which properties are necessarily associated with it would be to reverse the order of explanation between kinds and properties.[14] Kinds are *not* the kinds they are because they have certain properties associated with them; rather, they have certain properties associated with them because they are the kinds they are. This seems to suggest that the identity of kinds is independent of, and prior to, the properties that are necessarily associated with them. Presumably, Aristotle thinks that the defining features of a certain kind, i.e. the essential features that fall within the definition of the kind and so constitute its identity, are distinct from and explanatorily prior to the necessary, but non-essential properties that are associated with the kind. Such non-essential but necessary properties are somehow implied by the definition that spells out the essence of the kind. Since I want to

---

[13] This is the view in Lowe (2006).   [14] See again Brody (1973).

make much in the following of the notion of explanation, I prefer to take the second and more Aristotelian line and hence to explore the possibility of making the identity of a kind independent of the properties that are necessarily associated with it.

3. Why posit kinds in the first place?

Kinds are usually credited with providing a unified account of a series of phenomena concerning particular objects. Although I am not particularly interested in going into such well-known aspects of kinds theories, it may be useful to recall them in a few words.[15] (i) First of all, kinds are supposed to furnish both synchronic and diachronic criteria of *identity* for particular objects (John Locke was probably the first philosopher to draw attention to this aspect of our talking of kinds, species, or sortals). The basic insight here is that, from the synchronic point of view, we count particular objects on the basis of the kinds they belong to (with the result that there cannot be more than one object of a certain kind in one place at a time). As to the diachronic perspective, moreover, we can reasonably say that an object at t_1 is the same as an object at t_2 if it belongs to the same kind K and exhibits the sort of continuity that is required by the fact that it belongs to the kind K (so the kind K determines which changes an object can undergo without ceasing to be a member of K). (ii) Second, kinds are useful in handling the question of *individuation*. For kinds theorists, it is a fact about the world that instances of kinds, or, to be more precise, instances of genuine kinds, are individual objects provided with fixed ontological boundaries. In some sense, therefore, things are individual because they are instances of kinds.[16] Clearly, the 'because' here does not amount to strict explanation, for another legitimate way of phrasing the above claim would be to say that the individuation of substances, i.e. of instances of kinds, is primitive.[17] However, talking about membership in a kind helps us at least to give some content to the idea that the reason why substances are individual should not be sought for outside the fact that they are the kind of things they are. The same thought can be expressed by having recourse once again to principles for counting. The idea is that in virtue of falling under or belonging to its proper kind a particular object is marked out as countably distinct not only from the things of other kinds but also from

[15] For more on such issues see Lowe (1989) and (2009); Wiggins (1980) and (2001). For a defense of kinds that centers on mereology and restricted composition see Koslicki (2008: 200–34). Unfortunately, a consideration of mereological issues far exceeds the scope of this chapter.
[16] Cf. Loux (2006b: 102–17).   [17] Cf. Lowe (2005).

other things of the same kind. (iii) Finally, similar considerations could be applied to the problem of the *unity* of particular objects. It is an undeniable fact – kinds theorists insist – that some particular objects have a privileged degree of internal unity and cohesion. In this case as well, talking about membership in a kind may help to flesh out this general idea: instances of genuine kinds are things provided with a privileged type of unity and internal cohesion. It can be noted, incidentally, that considerations about the unity of particular objects can act also as determinants in our decision over which genuine kinds there are. We may decide, for instance, that no genuine kinds correspond to objects that do not display a sufficiently high degree of unity, even though, of course, determining what 'sufficiently' exactly means can turn out to be rather difficult in practice. This line of argument will naturally lead up to restricting genuine kinds to kinds of natural things or possibly living beings alone. For only natural objects or, possibly, only living beings – it can be argued – possess the required degree of unity and so only the kinds under which natural objects or living beings fall should be regarded as genuine kinds. Even though each of the three theoretical advantages of kinds theories is open to dispute, it cannot be easily denied that, all things considered, the introduction of kinds seems to provide a unified answer to several questions (identity, individuation, and unity) concerning the nature of sensible objects.

So, one natural rejoinder to the question 'Why posit kinds?' could simply be: 'Why not?' Opponents of the existence of kinds would typically say that kinds are dispensable: we can explain all the facts we want to explain without having recourse to a separate category of universals, distinct in character from the properties observed in ordinary experience or in scientific inquiry. These philosophers may well also concede that our ordinary talk of kinds of objects, kinds of stuff etc. is not arbitrary and that kinds outline the objective joints of reality. Still, they will insist that in order to explain our ordinary talk of kinds we do not need to introduce a separate category of universals, over and above the observable properties of particular objects. Since this general strategy to eliminate kinds needs some important refinement I shall take it as the starting point of my discussion and briefly examine the strong case that David Armstrong has made against the existence of kinds in his important book *A World of States of Affairs*.[18]

---

[18] In principle, we could and perhaps should distinguish between a reductionist and an eliminativist strategy. If kinds are reduced to something else, for instance conjunctions of necessary properties, sentences about kinds are true but can be paraphrased away as sentences about conjunctions of properties. Hence such sentences do not introduce a separate category of entities, but are still true. On an eliminativist strategy, by contrast, sentences about kinds talk about things that simply do not

One thing that is not sufficiently noticed is that Armstrong has two separate arguments against kinds: (i) one is directed against the existence of kinds of Aristotle-style substances, i.e. ordinary middle-size particular objects, while (ii) the second is an argument against the existence even of kinds of subatomic particles such as electrons. As a matter of fact, only the second argument can be taken as a genuine argument against the very distinction between kinds and properties, while all the first argument shows, if successful, is the dispensability of the kinds of middle-size particular objects without providing evidence against the existence of kinds of smaller-sized objects.

(i) In his argument against kinds of ordinary objects and in particular of living beings, Armstrong observes: 'Using once again the powerful truism that a universal must be strictly identical in each instance, it seems that there is no biological structure that will serve as the universal required' (Armstrong 1997b: 66), i.e., the universal *human being* existing identically in all human beings. Armstrong concedes that the genetic structure of the human DNA is what comes closest to an identical structure existing in all human beings and that there probably is a sufficiently abstract description that singles out the sufficient and necessary characteristics of the human DNA. However, we should posit in reality a universal (a very complex one) answering to such a description only if the universal in question could play a causal and nomological role in explaining the typical behavior of human beings. And – Armstrong thinks – no such role can be played by the universal *human being*, even biologically interpreted, for 'the causal work in producing and maintaining a human being is surely done by constituent molecules, and more complex structures, that act in virtue of their determinate properties' (Armstrong 1997b: 66). As the last quotation shows, Armstrong's argument displays the rather reductionist flavor of his scientific realism. The central idea is that the basic entities, the building blocks of the world, are the basic particles that are studied by modern physics. All the other entities, from simple atomic structures to complex living beings, can be somehow constructed out of

---

exist and so are, strictly speaking, either false or meaningless or devoid of truth-value, depending on the stance on takes on sentences introducing non-existent objects. It seems clear to me that Armstrong's perspective is reductionist: he clearly says that kinds make objective joints in reality thereby implying that sentences about kinds, when appropriately reinterpreted, turn out to be true. Since Armstrong, however, does not explicitly distinguish between the two strategies, I shall follow him in talking indifferently of reducing kinds to or eliminating them in favor of something else. After all, to reduce one *category* of things to another can be taken as a way of eliminating the category we wish to reduce. For a more sympathetic analysis of Armstrong's argument (and a criticism of the claim that kinds are fundamental) see Bird (2012).

the basic building blocks. Accordingly, all genuine, first-order universals are simple properties of basic particles (complex properties being analyzed in terms of states-of-affairs types) and relations among them. Thus, Armstrong's first argument is more a clear restatement of his physicalist and reductionist convictions than an argument against the very distinction between kinds and properties. The argument could be countered simply by rejecting Armstrong's *bottom-up* and reductionist explanation of the structure of familiar objects (especially living beings) and endorsing, instead, what Loux has called a *top-down* explanation, according to which the physical constitution of (at least) living beings is determined by the kind they belong to.[19] But, even if the argument is accepted as it stands, nothing of what Armstrong says prevents us from positing kinds for the elementary particles of physics in addition to their properties. For, as I said before, a theory of kinds is, at least at the beginning, neutral with respect to the size of the objects belonging to the different kinds.

(ii) As a matter of fact, Armstrong presents a second argument, which may be taken to be a general argument against the very distinction between kinds and properties. Armstrong explores the possibility that we should introduce kinds not for ordinary middle-size objects but for the particles that are studied by modern physics, the particulars, in other words, which he himself takes to be basic and fundamental. The hypothesis, therefore, is that besides the properties all electrons share we may consider introducing the kind *electron* (or *electronhood*, as Armstrong puts it), the universal indicating the kind of thing that possesses the characteristic properties of electrons. Armstrong rejects this hypothesis and insists that a reductive account can be provided also for the kinds of physical particles. On this account, the kind *electron* can be reduced to and hence should be identified with the conjunction of the fundamental properties of electrons. All there is to being an electron, for instance, is the possession of mass, charge, and spin, which are literally identical in all electrons. Therefore, the kind *electron* can be reduced to and identified with the conjunction of such three properties. By way of conclusion, Armstrong insists that there are, of course, different kinds of thing and that kinds make objective and fundamental joints in nature. All that he denies, however, is that we need to introduce 'an independent and irreducible category of universal,' i.e. kinds, to explain such objective joints.[20]

---

[19]   Cf. Loux (2006a).

[20]   Armstrong's formulation leaves open the possibility for someone to say that kinds exist but not as an independent and irreducible category of universal. Armstrong himself in fact dubitatively

It seems to me that Armstrong is here advancing some sort of dispensability argument, which is probably best understood as some 'scientific realism' version of Ockham's razor. The assumption underlying the reduction of the kind *electron* to a conjunction of the electrons' fundamental properties must be that we can explain the typical behavior of an electron and its standard causal interactions by having recourse only to its scientifically observable properties and nothing else. The first, preliminary thing to observe is that, although Armstrong focuses on his favorite candidates for kinds, i.e. the kinds of elementary particles, his argument is in fact quite general. If successful, the argument shows that all sorts of kinds we may be prepared to accept can be in fact dispensed with, provided that we come up with the right conjunction of characteristic properties. Armstrong's point, in other words, is that kinds are nothing other than conjunctions, clusters, or groupings of fundamental properties. Admittedly, the case of the kind *electron* is particularly favorable, because electrons, as Armstrong himself points out, have very few fundamental properties. But, in principle, nothing prevents one from regarding even more complex kinds as constructions out of fundamental properties, provided that one is able to come up with the right group of properties, the smallest group of properties that explain the phenomena one wishes to explain. Thus, even if I shall mainly concentrate on Armstrong's favorite choice of examples, my reply should be taken as general as Armstrong's point.

How react to the dispensability argument? To put things into perspective, let me say, first of all, that Armstrong's basic assumption, i.e. that the typical behavior of an electron and its standard causal interactions can be explained by having recourse only to its scientifically observable properties and nothing else, is not at all incompatible with the acceptance of kinds as a separate category of entities. For if there are kinds, one would naturally expect, given the account of kinds I gave in the previous section, that in

suggests that the existence of kinds may be understood in terms of supervenience (defined as follows: entity Q supervenes upon entity P iff it is impossible that P should exist and Q not exist, if P is possible, i.e. in terms of possible worlds, iff there are P-worlds and all P-worlds are also Q-worlds). Given all the states of affairs (where these are conceived of as containing particulars, their properties, and relations), all the kinds that there are supervene. On this account, kinds will not be completely eliminated from the ontology, but only thought not to constitute a separate and independent category of entity. I prefer to leave out of my consideration the supervenience version of Armstrong's argument, for it is not clear to me whether things that supervene according to Armstrong's definition can be said to exist in the same sense as the entities on which they supervene. Since I wish to avoid, if possible, talk of primary as opposed to secondary ways/senses of existing/'existing' I shall confine myself to criticizing Armstrong's dispensability argument. Possibly, the notion of supervenience is supposed to give content to a more clearly reductionist analysis of kinds (as opposed to an eliminativist one) according to which kinds somehow exist, but truths about kinds can be analyzed away as truths about something else.

some sense the typical behavior of an object and the causal interactions it enters into are completely explained by its properties. For we have seen that, according to kinds theorists, a certain kind brings along with it a set of necessary properties. Typically, such necessary properties will be dispositions, powers, and capacities, i.e. properties that are perfectly suited to enter into causal interactions. Thus, if all we mean by 'explanation' is 'explanation of typical behavior and causal interaction,' it is in a sense reasonable to suggest that properties explain all that we need to explain. Defenders of kinds, however, think that explanation can be pushed a step further. Can we explain why electrons have their fundamental properties or do we have to think that once we have reached the fundamental properties of electrons explanation should end? Armstrong holds that explanation should end because, once we have the fundamental properties of electrons we can provide a complete explanation of their causal behavior as well as their role in physical laws. Kinds theorists, by contrast, think that electrons have the fundamental properties they do because they are the kind of things they are. Here, clearly, intuitions fundamentally diverge.

One common strategy to defend kinds consists in weakening the sense in which the properties associated with a kind are necessary by distinguishing between physical and metaphysical necessity.[21] Electrons have necessarily the properties *mass*, *charge*, and *spin* as a result of the physical laws governing the actual world. But it is possible for there to be physical laws different from the ones governing the actual world. There are, in other words, possible worlds where different physical laws obtain. Physical laws, therefore, are not metaphysically necessary. Thus, there are possible worlds (the worlds where different physical laws obtain) where there are electrons lacking some or all of the properties that are associated with them in our world and in all possible worlds where the same physical laws hold as in our world. In such worlds what makes electrons electrons cannot be the possession of the properties that are associated with them in our and similar worlds. Therefore, the possession of such properties cannot be what makes electrons electrons in this world, either.

Since this line of argument, which also touches upon the semantics of natural kinds terms, has been and is still being disputed, I would rather have an argument in favor of kinds that does not commit one to the view that physical laws are metaphysically contingent, even if, of course, their contingency could be independently argued.[22] What is required, in other

---

[21] This line of argument seems to be sketched out, if I am not mistaken, in Lowe (2006: 26).

[22] The view that at least *some* laws of nature are metaphysically contingent is in many respects the traditional view. For a defense of the claim that laws of nature are metaphysically necessary see (among others) Shoemaker (1980) and (1998); Ellis (2001); Bird (2005).

words, is a way of distinguishing the kind *electron* from the properties associated with it even in the case in which *mass, charge,* and *spin* were thought to be metaphysically necessary properties of the electrons, that is, even in the case in which electrons were taken to have those properties in all possible worlds. Wherever there are electrons there is the conjunction of its three fundamental properties (*mass, charge,* and *spin*) and wherever there is such a conjunction there are electrons. Is this sufficient ground to eliminate the kind *electron*? Possibly not. For the following question can still be raised: Is it because they have mass, charge, and the absolute value of spin that things are electrons? Or do they have the mass, charge, and spin they do because they are electrons?

One line of argument in favor of the second alternative could be the following. We agree that electrons have, necessarily, the properties *mass, charge,* and *spin.* But *what* has these properties? It seems that there are just three alternatives: (1) a bundle of properties; (2) a bare particular; (3) a thing already falling under a certain kind. It can be shown that (1) and (2) will not do and hence we should prefer (3). (1) is not an option that Armstrong himself favors, but it may be useful, nonetheless, to see why it fails. The hypothesis here is that an electron is a bundle of the properties *mass, charge,* and *spin* and *no other property.* Since we are realists we also believe that each of these properties is a universal, i.e. an entity which can exist as identical in all the electrons. If this is the case, however, we will not be in a position to explain what makes two different electrons different; we will not be able, in other words, to explain how there are many distinct electrons. For each electron will be nothing but a bundle of the three *universal* properties and hence all electrons will be made of numerically the same universal constituents and nothing else. Thus, in option (1), there will be nothing that distinguishes one electron from another and, what is more, there seems to be nothing that could possibly do so. As can be seen, I am simply echoing here a familiar worry about the principle of the Identity of Indiscernibles. The principle seems to hold necessarily for universals. Thus, if particulars are just bundles of universal properties, it seems that particulars having as their constituents the same universal properties should be identical.[23] Since, by contrast, there seem to be – or at least there could be – distinct particulars sharing all their properties, particulars cannot just be bundles of universal properties. If (1) fails, *mass, charge,* and *spin* will not be the properties constituting a bundle, but rather the properties of *something,* of something, in other words, having such properties, as it were, conjunctively.

---

[23] For the claim that the bundle theory is compatible with the falsity of the Principle of Indiscernibles see Rodriguez-Pereyra (2004). For an overview of the debate on the principle see Forrest (2010).

If we do not want option (3), i.e. if the something that has the properties is not a thing already falling under a certain kind, we seem to be left with endorsing option (2), i.e. the view that the thing that has the properties is a pure individuator, a bare particular. But if this is the case, it is difficult to make sense of the view that mass, charge, and spin are the necessary properties of something. For, clearly, there is no necessary connection, but only a contingent one, between the bare particular and the properties it has. For it seems to be built into the notion of a bare particular that it does not have any of the properties that it bears necessarily, but only contingently. Thus, a bare particular cannot be necessarily associated with any of the properties that it has. It might be said, in response to this argument, that the thing with which the relevant properties are necessarily associated is the thing with the properties (the 'thick particular') and not the bare particular ('thin particular').[24] It is the bare particular plus the conjunction of *mass*, *charge*, and *spin* that has mass, charge, and spin necessarily associated with it. This response, however, will not do. For one thing, if the thing with the properties contains a bare particular as one of its constituents, it can be said to have the relevant properties only in a very derivative sense. For it is the bare particular and not the object with the properties that is the literal bearer of the properties. For another thing, even if it is conceded that in some sense the object with the properties can be said to have the properties necessarily, the fact remains that such properties are necessarily connected with the object only because a contingent connection obtains between them and the bare particular. The contingent character, in other words, of the connection between the relevant properties and their literal bearer makes it difficult to attach significant sense to the view that properties such as *mass*, *charge*, and *spin* are necessary properties of the electrons. (2), therefore, seems to fail too and so the only option we seem to be left with is saying that the thing that has the relevant properties is a thing already falling under a certain kind, in the case at issue the kind *electron*. It should be noted that (3) makes the kind *prior* to the relevant properties. For the metaphysical fact that explains why a certain thing has some relevant properties necessarily is precisely the fact that such a thing falls under a certain kind. The thing's falling under a certain kind, in other words, is the metaphysical ground or explanation of its possessing certain relevant properties necessarily. If (3) is true, a thing has certain necessary properties because it belongs to or falls under a certain kind and not the other way round. I think the argument I have just sketched out can be generalized,

---

[24] For the distinction between 'thin' and 'thick' particulars see Armstrong (1997a). See also Sider (2006).

being clearly applicable to any kind of object and any series of properties necessarily possessed by the object. Thus, the conclusion must be that the thing that has the relevant properties necessarily is a thing of a certain kind, which possesses such properties in virtue of their necessary association with the kind the thing belongs to. Kinds, therefore, cannot be eliminated or reduced to conjunctions of properties.

Of course, my argument, if successful, only shows that we should posit at least *some* kinds. It does not give indications as to which kinds in fact there are, and one's decisions on this particular point may be dependent on other considerations including one's general metaphysical intuitions about what is and what is not basic, what can and what cannot be explained away. It is to such intuitions that I wish to turn now.

4.   How many kinds are there?

There are various ways in which the question proposed could be understood and, consequently, different ways in which one could try to answer it. One road is to think that some putatively good examples of first-order kinds do not count as genuine kinds after all. The general idea here is that we may be prepared to put restrictions of some sort on what should count as a genuine kind. The distinction Armstrong makes between *human being* and *electron* may indicate one possible way of achieving the restriction desired. The suggestion might be advanced, in other words, that the only genuine kinds that there are, are the kinds of fundamental physical particles. If one accepts Armstrong's physicalist argument against the existence of the kind *human being* together with my argument for the ineliminability of at least some kinds, this is precisely the kind of view one ends up with. This strategy needs an argument (and a powerful one, indeed) to show that all the properties of macroscopic objects can be fully explained by having recourse to the properties of fundamental physical particles. Since it is dubious that such an argument can in fact be provided, this strategy is likely to find the opposition of anti-reductionists, who will probably insist that reductionists take things the other way round: material constitution should be explained in terms of the kinds and fundamental properties of macroscopic objects and not vice versa. Be that as it may, the option is open of restricting kinds to microscopic objects and insisting that all other putative examples of kinds are dispensable in that either they are reducible to kinds of microscopic objects or, at most, supervene on them.

Restrictions may also go, however, in a rather different direction. One might try to urge the point that, even if there are kinds corresponding to the macroscopic objects of our everyday experience, or even if there are only kinds corresponding to macroscopic objects, not to all sorts of macroscopic object there corresponds a genuine kind. One familiar thought in this area is that only natural kinds, as opposed for instance to artificial kinds, count as genuine kinds. This line of argument can be pushed even further to maintain that, among natural kinds, only biological kinds are genuine instances of kinds.[25] Thus, living beings or organisms are the only things for which we should posit kinds. If one takes this line, some of the arguments that usually serve a reductionist strategy may turn out useful, after all, for eliminating artificial kinds. Even if the fundamental properties and the typical behavior of living beings cannot be entirely reduced to the fundamental properties of their material constituents, such a reduction can be carried out, it might be thought, in the case of artifacts. The fundamental properties of a table, of a statue, or of a computer, so the suggestion goes, can be entirely reduced to the properties of their material constituents. Thus, while we need to posit kinds for at least some natural beings (and certainly for living beings) we do not need to do so for artificial ones. The result is that, unlike natural beings in general and living beings in particular, artifacts are mere aggregates of more fundamental objects. Thus, even if terms such as 'table' or 'computer' may exhibit, superficially, the logic of sortal or kind terms, their doing so is presumably only the result of human interests and needs. It is human beings, on account of their practical needs or artistic concerns, that need to treat artifacts as if they were unitary objects, even if they are not so in reality. At the end of the day, it is just our mind that somehow construes aggregates as unitary objects (a thought that, I think, Leibniz may have liked). This strategy for eliminating artifacts from the number of things for which we need to posit kinds may be usefully coupled with considerations about the unity of natural and artificial objects, respectively. After all, one of the reasons why we may think that kinds of artifacts are not genuine kinds is that such objects do not exhibit the sort of unity the explanation of which compels us to posit kinds. The unity of natural objects in general and of living beings in particular is a per se unity, i.e. a form of unity which cannot be explained as the combination or clustering of more fundamental objects: try as we may, we will never obtain the kind of unity characteristic of natural objects simply by putting together fundamental objects and gluing them up with some kind of relational tie, nexus, or superimposed structure. The unity of artifacts, by contrast, is, to use Aristotelian jargon, an accidental unity, a unity that can in principle be

---

[25] For a classic study of the ontological status of both living things and artifacts see van Inwagen (1990).

explained in terms of the artifacts' material constituents plus some kind of tie, nexus or superimposed structure which glue them up. In *Metaphysics* Z 17, for instance, Aristotle observes that we should restrict substances, i.e. per se existing objects, to things that are natural unities, where the prominent, if not the only examples of natural unities are living beings.[26] I do not think that what Aristotle means is that artifacts do not exist at all, but part of his view must be at least that artifacts are not genuinely per se objects because they lack the required degree of unity and are in some sense reducible to their material constituents plus some kind of connecting tie. No such reduction, on the contrary, is available for living things. One consequence of this view is or may reasonably thought to be that only the kinds of natural objects or, possibly, living beings, are genuine instances of kind.

Restrictions on what counts as a genuine kind are also mandatory if we want to preserve some of the advantages of kinds theories I have alluded to in section 3. I said there, for instance, that for kinds theorists, it is a fact about the world that instances of kinds, or to be more precise, instances of genuine kinds, are individual objects provided with fixed ontological boundaries. I also said, somehow equivalently, that in virtue of falling under or belonging to its proper kind a particular object is marked out as countably distinct not only from the things of other kinds but also from the things of the same kind. It is clear, however, that this is not true of all the putative examples of kind. Some count names, for instance, do not provide appropriate principles for counting and individuating. Terms like 'wave,' 'cloud,' or 'flame' are good examples of count names that do not provide principles for counting and individuating (even if things may come in degree when it comes to counting and individuating). If *wave* and *cloud*, therefore, are genuine kinds, it is simply not true that in virtue of falling under or belonging to its proper kind a particular object is marked out as countably distinct not only from the things of other kinds but also from the things of the same kind.[27] These considerations may incline one to restrict kinds to those under which ordinary particular objects fall, to kinds, in other words, that are accompanied by the appropriate principles for individuating and counting. If we have independent reasons (like the ones I have illustrated in the previous paragraph) for not believing in kinds of artifacts, considerations about principles for counting may induce

---

[26] Cf. Aristotle, *Metaphysics* VII. 17, 1041b27–31.
[27] For these themes see again van Inwagen (1990: 81–97). For other problematic examples see Wiggins (1980: 73) and (2001: 75), who calls attention to the case of homeomerous substances (e.g. *crown*), which seem to have clear identity criteria but do not provide as clear principles for counting.

us to posit, once again, kinds only for natural objects or, possibly, living things. Of course, opinions as to which restrictions on the notion of kind should be introduced may differ a good deal, but the general idea should be retained that we should be prepared to distinguish between *genuine* and *non-genuine* kinds and that biological kinds qualify as good candidates for being genuine kinds.[28]

There is another sense, however, we could give to the question 'How many kinds there are?' A particular human being belongs to the lowest-level natural kind *human being*. By being a human being, however, he or she is also an animal, a living thing, and a substance. Analogously, the red rose in my garden I am looking at right now belongs to the lowest-level kind *rose*. By being a rose, however, it is also a flower, a living being, and a substance. Thus, one might reasonably ask whether we should posit, in addition to lowest-level kinds such as *human being* or *rose*, a series of hierarchically ordered higher-order natural kinds such as *animal, living being*, or *substance*. My view is that there are good reasons to think that we should do without higher-order natural kinds and so go for the claim that for each substance there is only one natural kind it belongs to. The most important motivations for taking this view are reasons of ontological parsimony and explanatory simplicity: all that can be explained by positing a hierarchy of higher-order kinds can be explained simply by positing just one lowest-level kind for each substance. By being a human being, a particular object is also an animal, a living thing, and a substance. For being an animal, a living thing, and a substance is what being a human being (partly) consists in. So there is little reason to suppose that some

---

[28] It is sometimes thought that the defense of natural kinds is made hard by some of our most recent scientific discoveries or by the possibilities of our advanced genetic technologies. Examples of crossbreeding as well as those of genetic modifications call into question one of the fundamental assumptions of the theory of natural kinds, namely that the boundaries between one species and another are in all cases well-defined and stable. Zoology and genetics, it is urged, clearly show that such boundaries are in some cases not so clearly defined as the theory of natural kinds might wish. Although I do not want to go into these matters here, it should be recalled that theories of natural kinds are not without answers to these observations. The most important is that the commitment to natural kinds is the commitment to there being in nature some objective lines of demarcation between different kinds of things. Although we may have some pre-scientific intuitions about how such lines of demarcation should be drawn, a belief in natural kinds is not incompatible with our discovery that some of the lines should be redrawn or drawn differently from how we thought they should be drawn in the first place. After all, a good number of our pre-scientific intuitions about which natural kinds there are have not been completely superseded, as yet. In any event, although I have some sympathies for the advocates of natural kinds, I shall not pursue this topic any longer here. After all, decisions over what kind of first- or lowest-level universals there are depend, as I have tried to show, on one's reductionist or anti-reductionist intuitions concerning various kinds of objects and may also depend on some *a posteriori* scientific discoveries.

particular object is an animal, a living being, and a substance because it belongs to kinds distinct from the kind *human being*.

Before fleshing out the details of the strategy I am endorsing here, I wish to clarify how my appeal to 'reasons of ontological parsimony and explanatory simplicity' should be understood here. There are mainly two issues here. First of all, one natural objection is that my argument is only *conditional*: if we think that universals should be introduced to explain the fundamental characters of particular objects then we do not need higher-order kinds. For all that can be explained by introducing higher-order kinds can also be explained by introducing only minimally universal kinds. As it stands, however, the argument does not give any independent justification for believing that universals should be introduced to explain the fundamental characters of particular objects and for no other reason.[29] Although I think that such justification can be and has been provided,[30] my intent in this chapter is not to argue in favor of a character-based approach to universals. My point is rather that, since Platonists and Aristotelians fundamentally diverge in their approach to universals, they should also be at variance insofar as the existence of higher-order kinds is concerned. The details of why this is so will be given in the next section, but the general point remains that philosophers who share a character-based approach to universals may find in my considerations a further motivation to go Aristotelian about universals. Second, it might be objected to me that in section 3 I have rejected Armstrong's appeal to ontological parsimony in his attempt at eliminating kinds in favor of scientifically observable properties. In response to this, I will simply say that, in the case of Armstrong's argument, ontological parsimony was introduced to reduce one fundamental category of objects (kinds) to another (properties) and so cut down the number of ontologically fundamental categories, while what I am suggesting is just that we use the criterion of ontological parsimony and explanatory simplicity to reduce the number of entities within one and the same ontological category. While this move of mine can, of course, be regarded as dubious, it is not the same kind of move as Armstrong's.

A couple of historical examples may illustrate in more detail the sort of general strategy I am inclined to endorse. As is known, Aristotle in the *Categories* seems to think that in order to explain the fundamental characters of natural substances we must posit a hierarchy of kinds, which are related to each other as the less general to the more general up to the highest

---

[29] I wish to thank an anonymous referee for pointing to the problematic aspects of my argument and so allowing me to clarify this crucial point.
[30] See Loux (2007b) and Chapter 1 in this volume.

kind *substance*. Among the reasons why Aristotle takes this view in the *Categories* there must have been a certain understanding of realism about universals. Individuals belonging to different kinds have characteristics in common, for instance their being all animals or their all being substances, which exceed the boundaries of the lowest species they belong to. Thus – Aristotle must have thought – such cases of attribute agreement can be explained only by supposing that particulars of different species, besides belonging to their lowest species, also belong to higher-order kinds somehow distinct from lowest species. In the *Metaphysics*, however, Aristotle came to reconsider his view in favor of the more parsimonious one that the only real kinds that there are are the lowest kinds to which particular substances belong. In all likelihood, in the *Metaphysics* Aristotle also reconsidered his former view that membership in a lowest-level kind is a primitive fact about the world, which is in no need of explanation.[31] In the new setting, the membership of particular objects in natural kinds can be further explained by the fact that they possess a principle of structure and internal organization, their form, which explains why they belong to the kind they belong to. Forms have a direct connection with kinds the membership in which they explain: all the individuals belonging to a certain kind share one and the same form, one and the same constituent or principle of structure, which is made different by existing in different parcels of matter. Although the notion of form will be of some usefulness to us for understanding my second historical example, I am more interested here in Aristotle's motivations for doing away with higher-order kinds. Aristotle seems to think that our talk of higher-order kinds, the different genera to which particular substances belong, is just the result of our *conceptual* decomposition of the different lowest-level species.[32] If we consider the various powers, dispositions, and capacities that characterize the different particular substances, we shall see that some of them are common to substances belonging to different lowest-level kinds, while some others are shared only by individuals belonging to the same lowest-level kind. This, however, does not imply that the powers, dispositions, and capacities that are common to individuals belonging to different lowest-level kinds must be explained by positing higher-level kinds. The powers, dispositions, and capacities that are shared by individuals belonging to different species are entirely explained by their belonging to the lowest-level kinds or species

---

[31] For a full exploration of this theme in Aristotle see Driscoll (1981), Code (1984), Loux (1991), and Galluzzo (2013). See Loux (2006b) for an attempt at bringing out all the philosophical consequences of Aristotle's new approach.

[32] Cf. Aristotle, *Metaphysics*, VII, 12.

they belong to: a human being is a living being in virtue of being a human being and a rose is a living being in virtue of being a rose and there is nothing more to say. Thus, Aristotle seems to think that, in a hierarchical order, the more complex brings along it all the characters of the less complex and so we do not really need to posit higher-order kinds to explain why the most complex living things also possess characteristics that are possessed by less complex living things (why for instance a human being and a frog are both animals or a human being and a flower are both living beings). Possibly, behind Aristotle's position there is also the conviction that realism about universals should not be pushed to the extreme. It is certainly true that a rose and a human being are both living things but the kind of life they have is entirely different in the one case and in the other. Thus, to think that there is a common higher-genus which both human beings and roses belong to may seem to be not entirely justified, after all. Clearly, however, Aristotle does not think that the reasoning that can be applied to the relationship between species and higher-order kinds can be also applied to the relationship between the different individuals of a certain species and the common species they belong to. Even though it may be true in some sense that the different human beings are human beings in different ways, they do not differ in the way in which they are human beings. Another way of phrasing this point is to say that differences between one individual and another are material as opposed to formal differences: they are differences that fall outside the nature of the kind and so are in some sense accidental to it. While horses and humans differ, according to Aristotle, as animals, Socrates and Plato do not differ as human beings. This view implies, incidentally, that also differences of race and gender are not differences of kind: human beings differ in gender or race, but such a difference does not concern what they essentially are.[33] For people of different gender or different race do not differ in the way they are human beings.

The second historical example I wish to mention is the medieval debate over the unicity versus multiplicity of substantial forms. As we have seen, forms are not kinds, but rather the constituents or internal principles of natural things that explain their membership in a certain kind. However, some (even if not all) of the arguments against positing more than one substantial form in each substance can also be used to argue that we should not posit more than one kind for each substance and so are in keeping with the general strategy I am here endorsing. Pluralists about substantial forms maintain that to each level (or, at least, to many levels) of substantiality we

---

[33] Cf. Aristotle, *Metaphysics*, X, 9.

detect in a sensible substance there corresponds a different substantial form in the substance itself. For instance: a human being is also an animal and a living being. Pluralists maintain that these three characters of a human being, i.e. being a human being, being an animal, and being a living thing, must be explained by positing three distinct constituents, the form corresponding to being a human being (e.g. the rational soul), the form corresponding to being an animal (e.g. the sensitive soul, that is, the form characteristic of animals), and the form corresponding to being a living being (e.g. the vegetative soul, that is, the form characteristic of living beings). Thomas Aquinas, a staunch defender of the unicity of substantial form, leveled several objections against the pluralist view. One in particular is of much interest to us. Aquinas contends that the form characteristic of human beings virtually contains or includes also the forms characteristic of animals in general and of living things in general. What Aquinas means is that the functions, powers, and dispositions that are conferred upon something by its having the form of human being also include all the characteristics that we associate with higher-level forms such as the form of animals in general and the form of living things in general. If something is a human being, it will also have, by the only fact of being a human being, all the characteristics common to all animals as well as those common to all living beings, in addition of course to the characteristics which mark it out as a human being. Thus, we do not need to posit substantial forms other than the form of human being in order to explain why human beings have many characteristics in common with other animals or with other living things. Clearly, Aquinas' reasoning can also be applied to the case of kinds. If *human being* and *rose* are genuine natural kinds, we do not need to posit one extra natural kind, say *living being*, to explain why both roses and human beings are living beings. For roses are living beings only in virtue of being roses and human beings are living beings only in virtue of being human beings. In conclusion, for the Aristotle of the *Metaphysics* and for Thomas Aquinas, higher-order kinds are accorded no real existence outside the mind but only a conceptual role in unpacking the concept of first-order universals: the reason is that we can and so should do without them in the explanation of the phenomena for which we posit universals in the first place. My suggestion is that we follow their lead and share their concerns about economy of explanation. Unlike Armstrong, I think that kinds are needed to explain the fundamental characters of particular objects. Like Aristotle and Aquinas, however, I also believe that, if universals are introduced to explain the fundamental characters of particular objects, then we do not need higher-order kinds, as first-order kinds are good enough to do all the explanatory work.

5. Aristotelian and Platonist kinds

One interesting question in this connection is whether the elimination of higher-order kinds forces us to be Aristotelian about universals (i.e. to take universals to be immanent in particulars) and, conversely, whether the acceptance of higher-order kinds compels us to be Platonists. Logically speaking, the elimination of higher-order kinds is independent of Aristotelianism as much as their acceptance is independent of Platonism. In the *Categories*, for instance, Aristotle takes universals to exist in their particular instances but also admits of a number of higher-order kinds of increasing generality. On the other hand, nothing prevents one from maintaining that universals are transcendent, i.e. exist apart from their particular instances, and then insisting that we should not multiply entities unduly. However, dispensing with higher-order kinds is an option that is closer to the general spirit of Aristotelian realism and, moreover, one that Platonists cannot so easily avail themselves of. For it is difficult to see which motivations Platonists could possibly give to defend their doing away with higher-order kinds. From within the Platonist metaphysics, in other words, there seems to be no particular reason to hold that first-order kinds exist while higher-order kinds do not and so Platonists seem to be committed to or at least strongly inclined towards an 'all-or-none' view about kinds. This has to do with the way Platonists formulate the existence conditions for universals and so with their typical rejection of the Principle of Instantiation. According to Aristotelians universals are existentially dependent on their particular instances. Of course, the existence of a universal does not depend on the existence of one of its instances in particular but generically on the existence of some particular or other: for the universal *human being* to exist at least some human beings must exist, even though no human being in particular. Thus, typically, our reasons for introducing universals or for doing away with some putative universals will have to do with the explanation of the characters of particular objects, their attribute agreement, their causal interaction, and so on and so forth. Within this framework, it is rather natural to reason that the facts about particular objects the explanation of which encouraged us to posit universals can in fact be explained by positing fewer universals than the language or our conceptual apparatus invite us to posit. This line of argument applies in particular to higher-order universals: in order to explain the essential characteristics of particulars for which we thought it necessary to posit kinds in the first place we just need first-order universals and nothing more. An analogous line of argument is not easily available to Platonists. For Platonists universals do not existentially depend on their particular instances: universals exist whether or not their particular instances do. Typically, Platonists reject the Principle of Instantiation: some of the universals that exist are not instantiated now and, on a stronger version of Platonism, others have never been, are not, and will never be instantiated. If this is the general structure of the theory, our reasons for maintaining that some universals exist cannot be confined to the fact that universals explain certain basic facts about particular objects. For uninstantiated universals do not explain any of such facts: if there are no human beings, the universal *human being* still exists, but its function is not that of explaining the characters of particulars that do not exist. It might be said that uninstantiated universals would explain the characters of their particular objects, if they were instantiated. But, especially in the case of universals that are never instantiated, it seems odd to say that their existence is forced upon us by the fact that they would explain the characters of their particular instances if they were instantiated. Thus, the argument that higher-order kinds can be dispensed with because positing only first-order universals will suffice to explain all the facts about particulars that we need to explain is not easily available to Platonists.

More typically, Platonists will argue for the existence of universals on the grounds that our language is unintelligible if there are not universals. I can think of two main variants of this general strategy and neither seems to me to have the resources for eliminating higher-level kinds. The first variant centers on the traditional, semantic arguments for the existence of universals. Platonists, for instance, will urge that predicates have after all some referential import insofar they *connote* (i.e. indirectly refer to) universals. Moreover, they will also insist that the phenomenon of abstract reference introduces universals directly. Is there any room within this strategy for doing away with higher-order kinds? Things may seem not so bad with predicates. For in general, realists are well prepared to put restrictions on which predicates connote genuine universals. One might say, for instance, that being an animal is part of what being a human being means and so insist that being an animal is somehow implied by being a human being. The general conclusion might be, therefore, that we do not need to introduce universals for all the predicates that are part of the meaning of other (less general) predicates. But this strategy is highly problematic. For the elimination process might as well go the other way round. If 'animal' is part of the meaning of 'human being' (on definitional grounds) then 'animal' is a primitive predicate and 'human being' a derivative one, for the meaning of 'human being' is given in terms of 'animal' and not the other way round. Thus, one might reasonably say that first-order kinds such as those picked out by 'human being' and the like, are constructions out of higher-order kinds (plus, presumably, some properties restricting higher-order universals in the appropriate way). It is not by chance that, for instance, Plato seems to have taken some similar view by insisting in his late dialogues that the more general is also the more real. Thus, if no extra-linguistic reasons are provided for eliminating higher-order kinds, it is hard to see how this could be done on the basis of the analysis of predicates. Things are even worse with abstract reference. Take the sentence 'Animality is the capacity of perceiving the external world' and suppose it to be true. Realists who advance linguistic arguments for the existence of universals usually take abstract terms like 'animality' to refer directly to universals. So, if we do not want animality in our ontology, what does 'animality' refer to? The only option I can think of is that 'animality' refers distributively to all the different first-order kinds of animals, *human being, horse,* etc. and so the reference to animality could be paraphrased away in such a way as to make the sentence talk only about first-order kinds. But if one allows for distributive reference to do the job of eliminating the reference to higher-order kinds why should one not allow for it to eliminate the reference to first-order kinds too in favor of, for instance, the individuals belonging to such kinds?[34] Admittedly, there is some work to be done here, because the relation between higher-order and first-order kinds may not be analogous in all respects to that between first-order kinds and their members. However, appeal to distributive reference is a nominalist device and we had better not accord to it much force, if we are realists.[35]

---

[34] For this solution see Sellars (1963b).

[35] Possibly, the picture of Platonism I have presented here is a rather narrow one. Platonists may be driven to posit uninstantiated universals not only on the basis of semantic considerations, but also for other reasons including for instance a certain understanding of natural laws. From this different perspective, Platonists may insist, there is room for restricting kinds to first-order ones and hence not introducing higher-order kinds. The suggestion could be advanced, for instance, that there are physical phenomena that have never occurred so far, but could occur in the future. Even if these phenomena have not occurred so far, there are many things we could say about them, their causes and their effects. Such phenomena will presumably involve kinds as well as necessary properties associated with kinds. According to Platonists, therefore, both the kinds and the associated universal properties that are required to explain possible future phenomena exist, even though they are not instantiated at the moment. Thus, the point may be urged by Platonists that, just as the explanation of present phenomena does not require higher-order universals, neither will the explanation of future or possible ones. This line of argument is promising but something more is required to bring home the main point. For I do not see any reasons of principle why the explanation of possible phenomena, as opposed to actual ones, or of future phenomena, as opposed to present and past ones, should not turn out to require higher-order kinds. Since the phenomena in question have not occurred and the universals involved are not instantiated, the possibility cannot be completely ruled out that the phenomena in question are radically different from the phenomena we have observed so far and that they require for their explanation positing higher-order universals. For more on Platonism see Hoffman and Rosenkrantz (2005).

Another variant of the Platonist strategy, which has been recently advo-
cated by van Inwagen, consists in presenting universals as *unsaturated assert-*
ibles, i.e. things that can be said (whether truly or falsely) of something.[36]
Van Inwagen distinguishes between two types of assertibles, propositions
and properties, which include, I assume, both kinds and properties in the
more specialized sense I have been using throughout the chapter. Propositions are saturated assertibles, i.e. things that can be said *full stop*, but cannot
be said *of* something. Properties, by contrast, are unsaturated assertibles,
i.e. things that can be said of something. Thus, *that Socrates is a human*
being is a proposition, i.e. something that can be said but cannot be said
of something. But I can also say *of* Socrates that he is a human being and
the thing that I can say of Socrates, his being a human being, is a property.
In general properties are introduced by unsaturated expressions such as '_
is a human being,' where '_ is a human being' is something that can be
said (whether truly or falsely) of a plurality of things, x, y, z, etc. Conceived
as assertibles, properties are typical examples of Platonist universals: they
are abstract entities and are in no sense constituents of concrete objects or
things that exist in them. Suppose now that some of the properties in this
large sense of the term are kinds. It seems clear to me that, if we conceive of
properties in general as assertibles, we are forced to endorse an 'all-or-none'
strategy with regard to the existence of kinds. For, on the view in question,
a universal is introduced on the grounds that there is a thing, x, that can be
said of another thing, y. But we can say of Socrates that he is a man, that
he is animal, that he is a material object, and so on and so forth. Therefore,
the option is not open to us to say that '_ is a man' introduces a kind,
while '_ is an animal' or '_ is a material object' do not. For the expressions
'_ is a man,' '_ is an animal,' and '_ is a material object' all pick out things
that can be said of Socrates and hence all pick out kinds conceived of as
assertibles. Thus, there is no way, within this conceptual framework, to
say that the kind *human being* exists, while the kinds *animal* and *material*
object do not. Van Inwagen himself makes it clear that conceiving properties as assertibles amounts to endorsing an abundant, as opposed to a
sparse, theory of properties. This is only to be expected because this variant
of Platonism makes little or nothing of the claim that universals should be
posited in order to explain the characters of particular objects, but rather
hinges on the assumption that universals are indispensable to explain our
thought and language. This suggests, more in general, that arguments in
favor of universals that heavily rely on considerations about language and

---

[36] Cf. van Inwagen (2006).

thought do not normally have the resources to cut down the number of universals that we need to posit.

Admittedly, one may not be interested in cutting down the number of universals. And one may not believe in kinds, for that matter. What seems to be clear to me, however, is that, if we believe in kinds and we wish to admit as many of them as facts about particulars require us to, we had better conceive of universals as immanent and bid Platonism, as it were, a kind farewell.[37]

[37] I had the chance of presenting an earlier version of this chapter on the occasion of a reading group on the problem of universals in contemporary philosophy, which I organized at the Scuola Normale Superiore of Pisa in the course of the Academic year 2009–10. I wish to warmly thank all the participants in the discussion – Giulia Felappi, Michele Ginammi, Giorgio Lando, Laura Mari, Valentina Morotti, and Giacomo Turbanti – for their precious suggestions and criticisms. Special thanks go to Giulia Felappi for reading various drafts of this chapter and making a number of valuable suggestions. My deep gratitude goes also to Mike Loux for commenting extensively on a semi-final version of the chapter (and not only for that). I am finally indebted to two anonymous referees for CUP, who made a number of interesting suggestions and helped me to improve the quality of this chapter.

CHAPTER 5

Universals in a world of particulars
John Heil

All things that exist are only particulars.

(Locke, Essay, III, iii, 6)

1. *Comme il faut* philosophy

What is the nature of properties – intrinsic properties of occupants of the spatiotemporal world? Locke regards properties as modes, 'abstract particulars.' The redness of this apple and the redness of a distinct but similarly colored apple are similar – even precisely similar – but distinct ways each apple is. An alternative is to regard properties as universals: shareable, repeatable entities.*

These days, philosophers who look with favor on properties more often than not take it as given that properties are universals. The idea that properties might be particulars, strikes these philosophers as next to unintelligible. Peter van Inwagen, for instance, observes that

> a universal is supposed to be a thing that has 'instances,' and a property – redness, say – is a species of universal. One might suppose that 'instances' of the property redness would be things like red apples. According to those who believe in 'property instances,' however, this red apple and that red apple are not two instances of the property redness; there are, nevertheless two instances of redness in the vicinity (so to speak) of the two apples. Those who believe in these items call them 'the redness of this apple' and 'the redness of that apple.' These items, these 'particular rednesses,' are supposed to be two distinct things even if the two apples are of exactly the same shade of red. (Van Inwagen 2007b: 38)

---

* This chapter was written for a conference on Universals at the Scuola Normale in Pisa, July 2010. A version of the it appears as Chapter 5 of Heil (2012). The author is grateful to Jeffrey Brower and Eleonore Stump for help with medieval conceptions of properties, to John Bigelow, Daniel Nolan, David Robb, and Denis Robinson for discussion of Lewis on modality and to Martin Coleman, John Lachs, and Herman Saatkamp for assistance with Santayana.

Van Inwagen proceeds to heap scorn on the very idea of property instances regarded as particularized properties.

> Belief in 'property instances' must represent some perennial tendency of the human mind, since it has arisen independently in several philosophical traditions. I can find no trace of it in my own mind, however. Consider two apples that are exactly alike in every respect. To my mind, saying that 'the redness of this apple' and 'the redness of that apple' are names of two distinct things makes about as much sense as saying that 'the diameter of this apple' and 'the diameter of that apple' are names of two distinct things. (Van Inwagen 2007b: 38)

Jerrold Levinson echoes this sentiment in a discussion of 'tropes,' Locke's abstract particulars: 'tropes cannot be particularized properties, since the notion of a particularized property, or condition, is simply an oxymoron. Hence there are no tropes' (Levinson 2006: 564). And the Macdonalds, Cynthia and Graham, speak for many when they note that 'in standard philosophical usage, a property is construed as a universal and an instance of a property is not a trope of that universal but a thing that has (instantiates, exemplifies) that property' (Macdonald and Macdonald 2006: 547).

Such comments would give pause to anyone who has struggled to get first-year philosophy students to comprehend universals. Is it that students who go on in philosophy eventually catch on? Or is it that they simply learn to talk the talk and repress their initial misgivings? Becoming a licensed philosopher requires learning many things including what questions *not* to ask, what issues *not* to press, what battles *not* to fight.

Anthropological considerations aside, what is most striking about these comments is the extent to which they distort philosophical tradition. The suggestion is that only philosophical outliers and cranks would dream of regarding properties as particulars. Serious philosophers would not give such a conception the time of day. The idea that properties are universals has stood the test of time as the default view, the view to be accepted in the absence of compelling reasons against it. In this regard, the thesis that properties are universals resembles the heavyweight champ. The champ retains the crown unless decisively defeated.

Philosophy is in trouble when philosophers rely for their inspiration on what everyone knows, what is accepted by all right-minded – meaning like-minded – professionals, what is doctrinally *comme il faut*. In philosophy, everything is up for grabs; there are no default views, no heavyweight champs. The thesis that properties are universals is a substantive ontological proposal on all fours with the thesis that properties are particulars. In neither case is there any question of a decisive refutation of competitors. Fundamental ontology is a matter of give and take, a matter of weighing costs and benefits. On this score, I suspect that universals do not fare well. My aim here, however, is not to disparage universals but to explain why, despite various temptations to regard properties as universals, you might find the doctrine that properties are particulars more appealing.

2. Historical reminder

Before pressing ahead, a brief historical reminder is in order. To hear contemporary philosophers tell it, the thought that properties are not universals but particulars has a spotty philosophical history, a thought embraced here and there by the odd philosopher, the philosopher outside the mainstream, cut off from philosophy's deeper currents. Real philosophers, the great ones, would see through the idea quickly and move on.

To view the history of philosophy this way, however, is to view it in manifestly revisionist terms. Start with Plato, the supposed original friend of universals. Even if you think of Plato's forms as universals and not archetypal exemplars, you might accept that Plato left room for, indeed insisted on, the 'moving forms,' instances of universals in the objects. There is Socrates, there is archetypal paleness, and there is Socrates' paleness, paleness *in* Socrates. Aristotle might or might not have embraced universals, but he very definitely believed in 'individual accidents': the sphericality of this ball, the brownness of this horse.[1]

By the medieval period, many prominent philosophers rejected universals, regarding properties as 'modes' (ways) or 'accidents.' The list reads like a who's who of medieval philosophy: Boethius, Avicenna, Anselm, Abelard, Averroes, Aquinas, Scotus, Ockham, Buridan, Suárez. This attitude carries over into the Enlightenment. Descartes, Spinoza, Leibniz, Locke, Berkeley, Hume, and Kant accepted properties but rejected universals. Not until the nineteenth century did universals make a comeback of sorts, and even then Husserl, and the early Russell, resisted the tide. In the twentieth century, G. F. Stout, John Cook Wilson, D. C. Williams, P. F. Strawson, Wilfrid Sellars embraced particularized properties. This is scarcely a catalogue of fringe figures.[2]

---

[1] For discussion of Plato, see Demos (1948) and Morrison (1977); on Aristotle see Sellars (1957) and Albritton (1957); Mertz (1996: 83–117) addresses both. Although I shall not attempt to make it, a case could be made for Aristotle's embracing a conception of universals close to the one sketched here.

[2] See Mertz (1996: 83–162) and Bacon (2008). Williams (1953: 189–91; 1966: 106–8) cites – in addition to Plato, Aristotle, Locke, Hume, Descartes, Spinoza, and Leibniz – James, Santayana, the Cambridge

I mention all this not in hopes of currying favor for the view that properties are particulars, but merely to encourage doubts concerning the prevailing doctrine that conceptions of properties as particulars are found only in philosophical backwaters, promoted by poseurs and eccentrics. Many of the greatest, most venerated philosophers regarded universals with suspicion, found themselves attracted to the thesis that properties are particulars, and took themselves to have sensible reasons for doing so.

3. Terminological interlude

Perhaps I have said enough to convince you that a conception of properties as particulars deserves a hearing. One reason they are difficult to trace historically is that, unlike universals (or 'forms'), particularized properties have flown under a multitude of banners.[3] Plato's 'moving forms' became, for Aristotle, 'individual accidents,' and for medievals, 'real accidents' and 'modes.' G. F. Stout (1921, 1936) and Keith Campbell (1981, 1990) call them 'abstract particulars'; Gustav Bergmann (1967), 'perfect particulars'; Nicholas Wolterstorff (1970b), 'cases'; Guido Küng (1967), 'concrete properties'; Gareth Matthews and Marc Cohen (1968), 'unit-properties.' Van Inwagen, in the passages quoted earlier, speaks of 'property instances.'

Nowadays, many philosophers favor the term 'trope,' a label originally proposed by D. C. Williams.[4] Williams cites one of his Harvard predecessors, George Santayana, as the inspiration for his use of the term: 'Santayana... used "trope" to stand for the *essence* of an *occurrence*...; and I shall divert the word, which is almost useless in either his or its dictionary sense, to stand for the abstract particular which is, so to speak, the *occurrence* of an *essence*' (1953: 7; 1966: 78).

Santayana's *The Realm of Matter* (1930) includes a chapter, 'Tropes,' in which Santayana makes clear that he means the term to denote 'essences' or universals as opposed to their particular 'occurrences.' Williams' motive for inverting Santayana's usage is less than transparent. This is especially so in light of the fact that Williams' preferred ontology reflects central features of Santayana's (see below and Williams 1954).

---

realists, A. C. Benjamin, H. W. B. Joseph, Dickinson S. Miller ('R. E. Hobart'), William Savory, Wilfrid Sellars, and E. B. McGilvary as countenancing particularized properties.

[3] The list here owes much to Armstrong (1989a: 113). Mertz (1996) and Bacon (2008) catalogue additional labels.

[4] Williams' best-known discussion of tropes occurs in 'The Elements of Being,' which originally appeared in two installments in the *Review of Metaphysics*, 1953, and was subsequently republished in a modestly revised form in Williams' *Principles of Empirical Realism*, 1966. Citations are provided for both.

We are left with a pint-sized hermeneutic puzzle. Williams adopts Santayana's term 'trope,' but deploys it self-consciously to mean the opposite
of what his Harvard precursor meant. Why? The obvious possibilities –
that Williams was unaware of traditional labels or that he was poking fun
at Santayana, for instance – appear unlikely for several reasons.

1. Williams was certainly familiar with (and indeed explicitly mentions)
    terms used by other philosophers – Aristotle's 'individual accident,'
    the medieval 'mode,' Stout's 'abstract particular' – that meant what he
    seemed to mean by 'trope.'
2. Williams understood Santayana's use of the term.
3. Williams' ontology has much in common with Santayana's.
4. Williams is a perceptive and subtle wielder of language, not given to
    lexicographical carelessness or gratuitous flouting of tradition.

What then explains Williams' choice of terminology?

In reflecting on his use of 'trope' to mean 'abstract particular,' Williams
makes the following observation:

> That the category of abstract particulars thus indicated conforms to the
> logic of whole and part, or the so-called calculus of individuals, that they
> have logical sums and products, and so forth, and that being by definition
> finer or lesser parts than the concreta in which they occur they are in an
> important sense the 'elements of being,' I once argued in print in the *Review
> of Metaphysics* 2, where I called them 'tropes,' which has a nice historical
> connection with the Latin 'modes.' (1959: 4)

This connects tropes with modes or 'ways,' but what 'historical connection'
does Williams have in mind?

The *Oxford English Dictionary* tells us that a trope is 'a figure of speech
which consists in the use of a word or phrase in a sense other than that
which is proper to it; also, in casual use, a figure of speech; figurative
language.' So, whatever else he is doing, Williams is using 'trope' as a trope!
But the *OED* does not stop there. In addition to its familiar use, there is
an 'obs. rare' use in logic to mean 'mood' or 'mode' – as the mood of a
syllogism.[5] There is, then, a connection, albeit an 'obscure' one, between
Williams' 'trope' and the traditional 'mode.'

But why take the trouble to seek out a term with this tenuous relation to
a more familiar (or at least more traditional) term? Why not, for instance,

---

[5] Jonathan Bennett brought this reference to my attention. My source is the *Oxford English Dictionary
Online* (www.oed.com/).

settle for 'mode,' thereby refusing to contribute to a frustrating proliferation of terms?

I believe Williams was after a term that lacked potentially misleading connotations and historical associations. He notes explicitly that, by 'trope,' he means what others – Stout, for instance – had meant by 'abstract particular' (1953: 174; 1966: 92). He sees a problem, however, with the label 'abstract' which had, he thought, come to be used in a way that diverges from its 'true meaning': *partial, incomplete,* or *fragmentary,* the trait of what is less than its including whole' (1953: 15; 1966: 85; see also Williams 1959: 5).

> The many meanings of "abstract" which make it repulsive to the empirical temper of our age suggest that an *abstractum* is the product of some magical feat of mind, or the denizen of some remote immaterial eternity . . . Logical philosophers proclaim their "renunciation of abstract entities" without making clear either what makes an entity "abstract" or how one goes about "renouncing" an entity. (1953: 14; 1966: 84)

A particular billiard ball's sphericality is abstract, not in the sense of its falling short of being fully 'concrete,' but in the sense that its 'separation' from the ball is a matter of abstraction, Locke's 'partial consideration,' an exercise of our capacity for considering the ball's shape as distinct from considering its color or considering the ball itself. The idea is not that, in abstracting, we *manufacture* abstracta; abstraction (partial consideration) is what enables us to *apprehend* abstracta. Because philosophers have too often lost sight of this 'root meaning' and come to think of abstract entities as non-concrete, existing incorruptibly apart from or 'outside' space and time, Williams thinks the label 'abstract particular' is apt to sow confusion.

Fair enough. But why should Williams shy away from 'mode,' or 'individual accident,' or even Santayana's 'occurrence'? Here is one possibility. With few exceptions, philosophers who have used such terms have invariably embraced two-category, substance–attribute ontologies. A mode, for Aquinas, or Descartes, or Locke, is a way, a particular way, a particular substance is. The identity of a mode is bound up with the identity of the substance of which it is a mode. Williams, however, wants a one-category ontology. The role of substances is to be filled by spatiotemporally 'concurrent' particularized properties. What is called for is a new term that lacks inconvenient, even embarrassing, historical antecedents. 'Trope' serves this purpose nicely.

In speaking of particularized properties, I prefer 'mode' to 'trope' (as does E. J. Lowe; see his 1998, 2006) for two reasons. First, thanks to

Williams – and to Keith Campbell (1981, 1990), Peter Simons (1994), David Robb (1997, 2005), and Anna-Sophia Maurin (2002) – most self-described 'trope theorists' today are also 'bundle theorists,' conceiving of objects as bundles of 'compresent' tropes.[6] Williams himself defended an austere ontology of tropes and part–whole – mereological – relations. I side with C. B. Martin and Lowe in thinking of particularized properties as particular ways – from the Latin *modus*, way – particular substances are.[7] This places me in the camp of traditional substance–attribute theorists.

Second, by thinking of properties as modes – ways – it is easier to see them as dependent entities, items the identity of which depends on objects to which they 'belong.' Socrates' paleness is *Socrates'* paleness. There can be no question of Socrates' paleness migrating to Simmias. On such a conception, properties are not assembled to form objects; objects are not *made up* of properties. Objects – substances – are the basic particulars. Every substance is various ways. These ways are modes.

You can see why a philosopher attracted to the idea that properties are particulars might be attracted as well to a bundle theory. If you thought properties were universals, you would need some way of introducing particularity into the world. Bundles of universals would seem just to be complex universals. Particularity could be achieved by introducing substances as non-repeatable items that instantiate or exemplify universals. If properties themselves are particulars, however, the particularizing role of substance is superfluous. Why not economize and settle exclusively for properties? Why not opt for a supremely elegant one-category ontology?

G. F. Stout (1921, 1936) provides a convenient example of this line of thinking. Stout regards the conception of objects as substances – substrata – equipped with properties, hopeless. This pushes us toward a bundle theory of objects. As the reflections above suggest, however, bundles of universals are merely composite universals. If you are attracted to the idea that objects are bundles of properties, if you are suspicious of 'substrata,' you will want properties themselves to be particulars.

One difficulty is in understanding properties as parts that *add up to* objects. Some philosophers, Descartes for instance, have regarded this idea as self-evidently incoherent. If there is sphericality, there must be a spherical

---

[6] Most, but not all. See Martin (1980, 2008); Heil (2003). See also Sophie Gibb's contribution to this volume. Armstrong (1989a: 136) argues that 'we do better, with Locke and C. B. Martin, to hold the trope view in a substance–attribute form.'

[7] The conception of properties as 'ways' made explicit by talk of modes is common to most, but not all, conceptions of particularized properties prior to the twentieth century. Hume might be an exception. In recent years talk of ways was revived by Jerrold Levinson (1978, 1980) and Daniel Seargent (1985) and endorsed provisionally by D. M. Armstrong (1989a: 96–98).

something, some spherically extended substance; if there are thoughts, there must be something that thinks, some thinking substance. The conception is of properties as dependent entities, items the identity of which depends on the substance that bears them.

These observations are not meant to constitute an argument against the bundle theory. I provide them only to dispel the impression that belief in abstract particulars or modes or tropes is inconsistent with the acceptance of a traditional substance–attribute ontology. Nothing in what follows requires taking a stand on whether properties are parts of objects or ways particular substances are. I shall continue to speak of properties as 'ways,' however, in the interests of expository simplicity.

4. Similarity and identity

On the table is a conception of properties as modes, particular ways particular objects are. Modes, like substances, are numerically distinct. Socrates' paleness and Simmias' paleness, although exactly similar perhaps, are distinct palenesses. Socrates and Simmias could both have 'the same' mass, m; but when they stand on a scale it registers $2m$. (And two balls with 'the same' diameter, d, would not both fit into a cube-shaped box the sides of which were d.) Where does this leave us with respect to the venerable problem of 'the one over many'? We want to say of Socrates and Simmias, distinct individuals, that they have something *in common*, that they *share* a color, that they have *the same* color. This suggests that there is some one thing common to Socrates and Simmias (and anything else with *the same* color).

Thoughts of this kind afford one prominent motivation for regarding properties as universals. There is a single universal paleness, and there are endless (actual and potential) instances of paleness. Socrates and Simmias are *the same* color, they *share* a color, they have a feature, color, *in common* because they, Socrates and Simmias, are each instances of the selfsame universal, paleness.

A philosopher who takes properties to be modes and rejects universals would say that Socrates and Simmias' having the same color is akin to two debutants arriving at the ball wearing the same dress, or, Williams' example, a son's having his father's nose where sameness is not a matter of identity but of more or less exact similarity (Williams 1953: 5). Socrates and Simmias' sharing a color, on such a view, is not at all like their sharing an umbrella; their having a color in common is not analogous to their joint ownership of a vacation cottage.

Detractors of modes are apt to weigh in here and point out that, whereas a believer in universals can explain similarities as 'grounded in' identities, a proponent of particularized properties must appeal to 'brute,' 'ungrounded' similarities. Everyone needs identity, selfsameness, but a denier of universals needs, in addition, irreducible similarities. The suggestion is that identity, so to speak, comes for free, but 'ungrounded' similarity is an unseemly ontological whisker vulnerable to Ockham's razor.

Consider the similarity relation, however; in particular, consider precise or perfect similarity. Suppose that Socrates' paleness and Simmias' are precisely similar. Why think that this similarity requires grounding in some deeper, more fundamental feature of Socrates, or Simmias, or their respective palenesses? If you have Socrates' paleness and Simmias' paleness, these very palenesses, you *thereby* have these palenesses being perfectly similar. Similarity, no less than identity, is an *internal* relation, a relation that founded on its relata: if you have the relata, you *thereby* have the relation (see Heil 2009). To regard similarity, but not identity, as ontologically weighty is to mistake an internal for an external relation.

This mistake is all too easy to make because it is easy to misidentify the relata. Suppose an internal relation is one you have if you have the relata. You could have Socrates and Simmias without their being similar colorwise. God could create a universe containing Socrates and Simmias without its thereby being the case that Socrates and Simmias are similarly colored. In the case under consideration, however, Socrates and Simmias are relata only derivatively. If Socrates and Simmias are similarly colored, this is because Socrates is colored in a particular way and Simmias is colored in a particular way, and these two ways of being colored are similar. If God creates objects colored in these ways, God has thereby created similarly colored objects. The idea that appeals to unreduced 'brute' similarities are ontologically profligate is a red herring.

What goes for similarity goes, as well, for *dis*similarity. Dissimilarity must be 'brute.' When God creates the substances and endows them with properties, God *thereby* creates all the similarities *and* dissimilarities. Similarity and dissimilarity, alike, are ontologically undemanding.

5. Costs and benefits

Ontological theses are assayed, not by measuring them directly against reality, but by considering their relative power. One thesis trumps another if it is implied by an overall ontology that does a better job of making sense of our experiences of the world in light of our best scientific theories.

What of parsimony, Ockham's razor? Parsimony serves as a tie-breaker: other things equal, the more parsimonious theory is to be preferred. Things are never equal, however, not really. Parsimony figures in the endgame, not at the outset of theorizing. Parsimony wielded as a theoretical constraint is a straitjacket. The question in play is whether an ontology of particulars (tropes alone or substances and modes) could accomplish what an ontology of particulars plus universals could accomplish.

You might doubt that it could. The thought that the sciences are engaged in a project of uncovering universals appears promising. Universals would seem to afford a tidy explanation of natural laws and of regularities we find in nature.[8] Hume wondered how it could be reasonable to expect similar objects to behave similarly. A proponent of universals has a ready response: similar objects behave, or would behave, similarly because they encompass identical elements.

Suppose, however, this ball rolls owing to its sphericity and suppose that *this* ball's sphericity is distinct from *that* ball's sphericity. Why imagine *that* ball's sphericity would dispose *it* to roll? Were sphericity a universal, this question would not arise: that ball's sphericity *is* this ball's sphericity. If this ball's sphericity is in any way responsible for its rolling, and if that ball possesses the *very same* sphericity, then it is no wonder that it, or *any* ball, rolls or would roll.

This elegant solution to Hume's problem is not available to a philosopher who regards properties as particulars. This ball's sphericity and that ball's sphericity are entirely distinct ways distinct objects are. The same holds for the charge and mass of individual electrons. How could such unrelenting particularity yield the kind of generality characteristic of scientific theorizing?

Consider how a proponent of universals might be thinking of the relation between universals instantiated by objects and laws of nature. You could follow Armstrong (1978, 1989a, 1997b) and embrace an *externalist* conception of laws. Laws, according to Armstrong, are second-order universals. Suppose F and G are universals. There might be a law, $N(F,G)$, to the effect that the F's necessitate the G's. (In fact, matters will need to be considerably more complicated. All sorts of additional factors might be required for the necessitating of a G by an F, and all sorts of factors might intervene to inhibit or block the necessitating of an F by a G. Pretend, however, that such matters complicate the picture without changing its fundamental character.

---

[8] Recent proponents of such a conception include D. M. Armstrong (1983, 1997b), Brian Ellis (2001), E. J. Lowe (2006), and Alexander Bird (2007).

A conception of this kind leaves open the possibility that laws are deeply contingent. We discover that the F's necessitate the G's, but we recognize it could have been otherwise. In the idiom of possible worlds, there are worlds in which there are F's and G's, but the F's fail to necessitate the G's. These would be worlds lacking a higher-order universal linking F and G.

A rather different approach to laws builds them – or truthmakers for formulations of laws – into the first-order universals: it is of the nature of the F's, *qua* F's, to necessitate the G's, and of the nature of the G's, *qua* G's, to be necessitated by the F's (see, for instance, Ellis 2001; Bird 2007). On this conception, properties are *powers*. A property's identity is bound up with the contribution the property would make to what its bearers do or would do. 'Nomological necessity' collapses into 'metaphysical necessity.' Contingency survives, if at all, in the possibility that different worlds might include different properties.

Externalist conceptions of laws make laws out to be *players*, entities in the world – second-order universals – in addition to propertied objects. In creating the world, God must do more than create the objects and first-order universals. God must create the laws by folding in second-order universals.

In contrast, an *internalist* conception, a conception that regards properties as powers, encourages the thought that laws are more aptly regarded as linguistic items: generalizations that in effect codify the contribution made by particular properties to the dispositional makeup of their possessors.[9] Newton's law of universal gravitation, for instance, could be taken to express the contribution mass makes to what objects do or would do – how objects would affect one another – *qua* 'massy.' Externalists think of laws as governing objects and holding under 'ideal' circumstances. Internalists think of objects as self-governing and law statements as attempts to distill the contribution particular kinds of property make to objects' capacities.

What happens to laws if properties are particulars? In that case, it is hard to see how an externalist conception of laws – laws as higher-order properties – could get off the ground.[10] If properties are modes, it is much

---

[9] A conception of this kind is associated with Nancy Cartwright; see her (1989) and (1999). See also Chakravartty (2007) and Bird (2007), although Bird holds that laws 'supervene' on propensities, which he regards as transcendent universals.

[10] Indeed the idea of higher-order modes or tropes is difficult to credit. A property of a property, thought of as a particular way a particular property is, would seem just to be the property itself.

more natural to regard the properties themselves as powers.[11] Where does this leave the laws?

If properties are modes, not universals, similarity replaces identity. If properties are powers, however, similarly propertied objects will be similarly empowered. Here, identity fares no better than similarity in grounding the kinds of generalization important in scientific theorizing and everyday judgment. As I shall argue below, this fits nicely with an account of universals advanced by D. C. Williams, an account that finds modes or tropes pregnant with generality. In fact, it looks as though *any* advantages thought to be provided by universals will be matched by an ontology of modes. This, coupled with Williams' suggestion that thoughts of universals must be understood as being made true, not by 'general entities,' transcendent or immanent universals, but by particulars, provides all the reason you would need to abandon an ontology of universals. Locke was right, particularity rules: the deep story about the spatiotemporal world is that all things that exist are only particulars.

6. Williams on universals

D. C. Williams, a prominent source of current interest in particularized properties, distinguishes conceptions of properties as universals from conceptions of properties as modes or tropes by appeal to the principle of the Identity of Indiscernibles.[12] Where universals are concerned, the Identity of Indiscernibles holds: if universals F and G are indiscernible, F is G. Indiscernible – exactly similar – tropes, in contrast, can be distinct.

Williams dismisses the idea that universals might occupy a Platonic realm, independent of space–time. If properties are universals, if properties make perceptible differences to concrete spatiotemporal objects, how could they fail to be located where the objects are located? Indeed, if you separate universals from the objects, you will need representatives of the universals in the objects. In Plato's case, these are the 'moving forms.'

In general, however, philosophers who regard properties as universals have disdained particularized property instances.[13] This encourages the

---

[11] To say that a property is a power is *not* to say that this exhausts its nature, not to say that properties are *purely* powers. I believe that there are excellent reasons to think of properties as powerful *qualities*. I shall leave this matter in the background, however; see Heil (2003, 2010, 2012).

[12] See Williams (1959). As noted earlier, I prefer 'mode' to 'trope.' In discussing Williams, however, I shall defer to his terminology and speak of tropes.

[13] Plato and E. J. Lowe (2006) are notable exceptions. Perhaps Aristotle was as well. Williams (1959: 6) suggests that 'the Nayaya philosophy of India' might have countenanced both universals and particularized property instances.

view that universals are 'immanent,' universals are present 'in' objects that
instantiate them. The paleness of Socrates and the paleness of Simmias
are the selfsame universal paleness. Paleness is not a 'scattered' entity,
however; the two palenesses are not *parts* of the universal, they *are*, each
of them, the universal itself in its entirety. Thus we have the view, most
recently defended by David Armstrong, that a universal is 'wholly present'
in each of its instances: *universalia in rebus* (Armstrong 1975, 1978, 1989a,
1997).

The difficulty most of us feel when confronted with this idea is in
grasping what it could possibly *mean*. We understand the *words*, and we
understand that they paint a picture of spatiotemporal entities that could
be wholly present in distinct places at once. But what is this picture meant
to be a picture *of*?

Williams suggests one possibility. Start with the tropes and consider
classes or sets of exactly resembling tropes. These classes or sets will be
neatly coextensive with instances of the corresponding universal – where
'instance' denotes, not the object 'instantiating' the universal, but the
universal-in-the-object.

Many things are spherical. The individual sphericalities are modes or
tropes. Now consider the collection or set of these individual sphericalities.
This collection or set would be a functional equivalent of the universal
sphericality. To say that *this* sphericality and *that* sphericality are one and
the same sphericality is, on such a view, to say that both sphericalities are
members of a plurality, or collection, or set of exactly resembling sphericalities, each of which is, to be sure, *wholly* spherical. Such 'resemblance
classes' of tropes are what Armstrong (1989a: 122) calls 'ersatz universals.'
Speaking of the universal sphericality, then, might be understood as an
oblique way of speaking of the class, or set, or community of particular
sphericalities.

The trouble is that this appears to fall well short of what proponents
of universals take themselves to mean when they speak of the universal
sphericality as wholly present in each of its instances. Believers in immanent
universals evidently have something much stronger in mind. Williams
offers a subtle diagnosis.

Assume a trope ontology, and imagine that you are inspecting two balls,
more particularly you are attending to the sphericality of each ball. In
perceiving the first ball's sphericality, you might naturally describe what
you perceive by saying 'this is sphericality.' Turning to the second ball, you
might think, 'this is [sphericality] *too*... the whole entity all over again'
(Williams 1959: 8). Such thoughts call attention to an abstract entity, a
particular characteristic of each ball, rather than the balls themselves.

In considering entities of a particular kind – the two balls, for instance – we accept a principle that '*a* is "identical" with *b* if and only if every part of *a* is a part of *b* and conversely' (Williams 1959: 8). Identity in this sense, strict identity, 'entails but is not entailed by exact resemblance' and applies to particular balls. When you 'abstract' a ball's shape, however, when you engage in Locke's 'partial consideration' and observe that distinct balls have the *same* shape, you employ a notion of '"identity" which *is* just exact resemblance' (Williams 1959: 8). This is the sense of identity in play when you think of a father and son as having the same nose. The noses are identical in the sense of being exactly similar.

'Universals are not made nor discovered but are, as it were, "acknowledged" by a relaxation of the identity conditions of thought and language' (Williams 1959: 8). Williams draws a parallel with temporal parts of concrete particulars:

> Similar relaxations occur in our treatment of ordinary proper names of concrete particulars, especially in the common idiom which, innocent of the notion of temporal parts of a thing, finds the whole enduring object, a man or a stone, in each momentary stage of its history. For here and now, we say, *is* the person called "John," not just part but all of him, and now again is the same "John," all present at another instant, though in strict ontology the "John" of today is a batch of being as discrete from the "John" of yesterday as he is from the moon. The relaxation of conditions which acknowledges universals, however, . . . is much more firmly seated in the facts of language and its object than any other I know. (Williams 1959: 8–9)

The thought is not that universals are linguistic contrivances, but that we employ a linguistic contrivance, 'generization,' to mark off kinds: kinds of object kinds of property. These kinds are not exotic general entities; they are the individuals considered as ways many things are or could be.[14]

> That universals are determined by a "weaker" identity condition than particulars does not even mean that they have an inferior or diluted reality. A tabulation of universals is just one way of counting, as it were, the same world which is counted, in a legitimately different and more discriminating way, in a tabulation of particulars. (Williams 1959: 9)

One way to put Williams' point might be to say that truthmakers for assertions concerning kinds or universals are *cases*, particulars through and through.[15] This yields what Williams dubs a 'trope–kind theory.'

---

[14] This is evidently Locke's view in the *Essay*, III, iii. Reality is uniformly particular; general terms designate, not general entities, but particular entities falling under the term. Generality stems from our capacity to think indifferently about members of classes of similar individuals.

[15] What of classes and sets? Does the world include, in addition to particulars, classes or sets? Again, truthmakers for claims about classes or sets are just the particulars.

As there is nothing in anything which is not either a trope or resolvable into tropes, so every trope, of whatever level of complexity, manifests its universal or kind. Generization, moreover, does not even stop short of concreteness, and does not therefore in the least depend upon *de facto* similarity or the recurrence of kinds. That is, having a general readiness to contemplate, by the right quirk of attention or description, either the case or the kind of any given occasion, we can identify a universal once for all in a single instance, only conceiving *ipso facto* that it is capable of other instances. (Williams 1959: 10)

Williams, note, regards trope–kind theory as a flat out, albeit 'modest,' realism about universals,

in as much as it holds that universals are real entities, and it is an immanent realism in as much as it holds them to exist *in rebus* – to be present in, and in fact components of, their instances. To make plain the sense in which it holds that an abstract universal is "in" a concrete particular we need only make explicit the analysis of predication, characterization, or instantiation which has been barely implicit here all along. That Socrates is wise, i.e., that he is an instance of Wisdom, which is an "instantiation" or "characterization" in the full sense, is sufficiently expanded in the formula that the concrete particular Socrates "embraces" [an] abstract particular (trope) which "manifests" Wisdom. (Williams 1959: 10)

7.   Painless realism

Could this be right? Could a trope-kind theory yield a *realism* about universals? That will depend on what a 'realism about universals' amounts to. If realism requires that terms used to designate properties or kinds are made true by the presence in the world of general or universal entities intermingled with particulars, Williams is no realist. If realism requires only that thoughts concerning universals can be straightforwardly objectively true, however, Williams might be accounted a realist.

Whether previous immanent realists would recognize their view in this opinion that universals are immanent because they are, to speak crudely, the similarity roles (or "adjectival identities") of abstract occurrents, I have some doubt. I am sure, from experience with myself, that an immanent realist begins by thinking he means more, but can bring himself to see, or think he sees, that he *couldn't* mean more – that every attempt to state an alternative results in something verbally but not significantly different from just redefining "identity" by resemblance. (Williams 1959: 10)

Statements invoking universals can be true, but, in David Armstrong's words, universals are 'no addition of being' (1997b: 112–13). Given Socrates' paleness, a case or particular, we have a way Socrates is, a way other things might be in virtue of being exactly similar colorwise. Every case is a kind.

Keith Campbell (1990: 44) calls this 'painless realism,' a kind of realism perhaps endorsed by E. J. Lowe. First, consider 'abstract entities':

> Abstract entities are not denizens of some "Platonic" realm which is "separated" from the world of things existing in space and time. According to this view, to say that abstract entities do not exist "in" space and time is not to say that they somehow exist "elsewhere," a notion which is doubtfully coherent in any case. It is merely to say that when we speak of abstract entities we must "abstract away" from all spatio-temporal determinations and distinctions. (Lowe 2002b: 66)

Lowe appeals to sets by way of analogy:

> Although the planets are concrete objects, each one occupying some particular spatial location at every time during its existence, the set whose members are the planets cannot be assigned a spatial location and cannot be said to persist through, or undergo change in, time. A set of objects exists, timelessly and without spatial location, in any possible world just in case those objects exist in that world. Time and place simply do not enter into the existence- and identity-conditions of sets and that is why they qualify as "abstract" objects. (2002b: 66)

The same will be true of

> properties, conceived as universals, such as the property of being red or the property of being square. Even if the properties are, like these ones, properties exemplified by concrete things, such as flowers and books, the properties themselves are abstract entities because time and place do not enter into their existence- and identity-conditions. According to "Aristotelian" realism concerning universals, it is a necessary condition of a property P's existing in a world w that some object should exemplify P in w – and if that object is a concrete one, P will be exemplified by it at some time and in some place. But this does not imply that P itself exists at any time or in any place. By implication, then, I am rejecting here the doctrine, strangely popular just now, that universals exemplified by concrete objects are "wholly present" in the space–time locations of those objects – a view which I have elsewhere argued to be incoherent. (Lowe 2002b: 66; see also Lowe 1998: 155–56)

You can consider an object – this tomato, for instance – as a substance, as a bearer of properties, or you can consider ways the object is, its sphericality, its redness. You can consider ways this tomato is, as ways *it* is – *its* redness, *its* shape – and you can consider those ways purely as ways, as ways other things might be. In so doing you are 'generizing,' you are considering them as universals. And they *are*, so considered, universals.

Does this give us a realism about universals? Think of tables and trees. Does realism about such things require that the world includes, in addition to, the particles duly arranged (or space–time locally thickened or the quantum field in flux), tables and trees? Or might it be enough that thoughts of tables and trees can be, and often are, objectively true? Such thoughts could be true, yet their truthmakers be arrangements of particles or dynamic thickenings of space–time. The mistake is to imagine that irreducible distinctions in thought or language signal irreducible ontological distinctions (Heil 2003, 2005, 2012).

The issues here parallel a longstanding discussion that began with Aristotle and continued through the medieval period and into the nineteenth century concerning the status of *relations*. Relations are difficult to accommodate in an ontology of substances and attributes. Relations seem not to be substances. Might they be attributes? Attributes are anchored in particular substances, however, and it is unclear how a single attribute could be beholden to distinct substances (its *relata*). The thought that relations reside 'between' substances threatens to turn relations into substances, so looks unpromising.[16] Might we then dispense with relations? That seems crazy. Relational predications are apparently indispensable. Relational predications are not translatable or otherwise resolvable into predications that make no mention of relations. Attempts to substitute monadic 'relational properties' for relations smack of sophistry; talk of relational properties is evidently nothing more than an oblique way of talking of relations (Russell 1903; Moore 1919).

Perhaps, however, relational truths are made true by non-relational features of the world. This might be so if relations were invariably 'internal.' An internal relation is 'founded' on apparently unproblematic intrinsic features of the relata. Simmias is taller than Socrates in virtue of Simmias' being six feet in height and Socrates' being five feet. If God makes a world in which Simmias is six feet tall and Socrates is five feet, God has *thereby* made a world in which Simmias is taller than Socrates. The taller-than relation is 'no addition of being.' Suppose it could be shown that *all* relations were, in this sense, internal, founded. Would we thereby have 'eliminated relations' or gone over into an anti-realism about relations? That depends. Perhaps we would simply have shown that truthmakers for judgments involving relations are non-relational features of the world.[17]

---

[16] Reflections of this kind can be found, for instance, in Leibniz (1715, Fifth Paper, §47); for discussion, see Heil (2009; 2012: Ch. 7).

[17] See Heil (2009, 2012) for a more detailed discussion of relations and the history of philosophical accounts of relations; see also Parsons (2009).

The suggestion is that you could be a 'realist about relations' without supposing that the world contains, in addition to objects and their 'monadic' properties, distinctive relational entities. Similarly, you could be a 'realist about universals' without supposing that the world includes, in addition to particular ways things are, general, non-particular entities.

8 Coda: modes and tropes

I have described properties as ways substances are and indicated a preference for the traditional 'mode' over Williams' 'trope.' It is easy to think of 'mode' and 'trope' as equivalent, two terms with a common denotation. The thought would be that modes are best understood as at home in a two-category, substance–attribute ontology; modes are particular ways particular substances are. Tropes are modes minus the substance. This, I now believe, is a mistake of a fundamental sort. You cannot subtract the tomato from a way the tomato is. It is of the nature of a mode to be a mode, a modification, of some substance.

This feature of modes underlies medieval debates over whether modes are *res*. Ways the tomato is are *res*, at least in the sense in that the tomato's being the ways it is makes a qualitative and dispositional difference to the tomato. Is your smile an entity? Your smile is a real feature of your face, a way your face is, but calling it an entity is apt to mislead. Certainly, modes are not entities in the sense in which the tomato's substantial parts – its stem, its skin, its seeds – are entities, items that make up the tomato, constituents of the tomato. You might construct a tomato by assembling the right kinds of particle in the right way. But a tomato is not made up of an assemblage of modes together with a substance.

If tropes are kinds of entity that could, in combination, make up objects, then tropes are ontologically fundamentally different from modes. Properties, considered as tropes, are, as Williams says, *parts* of objects in the sense that they *make up* or *compose* objects: objects are nothing more than collections, or sums, or 'bundles' of tropes.

Although modes have been around since Plato, tropes are a twentieth-century invention. Trope theory emerged hand in hand with another dubious twentieth-century innovation, bundle theory.[18] Indeed, it is precisely because properties were widely regarded as modes, that bundle theories were never considered, much less discussed or defended. It would make

---

[18] It is, I believe, anachronistic to call Hume a bundle theorist. Berkeley regards material objects as collections of ideas, but ideas are mental modes, ways minds are.

no sense to regard objects as bundles of modes. The closest earlier philosophers came to a bundle theory was in discussions of the Eucharist. God
transforms the wine into the blood of Christ by miraculously eliminating
the substance and leaving the properties. The properties left, however, are
not modes. Not even God could eliminate a substance and leave ways the
substance is, its modes. Properties that can survive the miraculous subtraction of substance are a species of individual accident, the so-called real
accidents.

In a discussion of real accidents, Descartes notes that such entities would
be propertied substances. 'The human mind cannot think of the accidents
of the bread as real and yet existing apart from its substance, without
conceiving of them by employing the notion of a substance' (Descartes
1641: 176). The whiteness of the bread considered as a standalone entity is
something white, something that is the white way.

This is not the place to take up the troubled history of the metaphysics
of transubstantiation: metaphysics in the service of a specific theological
doctrine. The important point here is that tropes are very special kinds of
entity, utterly different from traditional conceptions of particularized properties as modes. For this reason, I now think it a bad idea to lump modes
and tropes together. Substance–attribute trope theories (Martin 1980,
2008; Armstrong 1989a: 136) are more perspicuously thought of as taking
properties to be modes.[19]

---

[19] The situation is complicated by the fact that self-styled trope theorists are not always as clear as
they might be on the nature of tropes. See Robert Garcia's contribution to this volume and Heil
(2015).

CHAPTER 6

Is trope theory a divided house?

Robert K. Garcia

Michael Loux draws an important distinction between 'tropes' and 'tropers' (Chapter 1, this volume). My aim in this chapter is to explore the significance of this distinction. Before introducing my main theses, it will be useful to provide a provisional gloss on the trope/troper distinction as well as some terminology.

Both tropes and tropers are 'particularized properties' in that they are non-shareable character-grounders. Tropes and tropers are *character-grounders* in that it is in virtue of having a trope (troper) that an object is charactered in some way. For example, it is in virtue of having a sphericity trope (troper) that an object is spherical. Tropes and tropers are *unshareable* in the following general way: Where f is a trope or troper, if f is had by object O at time t, then nothing wholly distinct from O has f at t. For example, if distinct spheres a and b exist at t, the sphericity of a and the sphericity of b are numerically distinct even if they are qualitatively exactly similar. (In contrast, on a theory of universals, properties are shareable and the sphericity of a and the sphericity of b are numerically identical.) The basic difference between tropes and tropers can be put as follows: If the sphericity of an object is a troper, then the sphericity is itself spherical; if the sphericity of an object is a trope, then the sphericity *is not* itself spherical. In effect, a troper is a singly-charactered object, whereas a trope is a singly-characterizing property.

According to Loux, the concept of a troper is relatively novel, whereas the concept of a trope corresponds to what most contemporary philosophers have in mind when they use the term 'trope.' I agree that there are two distinct concepts mapped by this distinction. However, although I previously held that the concept of a troper is novel, I now think otherwise.[1]

---

[1] In Garcia (2009) I explore the relative merits of tropes and tropers. Ultimately, I argue that troper theory is superior to trope theory. Although my working assumption there is that the concept of a troper is novel, my main arguments do not turn on this assumption.

As I show below, the notion of a troper is already at play in the literature. Arguably, in fact, it is the dominant concept of a 'trope.' Thus, Loux's distinction between 'trope' and 'troper' is best described as a distinction between two different concepts of a *trope*. Regrettably, then, using 'trope' and 'troper' to label the distinction is potentially misleading. Accordingly, below I introduce the terms *modifier trope* (for Loux's 'trope') and *module trope* (for Loux's 'troper'), and unless further qualified, 'trope' and 'trope theory' should be read as neutral between the two trope concepts.

In what follows, I argue that Loux's distinction has far-reaching significance. First, the distinction throws into relief an ambiguity and discrepancy in the literature, revealing two fundamentally different versions of trope theory. Second, the distinction brings into focus unique challenges facing each of the resulting trope theories, thus calling into question an alleged advantage of trope theory – that by uniquely occupying the middle ground between its rivals, trope theory is able to 'recover and preserve the insights of' these views.[2] Ultimately, the distinction suggests that trope theory is a divided house.

In section 1, my aims are to clarify the distinction between two concepts of a trope and to note the more fundamental distinctions that underwrite it. I do so by considering the interrelationships between trope bundle theory and two of its rival mono-category non-relational ontologies: austere nominalism and realist bundle theory. Here I consider the suggestion that trope bundle theory monopolizes a sweet spot, so to speak, between austere nominalism and a realist bundle theory, uniquely incorporating the strengths and avoiding the weaknesses of these rival views. Ultimately, I argue that there are two fundamentally different trope theories that occupy that spot. In section 2 I show how distinguishing these theories sours the sweetness of the spot.

1.   Splitting the sweet spot

I will begin this section by detailing the interrelationships between realist bundle theory, austere nominalism and trope bundle theory. To set the stage, I start with a preliminary sketch of each of these views. Since it will be useful to contrast trope bundle theory with these other two traditional views, I will sketch them first. I will then go on to draw two key distinctions. These distinctions box a logical compass that will serve to introduce the distinction between module tropes and modifier tropes.

---

[2]   This quote is from Molnar (2003: 23), who will be discussed below.

1.1 *Interrelationships among mono-category constituent ontologies*

Like other so-called constituent ontologies, a realist bundle theory accounts for the character of concrete objects by taking them to have metaphysical structure.[3] A concrete object is structured in that it is identical with a bundle of properties, where these properties are construed as universals. There have been recent defenders (e.g. O'Leary-Hawthorne and Cover 1998) of this view, but the Bertrand Russell of *An Inquiry Into Meaning and Truth* (1940) is perhaps its most well-known exponent. Note that according to this view, concrete objects have metaphysical constituents, and all of these constituents are universals.

In contrast, the austere nominalist denies that properties exist. On her view, there exist only concrete objects like persons, potatoes, or electrons. In addition, she insists that an adequate account of the character of these objects can be had within this limited explanatory framework. Indeed, she limits herself to only one explanatory resource: the concrete object itself, taken as a whole – that is, taken as a metaphysically unstructured, simple, entity. She holds that we can account for the character of a concrete object *without* postulating properties of any sort – whether particularized properties (tropes), immanent (Aristotelian) universals, or transcendent (Platonic) universals. This sort of view has been attributed to W. V. O. Quine (1954) and has recent defenders (e.g. Devitt 1980; Parsons 1999). According to the austere nominalist, if we want a truthmaker for the sentence 'This apple is red,' we need only point to the apple itself, qua metaphysical simple.

Trope bundle theory is said to strike an advantageous compromise between the above rival ontologies. Philosophers typically said to defend this view include D. C. Williams (1953), Keith Campbell (1990), Peter Simons (1994), Douglas Ehring (1997, 2011), and Anna-Sofia Maurin (2002). Some of its usual doctrines are as follows: There are properties. Properties are tropes – they are particulars (where 'being a particular' is subject to some ambiguity, but usually means something like 'not multiply-instantiable' or 'not possibly wholly located in more than one non-overlapping place at the same time'). Properties are fundamental metaphysical constituents of concrete objects. Every metaphysical constituent is a property. And, a concrete object is charactered as it is in virtue of having properties as metaphysical parts.[4]

---

[3] See Garcia (2014b) for a recent discussion of bundle theory and Loux (2006a) for a discussion of the distinction between a constituent ontology and relational ontology.

[4] One of the most promising versions of trope bundle theory is the so-called Nuclear Theory developed by Simons (1994) and Keinänen (2011). See Garcia (2014c) for discussion.

Both realist bundle theory and trope bundle theory affirm the existence of properties. On trope bundle theory, however, a property is not possibly multiply-instantiated. If there are two distinct round balls, the trope theorist insists that there are two numerically-distinct roundness tropes, one in (or for) each ball. Indeed, on her view, tropes are the only kind of constituents that go together (via 'compresence') to make up a concrete object. But tropes *also* go together (via similarity) to make up *ersatz universals*, or property-classes – sets of resembling tropes. These sets serve to provide semantic values for abstract singular terms, such as 'redness' and 'triangularity.' The latter, for example, would name the set of tropes that resemble in being triangularities. More on this below.

Having noted the interrelationships between the above views, we can now consider an alleged virtue of trope bundle theory. According to some prominent trope theorists, one advantage of trope theory derives from that fact that it uniquely holds the middle ground between rival mono-category ontologies. Maurin's comments are representative:

> To put it simply, when one considers the problems that have faced attempts to develop one-category ontologies without tropes one finds that, at least *prima facie*, these do not seem to be problems that a theory incorporating only tropes would ever have to face. Classical one-category nominalists – nominalists, that is, who postulate only the existence of particular concrete objects [i.e. austere nominalists] – run into trouble when trying to account for what we refer to as the 'properties' of these objects. It is as if concrete objects are simply too unstructured and too concrete to be the ultimate constituents of the world. One category universal-realists [realist bundle theorists] on the other hand, who postulate only the existence of universals, seem to run into trouble when trying to handle the world's concrete ingredients. The fundamental entities postulated by the universal-realist simply turn out to be too universal to allow us to deal with the apparent existence of concrete objects. Trope theory seems to fill the gap between these two positions. The trope is particular and thus suitable for dealing with concrete objects, but it is also qualitative and thus suitable for dealing with properties. All of this indicates that the prospects of a one-category trope theory are unusually good. (2002: 6)

Others have expressed similar thoughts about the virtues of trope theory.[5] The general claim here seems to be this: Trope theory is superior to both austere nominalism and realist bundle theory because its account of concrete objects incorporates the strengths while avoiding the weaknesses of these views.

---

[5] E.g. Molnar (2003: 23) and Beebee et al. (2011: 256).

Maurin's argument merits closer scrutiny. On her view, the problem with realist bundle theory is that its 'fundamental entities... simply turn out to be too universal to allow us to deal with the apparent existence of concrete objects.' The merits of this claim depend on what Maurin means by 'concrete' object. Although it is not entirely clear, presumably her thought is that objects are 'concrete' in that they are *particulars*, that is, not the sort of thing that can be wholly multiply-located. For example, at this moment this sheet of paper is wholly here and nowhere else. Yet, the realist bundle theorist tells us that a concrete object is nothing but a bundle of universals – each of which *can* be wholly multiply-located. Thus, on this reading, the problem with realist bundle theory is the difficulty of seeing why a bundle entirely comprised of wholly-multiply-locatable entities would not itself be wholly-multiply-locatable. The problem would be that universals do not provide a realist bundle theory with adequate resources to ground the particularity of concrete objects. Thus, the trouble with realist bundle theory is that it takes all of the constituents in a bundle to be universals, even though the bundle itself is supposed to be a particular. In contrast, trope bundle theory takes all of the constituents in a bundle to be particulars; so it is no surprise that the bundle itself is a particular.

So trope bundle theory fares better than realist bundle theory when it comes to grounding the particularity of concrete objects. Like trope theory, however, austere nominalism does not founder on particularity. It takes particularity to be a primitive fact about concrete objects and denies that those objects have any metaphysical parts – much less any *universal* parts which might threaten the particularity of the object. The trouble with austere nominalism concerns whether it can adequately account for phenomena attending the *character* of concrete objects. Indeed, there are reasons to think that austere nominalism is weak on this score. In large part, the trouble for the austere nominalist stems from her refusal to posit anything besides concrete objects, qua metaphysical simples. On the one hand, she refuses to postulate any immanent metaphysical structure – thereby rejecting a so-called constituent ontology. And on the other hand, she refuses to postulate any non-immanent, namely transcendent, sources of character – thereby rejecting a so-called relational ontology. The trope bundle theorist, in contrast, accounts for character by adopting a constituent ontology on which the concrete object has particular characteristics – tropes – as metaphysical parts.

Nevertheless, both austere nominalism and realist bundle theory have strengths, and it is said that these strengths are incorporated by trope bundle theory. According to George Molnar, what is right about austere nominalism is that it abstains from the 'needlessly reificatory move [of postulating] non-particulars over and above the particulars' (2003: 24). And, what is right about realism is that '[b]y including properties among the irreducible contents of this world, realism allows us to construct the robust explanations, of the facts of predication, of causation, or nomological connection, etc., that are blocked by [austere] nominalism' (2003: 24). The trope bundle theorist is supposed to uniquely preserve what is right about these views. First, she takes the basic entities to be properties (like universals) but particular (unlike universals but like the concrete objects of the austere nominalist). And second, she takes concrete objects to be structured (unlike those of the austere nominalist) out of more basic entities (like the objects on a realist bundle theory).

1.2   Two kinds of trope theory

So trope theory is said to be unique in its ability to salvage the insights of both realist bundle theory and austere nominalism (Molnar 2003: 23). However, the idea that trope bundle theory monopolizes a sweet spot between its rival mono-category ontologies is called into question by Loux's distinction between tropes and tropers, or what I will call modifier tropes and module tropes, respectively. The distinction shows that between realist bundle theory and austere nominalism there are two fundamentally different trope theories. This, I will argue, shows that the alleged sweetness of the spot occupied by trope theory is illusory, the result of conflating module tropes and modifier tropes.

We can see that there is room for two concepts of a trope by drawing two traditional and fundamental distinctions: the particular/universal distinction and the object/property distinction. Unfortunately, conflicting terms have often been used to label these distinctions and sometimes a single term has been used to range over more than one relevant concept. In what follows, I have chosen what I take to be appropriate labels, but I am not so much concerned to defend their aptness as the genuineness of the distinctions they label. As we will see, both kinds of tropes are supposed to be particular. Thus, for the sake of getting clear on the distinction between them, it is less important to get clear on the particular/universal distinction than it is to get clear on the object/property distinction.

In the literature, the *particular/universal distinction* is usually drawn in terms of whether something can be multiply-located. On this view, universals are possibly wholly multiply-located at non-overlapping places at the same time, whereas particulars are not (cf. Campbell 1990: 12 and

O'Leary-Hawthorne and Cover 1998: 211–12). I will continue to use the distinction in this way.

The *object/property distinction* concerns what J. A. Cover and John O'Leary-Hawthorne call '*impredicability* – on which condition an individual substance is not said of (does not inhere in) anything in the way that properties are said of (inhere in) substances' (1999: 11). One might say that this distinction marks the difference between the subjects of our discourse and what we say about them. However, putting the distinction this way can mislead one into thinking that the distinction is a linguistic one, or is at least justified only by an appeal to the structure or use of language. Loux's gloss on the distinction is not misleading in this way; according to Loux, the object/property distinction maps the categorial gap between a *property* and a *property-possessor* (Chapter 1, this volume). Unfortunately, this construal also needs some refinement.

First, it won't do to say that an object is simply a property-possessor. Arguably, if there are properties, some properties are themselves property-possessors. For example, it is reasonable to think that if there is such a thing as redness, then redness has the property of being a color. At the very least, the object/property distinction should accommodate those ontologies on which there are such higher-order properties. (Thus, first-order properties which have higher-order properties are not genuine objects, though they *function like* objects with respect to those higher-order properties.)

There is a second, more important worry about Loux's gloss on the distinction. His notion of a 'property-possessor' might suggest that it is impossible that there be objects but no properties. But, at least for our purposes, the distinction should not have this implication, since it would thereby beg the question against the austere nominalist. The latter will insist that her ontology is entirely populated by objects, where those objects are truly *charactered* even though there are no properties, or characteristics, per se. In other words, the austere nominalist claims that there are objects but no properties. This point is especially crucial for understanding the concept of a module trope. As we will see, in an important sense both the austere nominalist and the module trope theorist deny that there are properties while affirming that there are charactered objects.

Fortunately, there is a way to draw the distinction that should suit our purposes. Traditionally, some metaphysicians have taken the concept of a property to be a basic one, typically introduced via ostension. We are invited to consider, say, the hard and smooth apple on the table. We notice its hardness and smoothness as distinct from that which is itself hard and smooth. That is, we notice the properties, or characteristics, of

the apple and we notice the thickly charactered apple. The latter is not
a characteristic, or property, but a charactered, or propertied, thing – an
object. And so we arrive at the relevant conceptual distinction. On the one
hand, there is the concept of a *property* (characteristic, quality, etc.). And,
on the other hand, there is the concept of something which is *charactered
but not itself a property or characteristic*. I will call the latter the concept of
an *object*.

This way of drawing the distinction allows the austere nominalist to
affirm that only objects exist. In addition, this gloss on the distinction does
not entail that a property cannot itself be charactered. It is consistent with
there being some sense in which *sphericity is a shape, courage is a virtue*,
etc.

The goal so far has been to draw attention to two important distinctions –
the universal/particular distinction and the object/property distinction.
These distinctions generate the following four complex notions: *universal-
property, particular-property, particular-object,* and *universal-object*. Thus,
the object/property and universal/particular distinctions box the following
logical compass:

	Particular	Universal
Object	Box 1 *Particular-object*	Box 3 *Universal-object*
Property	Box 2 *Particular-property*	Box 4 *Universal-property*

I will refer to this compass to note the basic differences between austere
nominalism, realist bundle theory, modifier trope theory, and module trope
theory. I will first note the agreements and disagreements between austere
nominalism and modifier trope theory. I will then discuss module trope
theory and show how it falls in the theoretical space between the latter two
views.

The basic agreement between austere nominalism and modifier trope
theory can be put in terms of the universal/particular distinction. Both
views agree that the universal side of this distinction necessarily has an
empty extension. They thereby endorse *strict particularism*, the doctrine
that, necessarily, there are only particulars. So they agree that Boxes 3
and 4 are empty. However, while the austere nominalist and the modifier
trope theorist agree that there are only particulars, they disagree on what
kinds of particulars there are. The austere nominalist insists that among

the particulars there are only objects, whereas the modifier trope theorist thinks that among the particulars there are both objects and properties. In other words, the austere nominalist thinks that Boxes 2, 3, and 4 are empty, whereas the modifier trope theorist thinks that only Boxes 3 and 4 are empty.

For the austere nominalist, all entities fall into Box 1 and are primitively thickly intrinsically charactered, in that each can be described in a multitude of ways. Supposing that a given ball is a particular, the ball will be said to be of a certain color, size, and shape – it is thus a thickly intrinsically charactered object. (Of course, the austere nominalist will, ex hypothesi, deny that she is thereby committed to there being either properties expressed by those predicates or some sort of metaphysical structure in the ball.)

For the modifier trope bundle theorist, the entities in Box 1 are somehow constructed out of the metaphysically more basic entities in Box 2. That is, the particular-objects are entirely constituted by particular-properties, or, more specifically, by particular fully-determinate characteristics. With respect to the ball, a modifier trope theorist might say that the ball has numerous constituent properties, such as scarlet-redness and sphericalness – which, along with the ball's other tropes, together thickly characterize the object.

We can now see that there are two primary differences between austere nominalism and modifier trope theory, and that these differences turn on the object/property distinction. First, whereas the austere nominalist denies that there are properties, the modifier trope theorist claims that there are properties and that properties constitute the metaphysical ground floor of being. Second, while both views affirm that there are objects, objects are metaphysically basic on austere nominalism, whereas objects are metaphysically constructed (out of tropes) and hence derivative on modifier trope theory. The basic entities of the austere nominalist are particulars, but they are also objects – they are charactered things but not characteristics. The basic entities of the modifier trope theorist are particulars but *not* objects – they are characteristics. For the modifier trope theorist, every object is 'constructed' entirely out of basic particulars, namely out of particular properties. Specifically, an object is a bundle of compr
esent tropes. It is thus apt to describe a modifier trope as a 'maximally-thinly characterizing particular,' since each modifier trope endows the object (of which it is a constituent) with a single specific fully-determinate characteristic. Or, put differently, each modifier trope characterizes an object in a single fully-determinate way. For example, on the modifier view of tropes, if an object is spherical it is so in virtue of having a sphericity trope as a constituent – where that trope is not itself spherical.

So much for contrasting austere nominalism and modifier trope theory. We are now in a position to consider module trope theory, which occupies the theoretical turf between the latter two views. In fact, as we will see, module trope theory is closer in spirit to austere nominalism than is modifier trope theory. What I am here calling a module trope Loux introduces under the term 'troper':

> one might propose a nominalistic ontology that has as its metaphysical atoms what we might call 'tropers.' Whereas tropes are particular properties – things like this redness, this triangularity, this pallor, tropers are thin individuals – things like *this individual red thing, this individual triangular thing*, and *this individual pale thing.* The claim would be that familiar objects are bundles of compresent tropers. (Chapter 1, 31, this volume)

To fix on the concept of a module trope (troper), recall Box 1, which represents the concept of a particular-object. A module trope is a basic entity that would fall into Box 1. However, a module trope is not the *thickly*-characterized object of the austere nominalist. Rather, a module trope is a *singly-* or *maximally-thinly* characterized object.

We can get a better handle on the notion of a module trope by considering the upshot of austere nominalism's failure. For a philosopher who concedes this failure but wants to provide an adequate account of the character of concrete objects, the natural move is to expand one's explanatory resources by appealing to something besides the concrete object itself, taken as a metaphysically unstructured whole. Thus, one way to characterize the difference between the two versions of trope theory is in terms of the *extent* of their response to austere nominalism's failure. In short, a module trope theorist responds by taking one step away from austere nominalism, whereas a modifier trope theorist takes an additional, second step.

The first step the modifier trope theorist takes is to adopt a constituent ontology: she posits metaphysical constituents within the concrete object. The second step she takes is to construe these constituents as belonging to a different category than that of the whole, or concrete object. She takes the constituents to belong to the category of *property*. In effect, this is a significantly bigger step away from austere nominalism than the first, since it concedes something to the traditional realist: that the category of property needs to be populated after all. Indeed, this second step opens a categorial gap between the concrete individual qua *object* and its constituents qua *properties*. Although this is not the place to discuss them, arguably this sort of gap raises challenges for a modifier trope theory (for discussion see

Garcia 2009, 2014b, and MS a), and it is precisely this sort of gap that worries Loux in the above citation.

In contrast, the module trope theorist takes only *one* step away from austere nominalism. She, like the modifier trope theorist, adopts a constituent ontology and thus posits metaphysically more basic constituents out of which concrete objects are constructed. But unlike the modifier trope theorist, she does this without the concession to the realist – *without taking the further step of construing those constituents as properties.* Instead, the basic constituents are *objects.* To be sure, these are not the thickly charactered objects of commonsense – rather, we might describe them as one-dimensionally-charactered objects or maximally-thinly-charactered objects. But module tropes are objects nonetheless. And, in an important respect, a module trope is like the objects of the austere nominalist – each is a charactered object and not a characteristic. In other words, the austere nominalist and the module trope theorist both refuse to populate any box other than Box 1. Note that the single step taken by the module trope theorist does *not* seem to open a categorial gap between a concrete object and its constituents – both are objects, both are from Box 1. Rather, their difference is one of degree, in terms of the thickness of their character. By way of comparison, note that the basic particulars of the austere nominalist are also objects – they are charactered things which are not themselves characteristics. But the basic particulars of the *modifier* trope theorist are *not* objects – they are properties or characteristics (this is consistent with properties 'having' formal character such as being particular or being a property). Thus, while austere nominalism and module trope theory agree that all entities fall into Box 1, the latter theorist would say that some members of Box 1 are constituted by other members of Box 1. On module trope theory, while everything is a particular-object, concrete objects (*thickly*-charactered particular-objects) are constituted by module tropes (*thinly*-charactered particular-objects). It is in this sense that module trope theory has the virtue of being closer in spirit to austere nominalism than modifier trope theory. In virtue of eschewing properties altogether, module trope theory is a more thoroughgoing form of nominalism than modifier trope theory. (Indeed, elsewhere I argue that module trope theory threatens to collapse into austere nominalism.[6])

To flesh out these differences, consider how a trope bundle theory looks on each way of thinking about tropes. Consider what we would ordinarily describe as two hard spheres. Call them Orbo and Orba. On both theories, each of these objects is entirely composed of tropes. For example, Orbo

---

[6] See Garcia (MS b).

has hardness$_1$ and sphericity$_1$, whereas Orba has hardness$_2$ and sphericity$_2$ (the subscripts serve as a reminder that these are *non-shareable* character-grounders). And, on both theories, Orbo and Orba are similarly shaped in virtue of sphericity$_1$ and sphericity$_2$ being exactly similar. The theories differ as follows. On the one hand, modifier trope theory has it that sphericity$_1$ is not itself spherical and hardness$_1$ is not itself hard. More generally, none of the character-grounding constituents in Orbo is itself an object. Instead, these constituents somehow go together (via 'compresence') to *form* an object. Thus, on modifier trope theory, objects do not exist at the ground floor of being. On the other hand, module trope theory has it that sphericity$_1$ *is* spherical and hardness$_1$ *is* hard. Thus, Orbo is composed entirely of basic thinly-characterized objects including what might be more accurately described, following Loux, as spherical-thing$_1$ and hard-thing$_1$. In addition, Orbo is a non-basic object: It is an object because its parts are objects, but it is a non-basic object because it is characterized derivatively, in virtue of its constituents being (primitively) characterized. Thus, on module trope theory, ordinary, thickly-characterized objects have their character derivatively, in virtue of the primitively thinly-characterized objects that occupy the ground floor of being.[7]

2.   Souring the sweet spot

So far I have argued that there are two fundamentally different trope theories occupying the theoretical space between austere nominalism and realist bundle theory. The distinction between module tropes and modifier tropes calls into question the claim sometimes made on behalf of trope theory – namely, that by uniquely occupying the sweet spot between its rivals, trope theory is able to 'recover and preserve the insights of' these views. In this section, my aim is to show that the sweetness of this spot is soured by being split between module trope theory and modifier

---

[7] An insightful referee asked whether spherical-thing$_1$ is aptly characterized as non-hard, and if so, whether it would follow that Orbo is derivatively non-hard, as well. This is an important and probing question. Arguably, a module trope theorist will want to affirm that spherical-thing$_1$ is non-hard on pain of thickening up the module trope's primitive character to the point of collapsing module trope theory into austere nominalism (see Garcia MS b). But presumably, she needs to deny that spherical-thing$_1$'s being non-hard entails that Orbo is non-hard. The difficulty here stems from the fact that such a module trope theorist needs to affirm both of the following general claims, where *t* is a module trope had by object O: (i) O is derivatively characterized in virtue of *t*'s being primitively characterized; and (ii) It is *not* the case that every true description of *t*'s primitive character also truly describes O. However, affirming both (i) and (ii) seems to require that there is a principled way to distinguish between the trope level character that is conferred to the object (e.g. being spherical) and the trope level character that is *not* conferred to the object (e.g. being non-hard, being metaphysically simple, etc.). Whether such a distinction can be drawn in a principled way is beyond the scope of this chapter. Nevertheless, the difficulty here seems significant.

trope theory. To do so I will discuss two projects that have been central to the development of trope theory, what Maurin calls *the construction of things* (in section 2.1) and *the construction of property classes* (in section 2.2). With respect to each issue, I aim to show two things. First, the distinction between module tropes and modifier tropes throws into relief a widespread discrepancy and ambiguity within trope theory. And second, disambiguation results in a clearer picture of the unique challenges facing each version of trope theory.

2.1   Challenges concerning the construction of things

I now turn to issues concerning a trope-theoretic account of concrete objects, or 'things.' My aim here is twofold. First, I aim to show that because trope theorists have been less than clear about the role(s) that substrata are supposed to play on rival ontologies, there is a resulting ambiguity concerning the concept of a trope – an ambiguity that maps onto the modifier/ module distinction. Second, drawing this distinction shows that the resulting trope theories have different strengths and weaknesses when it comes to the task of 'thing-construction.' Indeed, each view seems to face significant challenges and these challenges have been obscured by conflating the two kinds of tropes.

Keith Campbell has argued that an ontology of tropes can do without bare particulars. The argument is that bare particulars are both undesirable and unnecessary. They are undesirable because they are thought to be mysterious and/or paradoxical. They are thought to be unnecessary on the grounds that whatever role they are supposed to play can be played by tropes. Call the latter claim the *Parity Thesis*. Arguably, the Parity Thesis is interesting only if accompanied by the thesis that tropes are metaphysically simple. Maurin (2002: 101–15), at any rate, appears to concede this point (though see John Bacon (1995: 2), who seems to want to remain neutral on it). Call the thesis that tropes are simple the *Simplicity Thesis*. As Chris Daly (1997) has argued, unless a trope is simple, a bare particular-cum-universal *complex* would count as a trope, in which case trope theory fails to represent a genuine alternative to rival views. Indeed, the theoretical advantage of trope theory is said to consist in the fact that what the realist takes to be a complex consisting of a bare particular tied to a universal (categorially different entities playing distinct roles), the trope theorist takes to be a *simple* trope (a single entity playing multiple roles). This prima facie advantage is enjoyed by trope theory only if tropes are simple. At any rate, I will assume the Simplicity Thesis in what follows.

By way of the Parity Thesis, the trope theorist assigns to the simple trope various roles played by the items in the realist's bare particular-cum-universal complex. In this way, the concept of a trope has been introduced and partly defined in terms of the roles that bare particulars are supposed to play. Unfortunately, however, there are discrepancies concerning what these roles are supposed to be. This results in an ambiguity concerning the nature of a trope. Resolving the ambiguity yields the distinction between modifier tropes and module tropes.

Campbell's writing is not always sensitive to the distinction between the two kinds of tropes. His language sometimes suggests that he had modifier tropes in mind. For example, Campbell is comfortable illustrating his theory by talking about a *courageousness* trope and a *being a bamboo eater* trope. But it is hard to see how these even *could* be module tropes. If they were, the courageousness trope would itself be disposed to perform heroic deeds in certain circumstances, and the being a bamboo eater trope would itself be able to savor and munch plants. Nevertheless, on the whole, the thematic concept in Campbell's writings is that of a module trope. And Campbell has confirmed this interpretation in conversation.[8] One interesting place where Campbell can be (mis)read as positing modifier tropes is his defense of the Parity Thesis. He says that substrata are supposed to play only one role, that of *particularizing*. As we will see, this leads naturally to thinking of tropes as modifier tropes. In the context of the following passage, Campbell is comparing trope bundle theory to a rival two-category constituent ontology that takes an object to be constituted by a bare particular and universals. On such a view, the bare particular plays a crucial role of grounding the particularity of the object, a role that cannot be played by its universals. Campbell argues that trope theory improves on such a view because the particularizing role can be played by the constituent properties (because they are particulars), thus making bare particulars unnecessary:

> A [bare particular] is a specialist at particularity: it is introduced into theory as that which performs the particularizing role and no other... Tropes are particular, but not bare particulars. Their role is dual: to be particular natures. (1990: 58)

As is made clear by the rest of this passage, Campbell is thinking of *particularity* in the sense of being non-repeatable (i.e. non-multiply-instantiable, or non-shareable), or having a unique dimensional location (here understood broadly, so as to include location either in time and space or in some

---

[8] I thank John Heil for discussing this issue with Campbell for me.

analogue to time and space). Thus, Campbell is arguing that if constituent properties are particular, then they can ground *both* the character and the particularity of the ordinary object – and so the uneconomical and embarrassing bare particular is unnecessary. On this understanding of substrata, they are only supposed to play one role – that of *particularizing*. The Parity Thesis, then, amounts to the claim that because tropes are *particular* properties, they ground the fact that a bundle of tropes is non-repeatable. Thus, on this understanding of substrata, if a trope is to be thought of as a simplified substrata-cum-universal complex, then tropes are simple non-repeatable properties, or *modifier tropes*.

It is true that some philosophers who have taken an ordinary object to be constituted by universals and a substratum have posited the latter in order to ground the particularity of the object. However, there is another reason philosophers have postulated substrata: *in order to provide an ultimate subject for properties, an entity that is characterized by properties*. The idea here is that unless there is, in a complex, a non-property constituent that is non-derivatively or fundamentally charactered by the constituent properties in that complex, the complex itself cannot be even derivatively charactered in the ways specified by those constituent properties. A bare particular is supposed to play this role; in terms of the above property/object distinction, a bare particular is an object – it is a charactered non-property. The claim that a *bare* particular is *charactered* might sound surprising, if not contradictory, since it is widely assumed that a bare particular is supposed to be something that essentially has no properties. But this assumption is mistaken, and arguably traces back to a footnote (!) by Wilfred Sellars (1963a: 282, fn. 1) in which bare particulars are caricatured in this way.[9] However, the bareness of a bare particular is supposed to lie in the fact that there is no property that it has essentially, not that it essentially has no property whatsoever. In addition, the bareness of a bare particular does not entail that a bare particular fails to satisfy any description. Rather, the predicates necessarily satisfied by a bare particular hold primitively, in that they do not name reified properties. Thus, the predicates 'being a bare particular,' 'being such as to have no property essentially' (etc.) do not name properties. J. P. Moreland and Timothy Pickavance (2003) have developed a theory of bare particulars along these lines. But the point here

---

[9] Sellars argues that the sentence 'Universals are exemplified by bare particulars' is self-contradictory, and that this becomes evident as soon as we translate it into logical notation. The sentence then becomes $(x)[(\exists\phi)(\phi\ x) \supset \neg(\exists\phi)(\phi\ x)]$, which means 'If a particular exemplifies a universal, then there is no universal which it exemplifies' – a self-contradictory statement. This quotation is from Sellars (1963a). The logical notation is from Robert Baker (1967: 211–12) and is different from Sellars' only in style.

is not to defend the coherence of bare particulars.[10] Rather, the point is that Campbell is mistaken in thinking that bare particulars are supposed to perform 'the particularizing role and no other.' There is another role that bare particulars are supposed to play – namely, that of the non-property haver of properties, which *has* properties in the sense of *being characterized by* them. The thought being that, for example, where the sphere is there is more than just *sphericalness*, there is also something that is *spherical, something charactered in a spherical way.*

In sum, there are at least two roles which bare particulars have been employed to play: First, a bare particular in a bare particular-cum-universal complex is supposed to *render the complex non-repeatable* (i.e. non-shareable or non-multiply-instantiable). Second, a bare particular in a bare particular-cum-universal complex is supposed to be *characterized by the universal* in that complex. The upshot is this. According to the Parity Thesis, tropes can play whatever roles bare particulars can play. Thus, if we think bare particulars play only the *first* role, then, via the Parity Thesis, we are led to think of tropes as modifier tropes. On this line of thought, for example, a sphericity trope is particular only in the sense that it is a *non-shareable property.* However, if we think bare particulars play *both* roles, then, via the Parity Thesis, we are led to think of a trope as both a non-shareable entity and (via the Simplicity Thesis) a primitively charactered entity – a module trope. On this line of thought, a sphericity trope is particular in that it is itself a (merely-) *spherical-object.*

To sum up, Campbell assigns to the simple trope various roles played by the bare particular in a bare particular-cum-universals complex. In this way, the concept of a trope has been introduced and/or partly defined in terms of the roles that bare particulars are supposed to play. However, there are discrepancies concerning what these roles are supposed to be. The result is an ambiguity that resolves into the distinction between module tropes and modifier tropes and which represents two versions of trope theory. We are now in a better position to get a sense for how these versions have different strengths and weaknesses when it comes to the task of 'thing-construction.'

As noted, an important role that bare particulars have been assigned is that of being that which is *characterized* or *propertied.* And it seems clear that *something* must play this role, otherwise, nothing would be (say) spherical. On pain of failing to account for the seemingly Moorean fact that there are charactered entities, a trope theorist who rejects bare particulars is under

---

[10] For a defense, see Garcia (2014a) and Pickavance (2014).

significant pressure to take tropes to play this role. That is, she is under pressure to take a trope to be a *simple* which plays the role of *that which is characterized by a property*, thereby construing a trope as a metaphysically simple, singly-propertied-object, or module trope. This theoretical pressure seems to be noticed by David Armstrong:

> An important advantage that [a modifier tropes plus substrata] position has over a bundle of tropes account is that it gets us away from the idea that properties [tropes, in this case] are like things. Properties exist, they are entities, but they are not things. Rather they are *ways* that things are. (1997b: 25)

As my bracketed insertions suggest, in this passage I take Armstrong to have in mind a theory on which *modifier* tropes are accompanied by substrata, a view he takes to have the advantage of not construing tropes as objects (i.e. taking tropes to be module tropes). Accordingly, for a trope theorist who takes tropes to be modifier tropes, tropes do not play the second role noted above for bare particulars. Tropes are the characteristics, or properties, rather than the entities that *are* characterized, or propertied. But if tropes do not play the second role, then presumably some other kind of entity does. Thus, a modifier trope theorist faces significant pressure to accept something like bare particulars or substrata.

The upshot is that the trope theorist seems to face a choice between two views:

(TT1)   Taking tropes to be module tropes, unaccompanied by bare particulars.

(TT2)   Taking tropes to be modifier tropes, accompanied by bare particulars.

The numbers in the acronyms represent the fact that TT1 is a 1-category ontology, whereas TT2 is a 2-category ontology.

With respect to TT1, opting for module tropes has the advantages of making bare particulars unnecessary and avoiding a poly-category ontology. However, as I will discuss below, this view is not without costs. We will see that it is precisely the assumption that tropes are module tropes that makes them vulnerable to Goodman-style objections. Now consider TT2. Many trope theorists seem to find bare particulars either unacceptably mysterious or plainly incoherent. Nevertheless, accepting substrata along with tropes is precisely what Michael LaBossiere (1994) and C. B. Martin (1980) seem to recommend, arguably for reasons similar to the ones considered here. Of course, to do so is to give up on the dream of a mono-category ontology.

In sum, with respect to the task of 'thing construction,' module tropes and modifier tropes have different strengths and weaknesses. Conflating the two types of tropes has obscured the challenges facing each.

2.2 Challenges concerning the construction of property classes

In this section, I will consider how the distinction between module tropes and modifier tropes bears on a second issue that has been central to the development of trope theory: the construction of *property classes*. On trope theory, a property class is a resemblance class of tropes, where membership in the class is defined in terms of degrees of resemblance. More specifically, a class Σ of tropes is a property class iff (1) each member of Σ resembles every other member of Σ to some specific degree, and (2) no trope that is not a member of Σ resembles every member of Σ to that degree (Manley 2002: 77). According to Williams and Campbell, property classes of tropes can provide the semantic values for abstract terms while avoiding both the occult universals of the realist and the powerful objections raised by Nelson Goodman against object-class resemblance nominalism. Thus, property classes play an important role in trope theory, a role described by David Manley as follows: 'In general, whenever we have irreducible need for reference to (or quantification over) a property, there is a class of objects called a "property class" suited to be the subject of our discourse' (2002: 75). As we will see, however, the choice between module tropes and modifier tropes bears significantly on whether and how trope theory might be immune to Goodman's objections. Indeed, we will see that a module trope theory is more vulnerable to these objections than a modifier trope theory – but opting for modifier tropes comes with significant costs.

To show this, I will consider David Manley's challenge to the claim that the property classes of the trope theorist are immune to Goodman's objections. Because space is limited, my aims are as well. My intention is neither to present all of Manley's arguments nor to assess any of them in a comprehensive way. Instead, I will discuss the arguments for which the distinction between module tropes and modifier tropes is most relevant. We will see that Manley seems unaware of this distinction. He takes the tropes of Stout, Williams, and Campbell to be thinly-charactered objects, or module tropes. However, the tacit assumption that tropes are module tropes is not innocuous – it is a crucial premise in most of his objections to trope theory. Moreover, we will see that there are reasons to doubt that Manley's objections would be as forceful if retooled to fit modifier tropes.

The primary target of Manley's objections is what he calls the 'standard' version of trope theory, on which both of the following hold:

(i)   Every trope is a determinate trope.
(ii) Property-classes are resemblance classes of tropes and not all property-classes are constructed out of exactly-resembling tropes; some are formed out of inexact or loose resemblance. (Manley 2002: 82)

In taking the standard view to accept (i), Manley seems to have in mind what Campbell says is a 'well accepted' principle:

> *Principle of Absolute Determinateness* (PAD): 'Nothing can have a determinable character without possessing *exactly one* fully determinate feature [under that determinable] . . . ' (1990: 83–84)

Campbell does not add the bracketed qualification, but presumably, it was tacit; without it, PAD would preclude *everything* from having more than one fully determinate character. PAD expresses the intuitive idea that nothing has the merely determinable characteristic of, say, *being colored* unless it has some fully determinate shade of color, such as *crimson blue*. This is an extremely plausible principle. What is interesting is that Campbell takes PAD to bear not just on ordinary concrete objects but on *tropes as well*. From PAD he infers that 'there are . . . no free-floating determinables' (1990: 84), clearly meaning to affirm what we might call the

> *Absolute Determinateness of Tropes* (ADT): Only fully determinate tropes exist; there are no merely determinable tropes.

The acceptance of ADT is what makes a version of trope theory 'standard,' in Manley's terms.

But notice that PAD entails ADT *only if tropes are construed as module tropes*. PAD bans entities that *have* a merely determinable character. Campbell is clearly thinking that a merely determinable trope, such as 'an instance of color' would itself have to *be colored* but somehow not colored in any specific way. It would be colored, but somehow neither scarlet, nor crimson blue, nor (etc.). Thus, in rejecting merely determinable tropes, Campbell is clearly working with the concept of a module trope.

Manley also thinks of tropes in this way. Throughout his paper, it is obvious that he thinks of tropes as thinly-charactered objects. This is clear in his objections and also from how he describes his examples of tropes (2002: 84–85):

- Some color tropes are reddish, some are bluish, and some are pale.
- Where A is shape trope of an equilateral triangle, A is itself equilateral.

- Where B is the shape trope of a square, B itself has perpendicular sides
  as well as an interior right angle.

To be sure, Manley is interpreting Campbell and Williams in a reasonable way. As indicated above, the thematic concept for both of these
philosophers is that of a module trope. Thus, as they stand, Manley's
objections are aimed at the module trope theorist. In what follows, I will
consider whether the modifier trope theorist can dodge or at least resist
Manley's objections.

Manley's first Goodman-style objection is the *Companionship Problem*
(CP):

> [T]he essence of CP is that resemblance classes conflate attributes that are
> intuitively distinct ... Standard trope theory falls prey to a version of CP
> that concerns coextension between specific and general attributes. Consider
> a possible world where all objects are red. Here the class of colored tropes and
> the class of red tropes coincide exactly. In the actual world, of course, they do
> not, so the trope theorist seems to have succeeded in distinguishing *redness*
> from *coloredness*. In a restricted possible world, however, these collapse into
> the same property. But they are necessarily distinct properties, since things
> can be colored without being red. (2002: 82–83)

Call this restricted possible world 'Ruby.' Notice that in Ruby, PAD by
itself does not entail that there is only one property class and thus a companionship problem. Rather, it is ADT that ensures that there is only one
property class. In other words, Ruby presents a companionship problem
only if there cannot be determinable tropes.

Notice, however, that a modifier trope theorist who accepts PAD can
consistently deny ADT. For example, she could, consistent with PAD, take
Ruby to contain both redness tropes and coloredness tropes. The existence
of coloredness modifier tropes is consistent with PAD because they are
not colored at all; a coloredness trope is not colored, just as a redness
trope is not red and a sphericalness trope is not spherical. In this way, the
modifier trope theorist can take Ruby to contain both fully-determinate and
determinable tropes, in which case there would be the requisite diversity of
property classes, and so no companionship problem. Of course, such a trope
theorist will be accused of populating her ontology with superfluous items.
This accusation may have some merit to it. But, because the introduction
of determinables is also a natural response to Manley's next objection
(the imperfect community), I will postpone discussion of the superfluity
charge. For now it will suffice to note that if determinable module tropes
are incoherent, then the module trope theorist does not even have the
option of being extravagant in this way.

Manley presents the problem of the *Imperfect Community* (IC) as follows:

> [T]he essence of IC is that the criterion for the construction of resemblance classes fails adequately to gather all and only things with a certain property together . . . Consider a world with only three objects: an equilateral triangle, a square, and a right triangle. (For simplicity's sake, they are planar figures.) Let the letters 'A,' 'B,' and 'C' name the shape tropes of these objects, respectively. On standard trope theory, A will stand in various resemblance classes, one for each property that can be applied to the equilateral triangle. So the property *triangularity* should be a class of loosely resembling tropes, one of which is A. (The same should be true of *equilaterality* and *shapedness*.) Now, intuitively each of these shape tropes resembles every other one: A and B are both equilateral; A and C are both triangular; B and C each have perpendicular sides (and an interior angle). None of these tropes, however, shares any of the relevant attributes with *both* of the others. So none of the shared properties can be constructed as a property class out of only two of the shape tropes in this world. (2002: 82, 84–85)

The world Manley describes has three objects in it, so call it 'Trio.' In Trio, because every trope resembles the other two to the same (loose) degree, there is exactly one resemblance class and it has tropes A, B, and C as members. Thus, there is no suitable property class for (to play the role of) *triangularity*, nor for *equilaterality* or *perpendicularness*. Thus, the problem for standard trope theory is that its 'conditions for constructing resemblance classes' are not sufficient to produce the requisite property classes (2002: 85).

Manley considers the following 'tempting reply':

> Posit tropes at every level of generality. Accordingly, take A, B, and C to each be a complex construction out of more fundamental tropes. Take A, for example, to be constructed out of 'a triangularity, an equilaterality, and many more such tropes, since we found that A could resemble other shape tropes in many different ways.' (2002: 85)[11]

Notice that this view posits determinable tropes, thereby rejecting ADT (and so is not a 'standard' version of trope theory). This reply also would work for the Companionship Problem, since on this view Ruby would contain both determinate and determinable tropes, in which case there would be the requisite diversity of property classes.

Against the above reply, Manley raises the charge of superfluity. '[I]f there is a trope for squareness, it would seem superfluous to have tropes for rectangularity and quadrilaterality as well' (2002: 85). By way of a response, I wish mainly to point to how the superfluity charge presents a different and

---

[11] Manley calls this 'Abundant TRN' (TRN is for 'trope resemblance nominalism').

arguably greater challenge for a module trope theorist than for a modifier trope theorist.

To begin, it is worth noting that the notion of a merely determinable module trope appears to be incoherent. If so, then the module trope theorist forecloses on exploring the potential importance and use of determinable tropes. Notwithstanding this point, the superfluity charge would seem to have different force on each kind of trope theory. Consider the square (concrete object) that exists in Trio. Call it 'Quad.' Quad is a bundle of tropes. If there are determinable module tropes, then it would seem that there is a multiplication of shaped objects, all falling at different places along the hierarchy under the determinable 'shaped' and all located where Quad is located. Within Quad, for example, there would be a shaped-thing, a rectangular-thing, and a square-thing; these are non-identical objects. Thus, where Quad is, there would be a multitude of shaped objects – not exact duplicates, but, so to speak, duplicates of varying degrees of resolution. That would be superfluity of a rather bizarre stripe. Postulating determinable modifier tropes does not have this result. If there are such tropes, the only shaped object in Quad's region is the fully-determinately shaped Quad. There would be no multiplication of shaped objects.

My aim here is neither to provide a comprehensive response to Manley nor to argue that a trope theorist must posit determinable modifier tropes. Rather, the point is this. With respect to the project of constructing property classes, the Companionship and Imperfect Community Problems pose significantly greater challenges for module trope theory than for modifier trope theory. The choice between module tropes and modifier tropes is a significant one.

3. Conclusion

The distinction between modifier tropes and module tropes throws into relief two fundamentally different versions of trope theory and brings into focus unique challenges facing each. With respect to the project of thing-construction, a modifier trope theorist faces significant pressure to abandon the bundle theory of substance and adopt a poly-category ontology that includes both tropes and substrata. Conversely, the aspiration for a mono-category ontology, or bundle theory, is better realized by taking tropes to be primitively charactered, thereby adopting a module trope theory. With respect to the project of constructing property-classes, it is precisely the assumption that tropes are module tropes that gives rise to the imperfect community and companionship problems. A modifier trope theory is better equipped to meet these challenges. In this way, the distinction between modifier tropes and module tropes calls into question an alleged advantage of trope theory: that by occupying the middle ground between its rival mono-category constituent ontologies – austere nominalism and realist bundle theory – trope theory uniquely incorporates the strengths and avoids the weaknesses of those views. Upon closer inspection, trope theory is a divided house.[12]

[12] An ancestor of this chapter was presented as 'Tropes and Tropers' at The Problem of Universals in Contemporary Philosophy: An International Conference on Ontology, Scuola Normale Superiore, Pisa, Italy, July 7, 2010. I have numerous friends to thank for their help with this paper. Most especially, I am grateful to Michael Loux – without his support, encouragement, and philosophical guidance, this paper would never have been born. I am also grateful to the other participants in the above conference, including Sophie Gibb, John Heil, E. J. Lowe, Fraser MacBride, Alex Oliver, Gonzalo Rodriguez-Pereyra, Peter van Inwagen, and Dean Zimmerman. For many hours of profitable discussion, I thank José Tomás Alvarado, Robert Koons, Chris Menzel, and Timothy Pickavance. Finally, I thank the two reviewers of the manuscript for their many helpful suggestions.

CHAPTER 7

Tropes and the generality of laws

Sophie Gibb

Are the red of this apple and the red of this vase, which exactly resemble each other in shade, numerically distinct? That is, are properties particulars, or, in other words, tropes? Or, do the apple and the vase both instantiate a single universal: a universal that is also instantiated by any other object that shares their shade? The great battle between upholders of tropes and upholders of universals is a multi-layered one that is impossible to disentangle from debates about the nature of powers, causation, and laws of nature. And it is on this last topic – the nature of a law of nature – that universals are generally presumed to have a serious advantage over tropes, some would argue a decisive one. David Armstrong (1993a, 1996, 1997b, 2004) has long argued that with tropes, unlike with universals, one cannot forge the required link between causes and laws. Peter Forrest (1993) claims that for upholders of tropes to make this link they must invoke unappealing meta-laws. And E. J. Lowe's (2006) main reason for admitting the category of universals in addition to that of tropes, is that he considers that without universals one cannot formulate a satisfactory account of the ontological status of a law of nature.

This chapter is concerned with a problem that Forrest and Armstrong both present as a central one for a trope account of laws – that of explaining the generality of laws. According to them, laws are general. The law that bodies do not accelerate unless acted on by a force implies that *every* body that is not acted on by a force will not accelerate. The law that water dissolves common salt implies that *every* quantity of water that comes into contact with common salt would, provided that nothing inhibits this, dissolve the salt.[1] But what explains this generality? Why couldn't some as yet unexperienced body accelerate despite not being acted on by a force?

---

[1] With Forrest and Armstrong, I shall assume that laws are general. But note, not everyone would wish to accept the generality of laws. Hence, for example, Lowe maintains that laws describe how an object *tends* to behave in various circumstances, not how it actually *does* behave. See Lowe (1987) and (2006: 131).

Why must water dissolve common salt in all times and places? Both Forrest and Armstrong claim that upholders of universals can, whereas upholders of tropes cannot, explain the generality of laws. In this chapter I shall argue that neither Forrest nor Armstrong successfully establish any such thing. If the conclusion of this chapter – namely, that universals have no advantage over tropes when it comes to accounting for the generality of laws – is correct, then this would be a significant victory for the trope-based approach.

1. Forrest's argument

Forrest's (1993: 48–50) argument for the claim that universals can explain the generality of laws goes as follows: Where F and G are universals, say that something causes there to be a G solely in virtue of instantiating F. In this particular case, the instantiation of F caused the instantiation of G because of something about F-ness. With Forrest, call whatever it is about F-ness that did this Ω, 'where "Ω" is a suitable predicate whose analysis need not here concern us' (1993: 49). Consider another instantiation of F. As F is a universal, it is identical across instantiations. Hence, given the Indiscernibility of Identicals, it will be true of F-ness in this further instantiation that Ω. Hence, in identical circumstances, this instance of F would also produce a G.

The generality of laws is therefore explained given the following combination of claims: (1) It is properties that make the causal difference. Hence, taking property-instantiations (where a property-instantiation is the instantiation of a property by a substance[2]) to be the causal relata as Forrest does, it is the property involved in the instantiation that makes the causal difference. For example, the flame instantiating the property of heat causes the copper sulphate crystals to instantiate the property of whiteness. It is the heat of the flame which enables it to bring about this causal effect; (2) properties are universals and, hence, repeatable; and (3) identical properties play an identical causal role in identical circumstances.

Although the generality of laws can apparently be explained by appealing to the nature of a universal, according to Forrest (1993: 49) – and Armstrong would agree (see, for example, Armstrong 1997b: 222) – a similar argument is not available for those who hold that properties are tropes. To demonstrate this Forrest starts with the observation that the latter account of

---

[2] No particular ontological account of substance need be assumed here. In particular, it need not be assumed that the category of substance is ontologically additional to the category of property; substances may be nothing other than bundles of properties.

properties treats 'the repeatable property F-ness as a class of particulars, and it is not by belonging to a class of particulars that one thing causes another' (Forrest 1993: 49).

To explain this claim let us assume the account of property-types advanced by trope-theorists such as Keith Campbell (1990), for this account is precisely the sort that Forrest considers himself to be attacking (Forrest 1993: 62, n. 10). It cashes out property-types in terms of sets of resembling tropes, with a set of *exactly* resembling tropes providing a substitute for a universal. Hence, the repeatable property F-ness is to be identified with a set of exactly resembling tropes. Resemblance is here to be understood as an internal relation: a trope is a member of a resemblance class because of what it is. Hence, whether two tropes exactly resemble depends entirely on their particular natures.

Now upholders of tropes agree that it is properties that make the causal difference – indeed, according to Campbell (1990: 22–23) and many other trope theorists, causes just are properties. But properties are tropes. They are therefore non-repeatable. For this reason, they cannot be numerically identical in different tokens of the same causal sequence. Furthermore, given the trope account, a trope does not make the causal difference that it does by belonging to a set of tropes. It makes the causal difference that it does in virtue of its particular nature and the other members of the set do not determine this nature and, hence, have nothing to do with its causal efficacy.

Applying these considerations, let us say that: (1) the substitute for universal F is the set of exactly resembling tropes 'f' and the substitute for universal G is the set of exactly resembling tropes 'g'; (2) f1 and g1 are tropes, where the first belongs to the set f and the second to the set g; and (3) f1 causes g1.[3] Now consider another trope that is a member of f, call it 'f2.' As f2 is not numerically identical to f1, what reason, Forrest would ask, is there to conclude that it would cause a trope that exactly resembles g1?

It is true that f1 and f2 exactly resemble each other, but the point, according to Forrest, is that they are not identical. Hence, rather than appealing to the meta-law that 'identical causes identical' as the upholder of universals can, the best, Forrest considers, that trope theory can do to explain the generality of laws is to adopt the meta-law that 'like causes like.' Causes that are like each other, in circumstances that are like each

---

[3] Note that Forrest's argument is not dependent on the claim that tropes are the causal relata, but rather that the properties that make the causal difference are tropes. Hence, for example, Forrest's argument is equally applicable to accounts that maintain that the causal relata are substances, where a substance is a cause in virtue of a trope that characterizes it.

other, will give rise to effects that are like each other. More specifically, exactly resembling tropes will play an exactly resembling causal role in exactly resembling circumstances. Forrest questions the plausibility of this principle, and in doing so is in agreement with Armstrong whose dislike of the principle spans many years (Armstrong 1993a: 67; 1996: 97–98; 1997b: 222; 2004: 132). According to Armstrong, '[i]ntuitively, this is a somewhat less compelling principle than the principle that identical causes give rise to identical effects' (1997b: 222) and one that 'is exposed to sceptical doubts when it is asked how it in turn comes to be justified' (1993a: 67). As Armstrong further objects, 'what truthmaker is there for this principle? It hardly seems a necessary state of affairs. That the principle should be flouted by actual singular sequences seems not self-contradictory' (2004: 132).[4]

Before responding to Forrest's argument, it is worth drawing attention to two initial points.

First, in section 3 it will become clear that the interpretation of Forrest's argument depends on whether it is embedded in a dispositionalist or a categoricalist account of properties. Forrest neglects to make this point or to state which account he is assuming. In this chapter I will consider both alternatives and show that under *neither* interpretation does Forrest establish that universals have any advantage over tropes in accounting for the generality of laws. If dispositionalism is accepted, then the principle that 'identical causes identical' and the principle that 'exactly resembling causes exactly resembling' are *equally* plausible. If dispositionalism is rejected, then the principles are *equally* implausible.

Secondly, observe that Forrest's account of laws does not appeal to higher-order relations among universals. According to Forrest there are particulars that instantiate universals and these property-instantiations stand in various causal relations to one another. Laws are not ontologically additional to these entities but instead universal generalizations which quantify over them. Although Armstrong considers Forrest's argument to reveal a serious problem for a trope account of laws (Armstrong 1993a: 67; 1997b: Ch. 15; 2004: 132), he parts company with Forrest in claiming that a satisfactory account of the generality of laws requires, not only a commitment to universals, but also to higher-order relations among them. In section 4

---

[4] To these general worries about the principle, Forrest (1993: 49) adds a more specific one, namely, that with such a meta-law one is unable to deal with functional laws. This chapter shall concentrate on worries of the first type. As Forrest and Armstrong both acknowledge, providing an account of functional laws is problematic regardless of whether properties are tropes or universals. The issue of whether one does a better job than the other deserves a separate discussion of its own.

I shall return to Armstrong's account, and consider whether it succeeds where Forrest's fails. The question that I wish to address first is whether, without an appeal to higher-order relations among universals, one really can establish that universals have any advantage over tropes in accounting for the generality of laws.

2.   A response to Forrest

Let me begin by pointing out one way that trope theory should *not* respond to the problem. On the one hand, the substitute for a universal, according to trope theory, is a set of exactly resembling tropes. On the other hand, the substitute for a trope, according to those who accept universals, is an instance of a universal, that is, the instantiation of a universal by a substance. The latter is a complex entity whose constituents include a substance (a particular) and a universal (a qualitative nature). Unlike it, a trope is not a complex of a particular and a qualitative nature. That is, it is not the case that a trope consists of a constituent that plays the role of particularizer and a further constituent that plays the role of characterizer. It is the trope (not any constituent of it) that is both particularizer and characterizer. To deny this by separating a trope's particularity from its qualitative nature is to admit that a trope is a complex that has a universal as one of its parts – assuming that the universal/particular distinction is an exhaustive one, a characterizing constituent that is not itself a particular can be none other than a universal. Consequently, one collapses tropes into instances of universals.[5] With such a model of tropes, one could, however, easily adopt a Forrest-style explanation of the generality of laws, arguing that causal relations between tropes hold in virtue of the 'characterizing constituent' of a trope. These characterizing constituents would be numerically identical amongst exactly resembling tropes and one could appeal to this numerical identity – invoking the 'identical causes identical' principle – to explain the generality of laws, in much the same way that Forrest does. This fails as a trope response to the problem, because it amounts to the adoption of a theory of universals in all but name.

The correct response to Forrest's argument is, I consider, to question why the principle that exactly resembling causes exactly resembling should be considered any less plausible than the principle that identical causes identical. I shall argue that the thought that it is less plausible is fostered

---

[5]   These claims are widely accepted by upholders of tropes. See, for example, Campbell (1990); Ehring (1997, 1999); Heil (2003); Maurin (2002); Robb (2005).

either by an inadequate understanding of the relationship of exact resemblance or by treating a trope account of laws less charitably than Forrest treats his own account of laws.

To develop this response it is first important to make explicit two features of the account of tropes that I am assuming. They are not ones that I take to be contentious amongst most upholders of tropes.

First, the only thing that differentiates numerically distinct tropes that exactly resemble is the fact that they are distinct particulars. (Universals are not particulars, and hence exactly resembling universals are not numerically distinct.)

Secondly, the particularity of a trope is not a property of it – it does not, in some way, characterize the trope. This point perhaps requires some justification. The reason is based on a priori considerations concerning the categories of being. Ontological categories, which I understand to be demarcated by their existence and identity conditions, form a hierarchical system. Hence, the claim that tropes are particulars is to be interpreted as the claim that tropes are an ontological category which falls within the more general ontological category of particular. In providing a hierarchy of ontological categories, the aim is to *structure* the elements of being. But as ontological categories structure the elements of being, they should not themselves be counted as elements of being. Hence, neither a trope nor the particularity of a trope are to be included alongside such things as tables and trees, and the greenness of a leaf or the scarletness of an apple, in a list of what there is. (For further defense of this point, see Lowe 2006: 6–7 and 40–44). From this it follows that the basis on which formal ontological predicates such as 'is a particular' apply to an entity differs from the basis on which empirical predicates such as 'is scarlet' apply to an entity. The apple is scarlet in virtue of its instantiating the property of scarletness. Unlike this, a trope is a not a particular in virtue of its instantiating the property of 'particularness.' Given the claim that ontological categories are demarcated by their existence and identity conditions, a trope instead falls within the category of particular in virtue of its existence and identity conditions. (For further defense of this point, see Lowe 2006: 98–200.) What this amounts to depends on one's understanding of what it is that distinguishes particulars from universals.[6]

---

[6] Hence, Lowe maintains that a universal is that which has instances, whereas a particular does not (Lowe 2006: 39). According to his four-category ontology, tropes are particulars because they lack instances, whereas a universal has tropes as its instances. This can be explained by consideration of the various ontological dependence relationships that the four categories stand in to one another, which in turn depends on each category's existence and identity conditions. Alternatively, one might

From all of this, we can draw a number of conclusions about exactly resembling tropes – conclusions that, once again, I take to be uncontentious amongst many upholders of tropes, but which need to be made fully explicit for the purpose of this discussion. These conclusions are as follows. The only possible *empirical* difference between exactly resembling tropes will be a spatiotemporal one. This is because all that distinguishes exactly resembling tropes is their particularity. 'Is a particular' is not an empirical predicate, but a formal one. The difference between exactly resembling tropes is therefore *ultimately* not an empirical one but a metaphysical one. I say 'ultimately' because one's account of what it is to be a particular might entail that different particulars, and hence exactly resembling tropes, could not exist in the same spatiotemporal location. Put slightly differently, there is no more of an empirical difference between two exactly resembling tropes than there is between two different instances of a universal.

Relatedly, a trope's particularity does not contribute to its powers. That is, it does not make a difference to the way in which it could affect an entity.[7] If the claim that a trope is a particular were to be analyzed in the same way as the claim that an apple is scarlet – that is, if one were ascribing a property to an element of being – it would be reasonable to raise the question of whether the particularity of a trope does contribute to its powers. This is because, returning to the plausible claim which Forrest's argument makes use of, it is properties that make the causal difference. But a trope is not an element of being and the particularity of a trope does not refer to a property that characterizes it. The ways in which a trope could causally affect an entity is wholly accounted for by the qualitative nature of the trope. The fact that a trope is a particular, and hence cannot characterize more than one entity at a time, makes no difference to these powers.

Indeed, those who support Forrest's argument for the claim that universals can explain the generality of laws, but wish to reject the claim that the particularity of a trope has no causal role to play can clearly be accused of inconsistency, for they themselves must hold that the particularity of a property-instantiation has no causal role to play. Say that particular P_1 instantiates universal F and that this causes P_2 to instantiate universal G. In this instance, the first instantiation produced the second because of something about F-ness, namely Ω. Now plug a different particular, P_3, into the

---

claim, with Forrest, that universals are repeatable whereas particulars are not. Hence, a trope is a particular in virtue of the fact that it could not exist in more than one place at a time. According to still yet another account, universals can characterize more than one substance at a time, whereas tropes cannot.

[7] Power here, of course, need not be interpreted according to the dispositionalist account.

first property-instantiation. Forrest assumes that it will still be true of this new instance of F that Ω, and hence that, in the relevant circumstances, P3's instantiation of F will produce an instance of G. The particularity of the instantiation does not affect F's ability to bring about an instance of G.

Given these considerations, let us return to Forrest's argument against tropes. With regard to exactly resembling tropes f1 and f2, if they did not cause exactly resembling tropes in exactly resembling circumstances, the only thing that distinguishes f1 and f2 – the fact that they are distinct particulars – could not be appealed to to explain this difference in their effects.

This provides an *initial* defense of the principle that exactly resembling causes exactly resembling. If f1 causes g1 and f2 exactly resembles f1, then, in exactly resembling circumstances, f2 must cause a trope that exactly resembles g1. This is because, given what has been argued above, the difference between f1 and f2 is not one that causation would be sensitive to. f1's and f2's qualitative natures will be indistinguishable, and hence their causal effects must also be indistinguishable.[8]

3. Dispositionalism and categoricalism

It is notable, however, that this defense smuggles in the assumption that having the qualitative nature that f1 does and causing g1 are intimately connected; that causing a g (that is a trope from the set of exactly resembling tropes to which g1 belongs) is built into the qualitative nature of f1, and hence that f1 wouldn't be f1 unless, in suitable circumstances, it caused a g. Certainly, given this understanding of the connection between f1 and g1, from what has been said above, it is reasonable to conclude that any trope that exactly resembles f1, and, hence, whose qualitative nature is indistinguishable from f1 will also, in suitable circumstances, cause a g. The power to cause a g flows from the qualitative nature of f1, and hence will also flow from the qualitative nature of any trope that exactly resembles f1. But, if one abandons the claim that there is any such intimate connection between f1 and g1, if f1's power to cause a g is not entailed by f1's qualitative nature, why should we assume that anything that exactly resembles f1 will itself cause a g?

---

[8] It should be remembered that at no stage is the suggestion that the distinction between f1 and f2's qualitative nature and f1 and f2's particularity a distinction between constituents of a trope. I would instead suggest that it is a formal distinction which can arguably be recognized by an act of partial consideration. See, for example, Campbell (1990: 56). I shall not defend this claim here, as it would detract from the main aim of my chapter.

For this reason, Armstrong, who rejects a dispositionalist account of properties, would presumably not consider that a satisfactory response to Forrest's problem has here been presented.[9] According to him, properties are not powers. This is true regardless of whether properties are universals or tropes. This leads to the rejection of the necessitarianism that dispositionalism engenders. If a property is wholly categorical then, as Bird puts it, its 'existence does not, essentially, require it to manifest itself in any distinctive fashion in response to an appropriate stimulus' (2007: 66). There is, therefore, no necessary link between a trope's having the qualitative nature that it does and its having a certain effect.[10] It follows that even though f_1 and f_2's qualitative natures are indistinguishable there is no reason whatsoever to infer from this that they will be causally indistinguishable. This has nothing to do with the thought that the particularity of a trope makes a difference to the way in which it affects an entity. Rather, it is because there is no necessary link between f_1's qualitative nature and the power to cause a g in the first place. Without dispositionalism, the problem that Forrest raises for tropes seems insoluble.

But matters are not as straightforward as they at first seem. On closer inspection, Forrest's argument for the principle that identical causes identical suffers from exactly the same kind of problem. According to Forrest, an instantiation of universal F brings about an instantiation of universal G because of Ω (F-ness). As F is identical across its instantiations, Forrest concludes that every instantiation of F will be Ω, and thus, in identical circumstances, would cause an instantiation of G. But on what basis should we assume that F will always have this effect in its different instantiations? One cannot respond that F's ability to cause an instance of G is part of F's nature, for we are operating on the assumption that dispositionalism is false. But, then, what is the truthmaker for the claim that F will cause an instance of G in different instantiations? What grounds the claim that identical causes identical?

Armstrong recognizes this problem for Forrest's version of the argument for the principle that identical causes identical. He considers that, given the desire to avoid dispositionalism, the best that Forrest can do is to say that the truthmaker is 'the nature of universality, what it is to be a universal, perhaps following this up with the claim that the identical universals→identical

⁹ Indeed, note that in more recent writing Armstrong (2004: 133) is not resistant to the claim that if tropes are embedded within dispositionalism, then the 'like causes like' principle becomes plausible. This claim is not one, however, that he explores in any detail.
¹⁰ See further Armstrong (1997b: 260).

effects principle supervenes upon what it is to be a universal' (Armstrong 1997b: 222).

What exactly this claim amounts to is unclear. According to the suggestion, it is a feature of the ontological category of universals that identical universals have identical effects. Is this supposed to be a brute fact about the category of universals? That is, is it simply true of universals that the principle that identical universals cause identical effects holds, where this principle is not itself explicable in terms of anything about the intrinsic nature of a universal? Surely the explanation cannot stop here! Certainly, if this is the suggestion, given the above observations about exact resemblance, it seems no more questionable or elusive to claim that it is a brute fact about the category of tropes that exactly resembling tropes have exactly resembling effects. If, on the other hand, the claim that identical universals have identical effects is not a brute fact about universals, but is true of a universal in virtue of something about the intrinsic nature of a universal, we are back where we started, for we have simply abandoned categoricalism for dispositionalism.

I should emphasize that if one does maintain that universal F will, in the relevant circumstances, always cause instances of G because of something about the intrinsic nature of F, exactly the same move will be available to upholders of tropes. Say that tropes f_1, f_2, etc. belong to a set of exactly resembling tropes that is a substitute for universal F and that tropes g_1, g_2, etc. belong to a set of exactly resembling tropes that is a substitute for universal G. Whatever it is about the intrinsic nature of F that links F to G, would also be something about the intrinsic nature of f_1 that links it to a trope from the set that is a substitute for universal G. To see this, compare the universal redness with a trope that belongs to the set of exactly resembling tropes that are red. A universal is nothing but a qualitative nature. Regarding tropes, in selectively attending to the redness of the trope, one has considered the qualitative nature of that trope in its entirety – the particularity of the trope is not some additional qualitative feature of it. Hence, a red trope has all of the qualitative nature that the universal redness has and no more. The one difference between a trope and a universal is that the qualitative nature of a universal exhausts its intrinsic nature, and hence the exact resemblance of two universals entails their numerical identity. The qualitative nature of a trope does not exhaust its intrinsic nature, and hence the exact resemblance of two tropes does not entail their numerical identity.

Given that a universal just is a qualitative nature, and that a trope has all of the qualitative nature that a universal has and no more, whatever it is about the intrinsic, and hence qualitative, nature of universal F which causes it to bring about an instance of G would also be something about the qualitative nature of trope f1 which causes it to bring about a g; the link between f1 and its power to bring about a g would be of exactly the same strength as that between universal F and its power to bring about of an instance of G. Having established this link between the qualitative nature of a trope and its effects, we can then return to our initial defense of the principle that exactly resembling causes exactly resembling.

To summarize, if properties are powers then upholders of tropes are just as able to defend the generality of laws as upholders of universals. If, on the other hand, one accepts categoricalism, then Forrest has failed to establish that a trope account of the generality of laws is any worse off than the account he offers in terms of universals. The stumbling block for both accounts is providing a strong enough link between a trope's or a universal's qualitative nature and its power to bring about a certain effect. If such a link could be provided, then, given a proper understanding of what distinguishes exactly resembling tropes, the principle that 'exactly resembling causes exactly resembling' would be no less plausible than the principle that 'identical causes identical.' Forrest's account and the trope account of the generality of laws stand and fall together.

4. A response to Armstrong

What if we were to abandon Forrest's claim that one does not need to appeal to higher-order relations between universals in order to explain the generality of laws? Certainly, the appeal to these higher-order relations is what Armstrong considers to be missing from Forrest's account (Armstrong 1997b: 222).

Let me briefly explain Armstrong's account of laws as presented in *A World of States of Affairs* (1997b). According to Armstrong, singular causation is a relation between first-order states of affairs; where S1 and S2 are thin particulars, and F and G are universals, S1 instantiating F brings it about that S2 instantiates G. For first-order states of affairs to be causally related, they must exemplify types that are lawfully connected. The lawfully connected types that the states of affairs exemplify are the universals that partly constitute the states of affairs. Thus 'S1's instantiating F causes S2 to instantiate G' is true if and only if F and G are lawfully connected. Crucially, unlike with Forrest's account, the lawful connection between universals is a direct one, it does not hold via their instances, that is, via first-order states of affairs. Furthermore, the nomic connection between state-of-affairs types (universals) is, according to Armstrong, a causal connection. That is, F and G are lawfully connected if and only if F brings about G. It is thus Armstrong's claim that causal connections are not merely between states-of-affairs tokens but also between states-of-affairs types (1997b: 225). Indeed, according to Armstrong, the *fundamental* causal connection holds at the type level. Singular causation is nothing other than the instantiation of this causal connection in a particular case (1997b: 227).[11]

Because Armstrong maintains that there is a direct causal connection between universals, his account of why universals explain the generality of laws differs from that of Forrest. If, in a particular case, an instance of F causes an instance of G, this is in virtue of the fact that F causes G – the first causal connection is nothing but an instance of the second. This direct connection between F and G entails, not only that this instance of F causes an instance of G, but that, in identical circumstances, every instance of F will cause an instance of G. Thus the truthmaker for the claim that F will cause G in different instantiations – a truthmaker which Forrest's account was arguably unable to provide – is the higher-order relation between F and G (Armstrong 1997b: 222). This is the real reason, according to Armstrong, why identical causes identical.

If Armstrong's account succeeds, then universals have a clear advantage over tropes in their account of laws, for a similar response is clearly unavailable to the upholders of tropes. Singular causation does not hold between tropes because of a more fundamental causal connection between type-level entities, that is, because of a causal connection between sets of exactly resembling tropes. Rather claims about type-level connections are true in virtue of claims at the singular level, that is, claims about singular causation.

But does Armstrong really provide a more successful account of the generality of laws? Given Armstrong's account, the strength of the inference

---

[11] In earlier work, Armstrong (1983) understands the lawful connection between universals to be the necessitation relation, laws having the form 'F-ness necessitates G-ness.' As the connection does not hold between universals via their instances, Armstrong took laws to be *second-order* necessitation relations between universals (1983: 88). (Laws are still contingent for Armstrong – there are possible worlds in which F-ness does not necessitate G-ness.) However, van Fraassen (1989: Ch. 5) objected that this account faces the 'identification problem' (the problem of how we should understand the relation of necessitation between universals) and the 'inference problem' (the problem of explaining what information the claim that one universal necessitates another gives us about regularities). Furthermore, solving one of these problems leaves the other insoluble. Armstrong's response to the identification problem is that the relation is the causal relation, and his response to the inference problem is that if the relation holds between state of affairs types it must hold between tokens of these types (Armstrong 1993b and 1997b: 227–28). Note, van Fraassen (1993) has questioned whether the relation between states of affairs type and the relation between tokens of these types can plausibly be identical.

that an instance of F would cause an instance of G depends on the strength of the connection between F and G. Now, of course, if the causal connection between F and G were a necessary one, then the relation between F and G could not change and the claim that, in the relevant circumstances, an instance of F always causes an instance of G would drop out of this. But Armstrong holds that the connection between F and G is contingent. This raises a question for Armstrong's account that he is all too aware of: 'Why may it not be that F has the nomic relation G at one time, but later, since the connection is contingent, this relation lapses, perhaps being succeeded by F's being related to H?' (Armstrong 1997b: 257). For Armstrong, there is no explanation of why F and G are causally connected in the first place which could then be appealed to to ground the claim that F and G will always be causally connected; although regularities among singular states of affairs are explained by causal connections between universals, and some of these connections might themselves be explained by appealing to more fundamental causal connections between universals, at the level of fundamental causal connections between universals the explanation stops, contrary to the dispositionalist. That said, Armstrong used to deny the possibility that the causal connection between F and G, if it obtains, might then cease to obtain; although the causal connection need not hold in other possible worlds, there is intra-world stability. But in more recent work, Armstrong (1997b: 257–62) has revoked this position, considering that, given his account, he is forced to admit that contingent relations between universals might change. To quote Armstrong, 'If F-ness produced G-ness, then F-ness has the power to produce G-ness. It may only have this power in a certain spatiotemporal area. It may at some point lose this power' (1997b: 261).

The resulting problem in accounting for the generality of laws is clear. If, in a particular case, an instance of F causes an instance of G, this is in virtue of the causal connection between F and G. But we cannot reason from this causal connection between F and G to the claim that a further instance of F will also cause an instance of G, because the causal connection between F and G may be space–time sensitive; that is, it might vary from space to space and time to time.

Now compare the problem facing Armstrong's account of the generality of laws with the problem facing the trope account of the generality of laws if dispositionalism is rejected. Of course, if causation is space–time sensitive, this will also present a problem for a trope account of the generality of laws. Exactly resembling tropes exist in different spatiotemporal locations and hence, in virtue of this difference, might, if causation is space–time sensitive, differ in their causal effects. However, the resulting problem facing the trope account of the generality of laws is none other than the problem facing Armstrong's account of the generality of laws.

The distinct, and additional, problem facing the trope account is that causal relations might differ from particular to particular, that is, that causation might be sensitive to particularity. (Note that depending on one's understanding of the distinction between a universal and a particular, if causation is sensitive to particularity, this might entail that causation is sensitive to space–time location.)

But what Armstrong fails to recognize is that if we grant that the world might be such that causal relations differ from particular to particular, an extended version of the problem facing his own account can be advanced. The original problem was that the causal relation between universals F and G might not obtain in different spatiotemporal areas – it might be space–time sensitive. But, if we are allowing that in the case of tropes, causation might be sensitive to particularity, then we surely have to allow that in the case of universals, causation might be sensitive to particularity. This raises the following problem for universals: If in a particular case, an instance of F causes an instance of G, this is in virtue of the causal connection between F and G. But we cannot reason from this causal connection between F and G to the claim that a further instance of F will also cause an instance of G, because the causal connection between F and G might not obtain for different instances of F and G, and this is not in virtue of the fact these different instances occupy a different spatiotemporal area, but simply in virtue of the fact that they are different instances, that is, that they involve different particulars. The resulting problem of how to move from the claim that universal F causes universal G to the claim that, in a particular case, an instance of universal F would cause an instance of universal G seems no less problematic than the problem of how to move from the claim that trope f_1 causes trope g_1 to the claim that a trope that exactly resembles f_1 would cause a trope that exactly resembles g_1.

Now Armstrong does have a reply to the point that causation might be space–time sensitive. In his defense of the claim that universal F would, as a matter of fact, stand in a causal relation to G in different spatiotemporal locations, he argues that F 'did have the power at a certain time. Is it not an attractive and simple hypothesis that it will continue to have this power at all times and places? (Power here, of course, does not have to be understood according to the Dispositionalist model.)' (1997b: 261). In other words, is it not an attractive and simple hypothesis that causation relations are not space–time sensitive? As Armstrong goes on to acknowledge, this justification 'may not be quite all one might hope for, but it seems to have real value.'

One would think that Armstrong would find the hypothesis that causal relations are not sensitive to particularity even more attractive than the hypothesis that causal relations are not sensitive to space–time. While 'is in spatiotemporal location x' is an empirical predicate, 'is a particular' is a formal predicate and thus, it is hard to see how nomic connections, which are empirical, could be sensitive to the difference between two particulars, qua particularity.

But if Armstrong allows that, in the case of universals, the causal relation is not sensitive to the particularity of the instantiation, how, if he is to be consistent, could he not allow that, in the case of tropes, the causal relation is not sensitive to the particularity of the trope? An empirical law would be no more sensitive to the difference between exactly resembling tropes than it would be to the difference between two different instances of a universal. As with Forrest's argument, so with Armstrong's – Armstrong's account of the generality of laws and the trope account of the generality of laws stand and fall together.

5. Some final remarks

The aim of this chapter has been to establish that neither Forrest nor Armstrong successfully demonstrate that universals do a better job of explaining the generality of laws than tropes. Given a dispositionalist account of properties, tropes and universals are equally successful in explaining the generality of laws. If, on the other hand, properties are categorical, universals are no better off than tropes, facing similar problems, which upholders of universals and upholders of tropes can attempt to respond to in similar ways. Contrary to Armstrong (2004: 132), to suggest that the principle that exactly resembling causes exactly resembling could be flouted in singular cases carries no more force than the claim that the principle that identical causes identical could be flouted in singular cases.

There is, of course, more work to be done in order to demonstrate that upholders of universals do not have an advantage over upholders of tropes when it comes to laws – discussions concerning the generality of laws are but one aspect, albeit a very important one, of this project. Universals might be thought to have an advantage over tropes in accounting for the link between laws and counterfactuals or in accounting for functional laws.[12] And the problem of how to distinguish law-like regularities from mere

---

[12] For the former problem, see Armstrong (1983: 103; 1996: 100–1; and 1997b: 261). As Armstrong (1996: 100–1) acknowledges, the problem is removed if there is a necessary connection between a trope and its effects. Equally, given Armstrong's denial of intra-world stability, it is not altogether

accidental regularities will not go away for those upholders of tropes who combine a regularity theory of laws with a regularity theory of causation, although clearly the problem is less pressing for those upholders of tropes who attempt to advance a less deflationary account of singular causation.

It is important to recognize that this discussion's focus has been on Forrest's and Armstrong's appeal to universals to account for the nature of laws of nature. Other ontological accounts may have a stronger case for the claim that one can provide a better account of the generality of laws with universals than one can with tropes. In particular, I have in mind Lowe's four-category ontology. Lowe (2006) considers that in order to provide a truly satisfactory account of laws one needs, not only universals, but also substantial kinds. More importantly for this discussion, unlike Armstrong, Lowe treats universals as abstract, that is as non-spatiotemporal entities. For this reason, Lowe understands laws (to the extent that they involve universals) to be timeless and placeless. The issue of whether this account is able to avoid the difficulties afflicting Armstrong's account has not been a topic of this discussion, but is one that deserves further exploration.

To raise a final point, this chapter has established that, at least as far as Forrest's and Armstrong's accounts of a law of nature are concerned, the universal-based approach and the trope-based approach are equally success-ful (or unsuccessful) in explaining the generality of laws. This equivalence in their explanatory power might raise the suspicion that the ultimate lesson to be learned is that there is not really any substantive difference between the two approaches. That is, to talk about multiply located *in re* universals and to talk about singly located exactly resembling *in re* tropes is to use two different languages to ultimately say the same thing – it is to make a distinction without a real difference. If so, it is no surprise that nei-ther theory has an explanatory advantage in explaining the generality of laws.

I would urge against this conclusion. There is a substantive difference between tropes and universals because they have utterly different identity conditions. While tropes are particulars, universals are not. In virtue of this difference, the exact resemblance of universals F and G entails their numerical identity, while the exact resemblance of tropes f1 and g1 does not entail their numerical identity. There is a substantive difference between tropes and *instantiations of* universals, because while the latter is a complex entity whose constituents include a substance and a universal, a trope does

---

clear that his own account of the link between laws and counterfactuals is entirely satisfactory, as Armstrong (1997b: 259–62) himself recognizes. For the latter problem, see Forrest (1993).

not have either of these entities as a constituent, indeed, it is not a complex entity. Although these differences between the two approaches do not entail any difference in their ability to explain the generality of laws, one would be incorrect to conclude that the two approaches were explanatorily equivalent in all respects. To mention but one of the resulting, well-known differences, those who maintain that universals are *in re* tend to consider that universals are 'wholly present' in the various substances that instantiate them. Hence, they accept that a universal can be wholly in two different places at the same time. The plausible objection that it makes no sense to say that anything, not even a universal, can be wholly in two different places at once, motivates the thought that universals cannot be concrete entities. *In re* tropes clearly face no such problem because they are not instantiated by more than one substance at a time.[13]

[13] This chapter was completed with support from the Arts and Humanities Research Council's Research Grant AH/F009615/1 'The New Ontology of the Mental Causation Debate.' I'm very grateful to James Clarke, John Heil, Valdi Ingthorsson, and Jonathan Lowe for their helpful comments on earlier versions of this chapter. I would also like to thank the participants of the conference on the problem of universals in contemporary philosophy held at the Scuola Normale Superiore in Pisa, Italy in 2010.

CHAPTER 8

On the origins of order: non-symmetric or only symmetric relations?

Fraser MacBride

1. Introduction

Non-symmetric relations abound, arranging things so that one is above another, arranging events so that one precedes another, and so on. Our manifest and scientific images of the world and their respective domains of thought and talk are thick with commitment to them and descriptions of them – spatial, temporal, causal, mechanical, mathematical, cognitive, the list is difficult to close off. It was the recognition of the reality of such relations that inaugurated the era of analytic philosophy; recognition that they exist and aren't reducible is what enabled Russell to decide against monism and idealism in favor of pluralism and realism (Russell 1925: 371).

Recognizing that non-symmetric relations exist and aren't reducible doesn't explain how relations pull off the feat of arranging things, events, etc. one way rather than another. Russell originally proposed to account for how non-symmetric relations do so by attributing the feature of 'direction' to them (Russell 1903: §218). Although Russell's commitment to this view subsequently wavered, it would be fair to say that many twentieth-century philosophers either took the view that non-symmetric relations have direction more or less unreflectively on board, or else simply took for granted the capacity of relations to arrange things one way rather than another, or, in fact, vacillated between these alternatives. Against the backdrop of this rather unsatisfactory state of affairs Fine has offered us a radically different account of how non-symmetric relations arrange things one way rather than another in terms of the interrelationships that obtain between the different states to which the application of non-symmetric relations give rise (Fine 2000). But really there is no need to embrace the consequence of Russell's appeal to direction or to undergo the intellectual somersaults that Fine's account requires of us. All we need to do is to embrace what might be described as a form of *Ostrich Realism*: the view that *how* a non-symmetric relation applies to its relata – one way rather than another – is ultimate and irreducible and that more substantive accounts of how relations apply to their relata yield no real explanatory benefits (MacBride 2013a).

Of course if there are no non-symmetric relations in the first place then this kind of deflationary realism goes by the board; without such relations there can no justification for enriching the ideology of our world-theory with the primitive vocabulary required to describe the application of relations. It has been suggested, or argued, by a number of recent philosophers, including Armstrong and Dorr, that there are neither non-symmetric nor asymmetric relations but only symmetric ones.

It seems *unlikely* that they're right about this. From a general methodological point of view it appears far more likely that an error is somewhere concealed in what are often labyrinthine and abstract arguments offered for the claim that there are only symmetric relations than that our cognitive systems, science, and mathematics should have portrayed to us a world of non-symmetrical relations when really there are none (James 1904). But, of course, acknowledging that Armstrong's and Dorr's arguments must be wrong doesn't relieve us of the philosophical task of locating where errors are to be found. So here I'm going to roll up my sleeves and take them to task. After laying out the basic motivation for adopting a kind of deflationary realism, I will argue that neither Armstrong nor Dorr's arguments give us anything like a good reason to say anything *less* about relations.

2. Non-symmetric relations: for deflationary realism

Relations such that xRy whenever yRx are symmetric. Relations that fail to be symmetric are non-symmetric – if xRy fails to guarantee that yRx. Asymmetric relations are a species of non-symmetric relation such that xRy excludes its being the case that yRx. But it can only be the case that xRy fails to guarantee that yRx, or excludes its being the case that yRx, if its being the case that xRy is genuinely different from its being the case that yRx. Otherwise xRy will guarantee yRx after all. So it is a basic requirement upon a relation's being non-symmetric, whether asymmetric or otherwise, that there are different ways in which the relation is capable of applying to the things that it relates. There are two ways in which a binary non-symmetric relation may hold between two things, six ways in which a ternary non-symmetric relation may hold between three things, twenty-four ways in which a quaternary relation may hold between four things, and so on. This basic requirement is the least we must allow if we are to make sense of the distinction between symmetric relations on the one hand and non-symmetric and asymmetric relations on the other.

Many philosophers, following Russell, have discerned a need to impose further requirements upon non-symmetric relations in order to make sense of their satisfying this basic one. Presupposing that the capacity of a non-symmetric relation to apply in a plethora of different ways isn't the kind of capacity that should be taken as primitive, they have set out to explain how it is possible for a relation to be endowed with such a capacity. Many of them, also following Russell, have done so by attributing to each non-symmetric relation a 'direction' or 'order' whereby it proceeds *from* one thing it relates *to* another. The difference between a non-symmetric relation applying one way rather than another thus arises from its proceeding in one direction or order rather than another: the relation such that xRy rather than yRx is the relation that proceeds one way rather than another between x and y. But it also appears to be a consequence of this explanation that each non-symmetric relation has a distinct converse too. For any relation such that xRy, its converse may be defined as the relation such that yR^*x, relations which differ only with respect to the direction in which they proceed from one thing they relate to another. Since it would be arbitrary to admit that one of these relations exists but not the other we appear beholden to admit both of them.[1] So now it appears that we are forced to recognize a further requirement upon non-symmetric relations: that each such relation has an existential partner, a converse that's distinct.

If the admission of distinct converses is an inevitable existential consequence of employing direction to explain how it is possible for a relation to fulfill the basic requirement upon its being non-symmetric, this provides a reason to be doubtful of the theoretical appeal of explaining what it is to be a non-symmetric relation in such terms. This is because admitting converses appears to have as a corollary a commitment to including additional states in our ontology to house them. But this commitment clashes with the established, commonsense beliefs about how many states there are. Consider that if we accept this commitment there will not only be the state arising from a given binary non-symmetric relation such that xRy to concern us. There will also be the state that arises from the converse of the given relation such that yR^*x. So there won't just be the state of the cat's being on top of the table to worry us but also the further state of the table's

---

[1] This line of thought, advanced by Fine (2000: 2–3), may be traced back to Russell (1903: §§218–19). For an account of the development of Russell's engagement with the issue of how relations apply see MacBride (2013b).

being underneath the cat. But surely there's only one state here, albeit a state that falls under two descriptions.[2]

To avoid our being overwhelmed by the superfluity of states that appears to result from the admission of converses, Fine has argued that we need to reject the assumption that led to the admission of converses in the first place (Fine 2000: 16–32). This was the assumption that the capacity of a non-symmetric relation to hold in a plethora of different ways is to be explained by the direction whereby it proceeds from one thing it relates to another. What makes this explanation initially appear compelling is that it answers to the (apparently) naïve preconception that relations apply *directly* to the things they relate. What distinguishes a non-symmetric relation being such that xRy rather than yRx depends solely upon its proceeding from x to y rather than from y to x – nothing else intervenes in the mechanism whereby a relation applies the things it relates. Fine argues that once we give up the naïve preconception that makes this explanation appealing to us, an alternative explanation comes into view of how it is possible for a non-symmetric relation to apply in a plethora of different ways. According to Fine what distinguishes a non-symmetric relation being such that xRy rather than yRx depends upon how xRy is interconnected with zRw. But this gives rise to a problem for Fine's account. Surely it's possible that a relation R be such that xRy even though there is no z and w such that zRw. Fine's explanation of what distinguishes R being such that xRy rather than yRx precludes this possibility, thereby ruling itself out. The preconception that relations apply directly to the things they relate, it turns out, isn't really naïve at all, it because it enables us to make ready sense of a non-symmetric relation being such that xRy even in the absence of some z and w such that zRw.[3]

It is also questionable whether, as Fine claims, an explanation in terms of direction of the capacity of an asymmetric relation to apply in a plethora of different ways really does require us to overcommit to converses and states to house them. It doesn't follow from the fact that such an explanation furnishes us with the ideological wherewithal to *define* the notion of a converse of a non-symmetric relation that we are compelled to admit something that answers to the definition. It doesn't follow either that because it would be arbitrary for us to select a non-symmetric relation

---

[2] Williamson (1985) offers a related semantic argument that if we admit converse relations then it will be irredeemably inscrutable which predicates express which relation.

[3] Further objections to Fine's approach are raised and developed in MacBride (2007: 44–53).

at the expense of its converse that we have reason to affirm a theory of relations that incorporates a commitment to both of them. It may exceed the evidence we have for our theory to suppose that whenever there is one non-symmetric relation there is more than one – its converse partner or partners too – because a commitment to one of them may suffice to satisfy the demands of the theory. We may only need to believe that one of them exists to account for things' being arranged thus-and-so rather than so-and-thus.

But in fact we should reject any explanation of what it is to be a non-symmetric relation in terms of direction because of another seemingly innocuous consequence that Fine doesn't make out. If a non-symmetric relation is such that xRy rather than yRx because it proceeds in one direction rather than another between x and y, then there must be a fact of the matter about whether R proceeds from x to y or from y to x. But we can't logically wring out of our ordinary and scientific descriptions of the application of non-symmetric relations anything to settle whether these relations proceed one way rather than another amongst the things they relate – such facts of the matter, if there are any, do not admit of detection by our logical radar but must somehow sneak underneath. Take the state S_0: Jeanette is to the left of Melanie. Does this state consist in a relation proceeding from Jeanette to Melanie or from Melanie to Jeanette? There is nothing in our description of S_0 to determine an answer one way or another. So even with regard to the application of a single relation to give rise to a given state, an explanation in terms of direction commits us to an unpalatable choice amongst unfathomable facts of the matter concerning how that relation proceeds between the things it relates to give rise to that state. The problem is only exacerbated when we compare S_0 with another state T_0: Jeanette loves Melanie. Does T_0 consist in a relation proceeding in the same or a different way between Jeanette and Melanie than the relation in whose application S_0 consists? If the application of non-symmetric relations is really to be explained in terms of direction there must be a fact of the matter about how these relations proceed between the things they relate. Because the descriptions of S_0 and T_0 provide no basis whatsoever for answering such questions we have reason to be doubtful that these states consist of non-symmetric relations that proceed from one of the things they relate to the other.

It is easy to be misled at this point if we don't take care to distinguish between the different degrees to which we may allow our metaphysics to embrace the idea of relatedness. The requirement that non-symmetric relations be capable of applying in a plethora of different ways is the least or *first degree* to which we must accept the idea of relatedness if non-symmetric relations are to be distinguished from symmetric ones. It is a further logical step beyond the first to embrace the *second degree*: the requirement that every non-symmetric has a distinct converse. And it is another distinct step to embrace the *third degree*: the requirement that there be a fact of the matter about whether the non-symmetric relation such that *xRy* rather than *yRx* proceeds from *x* to *y* or from *y* to *x*.

We cannot avoid embracing the first degree if we admit non-symmetric relations at all. But it is not logical succession that leads us ineluctably from embracing the first to the second and third. The second degree may be avoided altogether because the notion of a converse may be definable even though nothing answers to it; whilst the necessity to embrace the third is only conditional upon an explanatory hypothesis we don't have to adopt, i.e. a repercussion of explaining how the first degree is possible in terms of direction. The execrable consequences of embracing the third degree provide us with a reason to reject such explanations of the first (even if the consequence of the second didn't already do for direction).

Appreciating this leaves us with a choice. Either we can reach out again into the darkness for an alternative explanation of the first degree or we can recognize that the capacity of a non-symmetric relation to relate in a plethora of different ways isn't the kind of fact that admits of a discursive explanation but must be everywhere presupposed. But if we don't already think that an account of relations in non-relational terms is needed why suppose that an explanation of the first degree in other terms is needed in the first place? The failure of earlier attempts, such as Russell's or Fine's, to provide any credible discursive explanations provides corroborative evidence in favor of the view that the first degree doesn't admit of further explanation, i.e. deflationary realism.[4] It's time that we take seriously the neglected possibility that the first degree should be embraced as primitive without need of any discursive explanation, as capturing the very idea of a non-symmetric relation once the extraneous trappings of the second and third degrees have been stripped away.

3.   Armstrong: non-symmetric relations and unwanted necessities I

Descriptions of non-symmetric relations and their applications appear throughout the scientific and mathematical theories we routinely endorse.

---

[4] For additional arguments in favor of taking the first degree of relatedness as primitive see MacBride (2013a: 8–14).

But Armstrong has argued that a significant proportion of these descriptions, the ones that appear to pick out asymmetric relations, are inherently misleading. Such descriptions mislead us, if Armstrong's argument has it right, because there are no asymmetric relations out there to describe. Dorr has gone even further and argued that *any* description that appears to pick out a non-symmetric relation misleads us because there are no non-symmetric relations *whatsoever*; all our descriptions of non-symmetric relations are empty. Obviously if Armstrong and Dorr are right there really is no need to take the first degree as primitive – because only non-symmetric relations admit relatedness in the first degree. Both their arguments officially rely upon the Humean principle that there are no 'brute necessities' to be found in nature.

The brute necessities against which Armstrong inveighs link 'distinct existences,' necessities that cannot be rendered transparent to the intellect by appealing to overlap between the items linked. If we embrace the idea of relatedness in the second degree then we will find that Armstrong's view is straightaway compromised. This is because a non-symmetric relation's being such that xRy will entail that it has a distinct converse such that yR^*x. To safeguard the Humean principle that there are no brute necessities Armstrong responds by rejecting the second degree. He insists that the appearance of two states here, arising from the application of two distinct (converse) relations, is merely linguistic. Consider a's being before b and b's being after a. 'Fairly obviously,' Armstrong reflects, 'this is just one state of affairs,' a state that arises from the application of a single relation, albeit a state that may be 'described in two different ways' (Armstrong 1978: vol. II, 42; 1989b: 85). But even if the second degree is rejected, asymmetric relations, if there are any, present a further challenge to the denial of brute necessities. An asymmetric relation such that xRy excludes its being the case that yRx. But, Armstrong asks, how could this be without a brute necessity obtaining whereby one state excludes another? Armstrong saves the Humean denial of brute necessities by simply denying that there are any such asymmetric relations to be found out there. We might have naïvely thought that an event A's being before an event B excludes B's being before A. But, Armstrong maintains, it's not a necessary truth at all. It's possible that time is circular – its being so is compatible with the equations of General Relativity – so A's being before B doesn't exclude B's being before A. In a similar spirit Armstrong dismisses any other candidate for being an asymmetric relation (Armstrong 1989b: 85; 1997b: 143–44).

We shouldn't allow ourselves to be lured by Armstrong's choice of scientific example into generalizing hastily from the fact that some candidates for being asymmetric relations have turned out to be non-symmetric that no candidates are ever fitting. Nor should we allow ourselves be lured into thinking that Armstrong's denial of brute necessities is genuinely thorough-going. It appears to be so because he relies upon this Humean denial to discredit converse relations and asymmetric ones. It seems that Armstrong has the courage of his convictions, following his argument where it leads. But closer inspection reveals that Armstrong's theory of relations remains riddled with brute necessities – even when converses and asymmetric relations are sent packing.

According to Armstrong, the world is the totality of existing states of affairs where 'A state of affairs exists if and only if a particular (at a later point to be dubbed a *thin* particular) has a property, or, instead, a relation holds between two or more particulars' (Armstrong 1997b: 1). Even this most general and abstract characterization of Armstrong's ontology incorporates commitment to a battery of brute necessities. Were necessary connections fully absent from his ontology then its pieces ought to be, in Hume's phrase, 'entirely loose and separate'; it ought to be possible to throw them up into the air and let them fall wherever the breeze takes them. But the pieces aren't entirely loose and separate; they can't float down entirely independently from one another. There's a rigid network of necessary connections that controls their relative placement. It isn't possible for a state of affairs to exist in which a monadic property is such that none or more than one particular has it. It isn't possible for a state of affairs to exist in which a dyadic relation is such that one or none or more than two particulars are related by it. It isn't possible for a state of affairs to exist in which there isn't a property or a relation that's had by one particular or holds between two or more particulars. It isn't possible for a state of affairs to exist in which there is more than one property or relation. And this doesn't exhaust the list of necessary connections that exert a controlling influence on the pieces of Armstrong's ontology. (Exercise for the reader: find more examples.)[5]

Armstrong urges us to renounce asymmetric relations and the converses of non-symmetric ones in order to avoid brute necessities. But his ontology of states of affairs, particulars, properties, and relations incorporates commitment to plenty of brute necessities. The bottom line: this undermines his argument for renouncing asymmetric relations and converses in the first place.

---

[5] For further examples of necessary connections to which the theory of universals is committed see MacBride (1999: 484–93).

4.   Dorr: Non-symmetric relations and unwanted necessities II

Dorr goes further than Armstrong, urging us to renounce not only asymmetric but all non-symmetric relations in order to avoid brute necessities. But his argument is also undermined by the fact that his ontology doesn't avoid commitment to brute necessities either.

Dorr provides a more exacting account than Armstrong of what it is to be a brute necessity. Call a sentence S a brute necessity iff (i) S is not logically true, (ii) the only non-logical vocabulary in S consists of primitive predicates, (iii) all quantifiers in S are restricted to fundamental entities, (iv) S is metaphysically necessary.[6] According to Dorr the thought behind the principle that there are no brute necessities is just that 'metaphysical necessity is never "brute"': when a logically contingent sentence is metaphysically necessary, there is always some *explanation* for this fact' (Dorr 2005: 161). But such explanations are typically only possible when a sentence contains some non-primitive expressions that admit of analysis or expressions that are rigidly referring. Since the only non-logical vocabulary of a brute necessity S consists of primitive predicates – that are neither analyzable nor referential – such explanations of S's being metaphysically necessary are ruled out. Dorr surmises that unless an alternative explanation of S's being metaphysical necessary can be provided we should look askance at the claim of S to be a brute necessity. If Dorr is right that there can be no brute necessities, then to demonstrate that there are no non-symmetric relations Dorr need merely show that there is no admitting non-symmetric relations without also acknowledging brute necessities about them.

But is it really at all plausible that there are no brute necessities in the very exacting sense that Dorr prescribes? (Of course Wittgenstein held in the *Tractatus* that the only necessity is logical necessity (6.37) but, famously, things didn't work out well for him there.) If we think that the world is fundamentally composed of different categories of entity but we don't think that this is just a cosmological accident then it is difficult to see how brute necessities are ultimately to be avoided. Suppose, for example, that the world is fundamentally composed of particulars and universals, that behave in the coeval but nevertheless quite different manners suited

---

[6] In fact Dorr adds the stronger condition that a brute necessity S can be known for certain a priori to be true. He argues that there are no brute necessities in this stronger sense because sentences that are known for certain a priori require to be built up from non-primitive predicates or referring expressions and, *ex hypothesi*, the non-logical vocabulary of S consists only of primitive predicates. Since this stronger condition performs no additional role in Dorr's argument that isn't already performed by the weaker condition that a brute necessity is metaphysically necessary I will omit this complication.

to their respective categories. If this isn't just how the world happens to be then there must be brute necessities that describe how particulars and universals behave differently.

Armstrong didn't succeed in putting brute necessities behind him, never could have done, because his world is fundamentally composed of three different categories, states of affairs, particulars, and universals, entities that essentially exhibit quite different forms of behavior. But Dorr doesn't succeed in avoiding brute necessities either because he still admits two categories. It's a brute necessity that falls out of Armstrong's system that no state of affairs has more than one universal constituent. To avoid this brute necessity Dorr recommends that we jettison states of affairs and favor instead a theory in which there is just one primitive predicate '... holds among...' that takes one singular term and one plural term as its arguments (Dorr 2005: 189–91). Introducing this predicate has the consequence that we don't need to report upon the application of a symmetric relation r by saying that there is a state of affairs in which r is borne by x to y. We need merely report that r holds amongst x and y, a report which doesn't commit us to a state of affairs. Never mind the (extremely important) question whether a theory with just this primitive has the capacity to account for everything that a theory that posits states of affairs explains. If particulars cannot do what is typical of symmetric relations, nor symmetric relations what is typical of particulars, then brute necessities must still lurk within his system – the particulars and universals that compose Dorr's world just can't be entirely loose and separate.

What are examples of such brute necessities? If we forbid particulars and universals from existing outside of their permitted combinations, there can be neither 'bare' particulars nor relations that don't relate. Then it will be necessary that (S_1) it's not the case that there is an x such that there is no r which holds among x and some other things. Whilst relations can hold among the things they relate, presumably particulars are incapable of doing so. So it's also necessary that (S_2), if there is anything at all, there are some things (the particulars) such that they do not hold among other things. But even though they're necessary, S_1 and S_8 aren't logical truths and their non-logical vocabulary doesn't admit of further analyses; so they're brute necessities of just the kind that Dorr is committed to denying because he holds that the only intelligible necessities are analyzable. We don't need any more examples to appreciate that the denial of brute necessities fits ill with a fundamental ontology of particulars and universals.[7] Dorr bases his case

---

[7] Of course a 'way out' here for the Humean to take would be to deny that the categories of particular and universal are fundamental. See MacBride (1999: 497–99) and (2005: 124–26). One option would

against non-symmetric in favor of symmetric relations on the grounds that the former but not the latter give rise to brute necessities. Even before we negotiate the details of Dorr's argument it is apparent that his case cannot be effective.

5. Dorr: Do non-symmetric relations generate spurious possibilities?

The verb 'bears' provides a significant linguistic resource for describing how relations apply to the things they relate. Using this verb we can distinguish a relation r which is symmetric (because x bears r to y whenever y bears r to x) from a relation s which is non-symmetric (because x bears s to y even though y doesn't bear s to x). Dorr draws upon this resource to articulate what he takes to be a plausible sounding principle about relations:

CONVERSES: For every r, there is an r^* such that for any x and y, x bears r^* *to* y iff y bears r to x.

Evidently this principle isn't a logical truth. But suppose that CON-VERSES is metaphysically necessary, that the only non-logical predicate that appears in CONVERSES ('bears') is primitive and that its quantifiers are restricted to fundamental entities. Then CONVERSES qualifies to be a brute necessity. But if there are no brute necessities then this principle must somehow fail to meet the standard. If 'bears' is primitive then something else must be responsible for CONVERSES falling short. Suppose that its quantifiers are restricted to fundamental entities. Since CONVERSES isn't a logical truth, the only remaining explanation is the failure of CON-VERSES to be metaphysically necessary (Dorr 2005: 159–61). So if we grant Dorr that there are no brute necessities this establishes the first premise of his argument:

(1) If 'bears' is primitive then CONVERSES isn't metaphysically necessary.

The second premise of Dorr's argument is a disjunction:

(2) CONVERSES is metaphysically necessary or 'bears' is not primitive.

To establish this key premise Dorr relies upon a thought experiment about alien relations.

---

be to explain away the necessary connections found between particulars and universals by using counterpart theory. See MacBride (2005: 139–40).

Before we head into the laboratory it will help prevent future disorientation if we first get a firm strategic fix upon where Dorr is heading with his argument. If (2) is true then one of its disjuncts must be true. If the former disjunct is true, i.e. if CONVERSES is metaphysically necessary, then the consequent of (1) is false. So by *modus tollens*, the antecedent of (1) is also false, in other words, 'bears' is not primitive. If the latter disjunct is true, i.e. if 'bears' is not primitive then, of course, 'bears' is not primitive. Either way it follows from (1) and (2) that:

(3)   'bears' is not primitive.

If 'bears' isn't primitive then it must be analyzable in more fundamental terms. So Dorr surveys a variety of different candidate analyses of 'bears' in such terms – that appeal to such notions as *state of affairs* and *argument position*. But Dorr finds himself unable to find a credible analysis of 'bears' that isn't afflicted by such ailments as committing us to further brute necessities or that doesn't also have the consequence that 'if x bears r to y then y bears r to x' is equivalent to a logical truth. This leads Dorr to conclude:

(4)   There are no non-symmetric relations.

We needn't dwell upon the intricate sub-structure of the reasoning that leads Dorr from (3) to (4) because the thought experiment Dorr provides earlier in his argument fails to support (2).

Dorr doesn't argue directly for (2). Instead he uses the aforementioned thought experiment to establish that the following claim is false:

(5)   'bears' is primitive and CONVERSES is not metaphysically necessary.

Since the negation of (5) is truth functionally equivalent to (2), Dorr's thought experiment, if it's robust, indirectly supports (2). The problem that Dorr purports to find with (5) is that this combination of views 'forces us to draw *spurious distinctions* between the possibilities (metaphysical or epistemic possibilities – it doesn't matter which) in which CONVERSES fails' (Dorr 2005: 164). The design brief of the thought experiment Dorr constructs is to convince us that the distinctions between possibilities that (5) requires us to draw really are spurious.

Suppose for the sake of *reductio* that 'bear' is primitive and that CONVERSES is not metaphysically necessary. Now consider a possible world in which there is a series of simple particulars, linearly ordered by exactly two independent non-symmetric relations r_1 and r_2. Dorr asks: do the relations arrange this series in the same or in opposite directions? Philosophers reflecting upon relations, such as Russell or Fine, have used the expression 'direction' to mean a variety of different things but Dorr means something else quite specific by this question. He wants to know which of the following hypotheses is the case:

(i) For any distinct x and y in the series, x bears either r_1 or r_2, but not both, to y.
(ii) For any distinct x and y in the series, x bears both r_1 and r_2 to y, or bears neither r_1 nor r_2 to y.

Prima facie each world that features such a series ought to provide us with the materials to furnish a determinately right answer to the question 'Which hypothesis is true at that world?' But Dorr denies this to be the case: 'I say there can be no determinately right answer, because the question is not a legitimate one. There is nothing for us to be ignorant about; no genuine respect in which two possible worlds might be dissimilar' (Dorr 2005: 164).

Dorr offers us the now long-awaited thought experiment to persuade us that the distinction between these hypotheses is spurious. He invites us to imagine that our talk of charge turns out to concern two different magnitudes: charge and charge*. Our scientists assign numbers to charge and charge* in such a manner that the charge and charge* of a particle in our region of the universe are always the same whilst the charge and charge* of a particle in a distant region are of different signs. When scientists assign these numbers they are really coding the application of two fundamental physical relations, one for the comparison of charge, the other for comparison of charge*. Because we are supposing that (5) is true, i.e. CONVERSES is false, these comparative relations lack converses.

Now does this correlation of charge and charge* amongst particles hereabouts ultimately consist in the fact that these relations 'point in the same direction,' i.e. for any x and y in our region, x bears both relations or neither to y, or do they 'point in the opposite direction,' i.e. x bears exactly one of these relations to y? Dorr endeavors to persuade us that this question has no answer by adding a twist to the plot. It turns out alien scientists that inhabit this distant region assign numbers to charge and charge* differently to our scientists. They assign numbers in such a manner that the charge and charge* of particles in their region are equal whilst the charge and charge* of particles in our region are opposite. Dorr reflects: 'One need hardly be a verificationist to feel that this difference is purely a matter of convention: neither system of notation is in any way "better" than the other, as far as the metaphysics of the situation is concerned' (Dorr 2005: 165).

Dorr is surely right that the difference between the terrestrial and alien scientific communities is purely a matter of convention. The different communities have simply adopted different conventions for assigning numbers to particles to code the application of two fundamental relations. But it doesn't follow from the fact that these communities code the application of these relations differently that there is no fact of the matter concerning whether these relations whose application they code 'point in the same direction or in opposite directions.' Imagine two different gaming communities that differ with respect to whether they adopt the convention of assigning 0 to a winner and 1 to a loser or the convention of assigning 1 to a winner and 0 to a loser. It doesn't follow from the fact that it's arbitrary what code they use that there isn't a fact of the matter about which players are winners and which players are losers.

Keep at the forefront of your attention that Dorr's thought experiment is intended to convince us that (5) is incredible: that 'bears' can't be primitive and CONVERSES false because this combination of views requires us to draw spurious distinctions between possibilities. If Dorr's science fiction indeed convinced us that (5) was incredible then the perplexity that the contemplation of (5) is supposed to occasion ought to be relieved by restoring the metaphysical necessity of CONVERSES. But perplexity with regard to the question of how to code with numbers but without arbitrariness the application of comparative relations of charge and charge* certainly isn't restored by doing so.

Imagine that a community of super-philosophers occupying an even more remote region of the universe make contact to tell us that CONVERSES is metaphysically necessary after all. Suppose the terrestrial and alien scientific communities are alike convinced by the arguments of the super-philosophers. This leads everyone to conclude that there aren't just two fundamental physical relations responsible for the correlation of charge and charge*, there are two others, converses of the relations originally recognized. Should the discovery of the super-philosophers that CONVERSES is metaphysically necessary lead terrestrial and alien scientific communities to resolve or dismiss their former differences with regard to the question that Dorr describes as originally dividing them: whether it is correct to assign numbers in such a manner that the charge and charge* of particles in our region are equal whilst the charge and charge* of particles in the region of the alien scientists are opposite or the other way around? The story couldn't intelligibly climax with a terrestrial (or an alien) scientist winning a Nobel prize for discovering that only one assignment of numbers to charge and charge* is scientifically respectable.

What this shows is that the arbitrariness of numerical coding isn't really the issue; because it's always arbitrary how we code with numbers. What is germane is whether the comparative relations of charge and charge* point in the same direction or in opposite directions. But note that restoring CONVERSES and insisting upon four non-symmetric relations, instead of two comparative relations, doesn't provide the scientists from either community with any more purchase upon whether the relations point in the same or opposite directions than they had when they started. The super-philosophers have persuaded them to recognize the existence of two additional relations whose behavior *depends* upon the behavior of the two mutually independent relations from which we began. They're dependent, rather than independent, because they're introduced as the converses of the two original relations. But adding more dependent relations doesn't subtract from the number of possible ways that mutually independent relations can arrange the things they relate in a series. If CONVERSES is metaphysically necessary, there are still two possibilities to be distinguished: the possibility in which two mutually independent relations relate some things in the same direction whilst their converses both relate the same things in the opposite direction; and the possibility in which they relate things in opposite directions whilst the converse of each relates things in the opposite direction to it. So restoring CONVERSES does nothing to settle in which direction independent non-symmetric relations point; we only know that the converses we now recognize will point in the opposite direction to them. Nor does restoring CONVERSES enable us to avoid distinguishing between the possibility in which two independent relations point in the same direction and the possibility in which they point in the opposite direction.

Dorr's thought experiment doesn't establish that admitting non-symmetric relations whilst denying CONVERSES is an untenable combination of views – not unless admitting non-symmetric relations was already untenable by itself, in which case adding CONVERSES doesn't help. It follows that CONVERSES can't really be to the point either. What we need to know is whether we can make sense of non-symmetric relations applying in the same or opposite directions in the first place.

'Direction' is a term of art but remember that Dorr intends to mean something quite specific when he uses it. The expression is defined in terms of the verb 'bears': two relations point in the same direction if for any distinct x and y in a series, either x bears both or neither to y; whilst two relations point in opposite directions if x bears one of these relations, but not both, to y. These definitions will not enable us to settle whether two relations point in the same direction or opposite directions unless we already understand the verb 'bears.' But we won't be able to understand what this verb means if we dwell solely upon the significance of contexts in which 'bears' features whilst ignoring the relevant local holism. If we think of the significance of 'bears' in isolation then it is unclear that any substantial constraints discipline its use. But the verb does have a disciplined use because the contexts in which it features don't occur in isolation. Contexts of the form 'x bears r to y' typically have a traveling companion of the form 'x rs y.' To move from one context to the other we grammatically transform a noun into a verb or a verb into a noun, where the arrangement of the proper names that flank the 'bears . . . to' construction and the verb 'rs' bear a coordinated significance. For example, we can move from an ordinary predicative construction such as 'Thetis is the parent of Achilles' to the rarefied 'bears' construction 'Thetis bears parenthood to Achilles' by transforming the verb 'is the parent of' into the noun phrase 'parenthood' and preserving the right–left orientation of the flanking proper names. The predicative context constrains the proper use of the corresponding 'bears' constructions. We are entitled to say 'Thetis bears parenthood to Achilles' only if we're already entitled to say 'Thetis is the parent of Achilles.'

It is because the uses of 'bears' constructions are disciplined by corresponding uses of ordinary predicative constructions that their employment bears empirical significance. This enables us to distinguish between hypotheses about non-symmetric relations that Dorr finds spurious – to make verifiable claims concerning whether non-symmetric relations point in the same direction or different directions. Recall that what ultimately drives Dorr's argument is the concern that if 'bears' is primitive and two independent non-symmetric relations arrange a linearly ordered series of simple particulars then we are forced to distinguish between two hypotheses about how these relations apply.

(i)   For any distinct x and y in the series, x bears either r_1 or r_2, but not both, to y.

(ii) For any distinct x and y in the series, x bears both r_1 and r_2 to y, or bears neither r_1 nor r_2 to y.

Dorr denies that we can make any sense of the difference between these hypotheses. But, relying upon their transformational equivalences, we can derive from the 'bears' construction whereby r_1 and r_2 point in the same direction, hypothesis (i), and the 'bears' construction whereby r_1 and r_2 point in the opposite direction, hypothesis (ii), two corresponding predicative constructions, where relation-nouns are transformed into relational verbs,

(iii) For any distinct x and y in the series, $(x \, r_1 s \, y \land \neg \, x \, r_2 s \, y) \lor (\neg x \, r_1 s \, y \land x \, r_2 s \, y)$

(iv) For any distinct x and y in the series, $(x \, r_1 s \, y \land x \, r_2 s \, y) \lor (\neg x \, r_1 s \, y \land \neg x \, r_2 s \, y)$.

Suppose that r_1 is the relation *being taller than* and r_2 is the relation *being heavier than*. Then by tracking these transformations it's easy to see that a world where hypothesis (i) comes out true is very different from a world where hypothesis (ii) comes out true. In worlds where (iii), and therefore (i), is true, if someone is taller than someone else they will also be heavier than them (and vice versa). Whereas in worlds where (iv), and therefore (ii), is true, if someone is taller than someone else they won't be heavier or if they're heavier they won't be taller. Different scenarios indeed!

Dorr argues that because we can't distinguish between hypotheses (i) and (ii) we have to reject the assumption that 'bears' is primitive. But we can distinguish between these hypotheses even if 'bears' is primitive. This is because, even though 'bears' cannot be analyzed, 'bears' constructions may be transformed into equivalent empirical claims that are expressed using ordinary verbs, claims that are typically testable. So Dorr fails to establish that 'bears' isn't primitive, because admitting 'bears' is primitive doesn't require us to admit spurious possibilities. Since Dorr's case against non-symmetric relations relies upon the claim that 'bears' isn't primitive, his case collapses.

6. Dorr: Is life possible without non-symmetric relations?

The arguments against non-symmetric in favor of symmetric relations that we have considered so far aim to establish that we should avoid commitment to non-symmetric relations because of the unpalatable consequences of undertaking such a commitment – our having to admit brute necessities or draw spurious distinctions between possibilities. These arguments have been found to be wanting in one or other respect. Ultimately we cannot avoid brute necessities and the distinctions between possibilities that we are forced to draw if we admit non-symmetric relations don't turn out to be spurious after all. But if all statements putatively about non-symmetric relations could be paraphrased away in favor of statements about symmetric relations then it would appear that we could dispense straightaway with commitment to non-symmetric or asymmetric relations without the detour via brute necessities and spurious possibilities.

In *The Structure of Appearance* Goodman took an important logical step towards legitimating such a paraphrase strategy when he sprung upon the following equivalence between contexts in which the non-symmetric predicate 'is part of' occurs and contexts in which the symmetric predicate 'overlaps' occurs:

$(>)$ x is a part of y iff whatever overlaps x overlaps y (Goodman 1966: 47–49).

In the light of this equivalence Goodman proposed to define 'is part of' in terms of 'overlap'. Dorr draws upon this proposal to suggest that the *prima facie* commitment of mereology to a non-symmetric relation of parthood can be paraphrased away. Dorr goes on to outline a number of other piecemeal paraphrases for obviating commitment to non-symmetric relations. Dorr suggests that the three-place non-symmetric predicate 'between,' found in formalizations of Euclidean geometry, may be paraphrased away in favor of a binary symmetric relation 'overlap' and quantification over line segments using the following equivalence:

(L) x is between y and z iff every line segment that overlaps both y and z overlaps x.

Drawing upon unpublished work of Hazen's, Dorr also suggests that the non-symmetric set-theoretic predicate 'is a member of' may be paraphrased away in terms of two binary symmetric predicates. According to orthodox set theory there are sets, called ranks, such that whenever x is a member of y, there is some rank that contains x and not y, but no rank that contains y and not x. Relying upon the established idiom of set theory, Dorr introduces two symmetric predicates 'overlaps set-theoretically' and 'are of the same rank' by the following definitions:

(D1)   Two things *overlap set-theoretically* iff one of them is a member of the other.

(D2)   Two things *are of the same rank* iff they are members of exactly the same ranks.

Appealing to Hazen's unpublished result, Dorr tells us that the following equivalence is a consequence of orthodox set theory:

$(\in)$ a is a member of b iff a overlaps b and there is something of the same rank as b that overlaps everything of the same rank as a.

Dorr concludes that, 'we can adopt this biconditional as an analysis of "is a member of" in terms of "overlap" and "is the same rank as", and posit a symmetric binary relation corresponding to each of these two predicates' (Dorr 2005: 181–82).

Don't forget that the single primitive of Dorr's own preferred system is a non-symmetric predicate, '– holds among . . . '. It is possible to permute singular terms that occur in the plural argument of this predicate without disturbing the truth-value of a sentence in which it occurs: '*r* holds among *x* and *y*' is analytically equivalent in Dorr's theory to '*r* holds among *y* and *x*.' But the predicate is non-symmetric because permuting the singular term that occupies the singular argument position of the predicate with its plural term or any singular terms that occurs in its plural argument position isn't guaranteed to preserve truth-value: it doesn't follow from *r*'s holding among *x* and *y* that *x* holds among *r* and *y*. Since Dorr provides no strategy for paraphrasing away this non-symmetric predicate, this undermines his claim to have shown that the view according to which 'there are relations all of which are necessarily symmetric could be a defensible one' (Dorr 2005: 180). Once it is admitted that one non-symmetric predicate cannot be eliminated it is difficult to see what motivation there could be for adopting the recherché paraphrases Dorr recommends to avoid using other non-symmetric predicates – to privilege a metaphysical predicate we scarcely understand at the expense of geometrical and set-theoretic predicates that have an established usage.[8]

Nonetheless there is doubtless scientific interest in establishing how far a program for paraphrasing away commitment to non-symmetric relations can extend. Certainly the equivalences $(>)$, (L), and $(\in)$ provide necessary

---

[8] An anonymous referee suggests the following response on Dorr's behalf. Define a symmetric predicate, 'proto-hold each other,' in the following terms:

(P-H) $x_1, x_2, \ldots x_n$ proto-hold each other iff any of them hold among the others.

Next make the following stipulation:

(S) r holds among $x_1, x_2, \ldots x_n$ iff r, $x_1, x_2, \ldots x_n$ proto-hold, r is a relation, and $x_1, x_2, \ldots x_n$ are not.

Now 'reverse' the direction of the definition so that the non-symmetric 'hold among' is defined in terms of the symmetric 'proto-holds' plus stipulation (S). As the referee also points out this definition of 'hold among' won't work if there are relations that hold among other relations. This is a serious problem, but there is another more immediate difficulty. (P-H) fails to guarantee that when $x_1, x_2, \ldots x_n$ proto-hold each other, one of them holds amongst all the others. As a consequence (S) allows r to hold amongst $x_1, x_2, \ldots x_n$ even in circumstances where x_n fails to stand in any significant relation to $x_1, x_2, \ldots x_{n-1}$. Another difficulty concerns the fact that it may only be possible to explain what it means for r to be a relation in terms of r's being an item that holds among other things. So even if (P-H) is emended the proposed reduction may end up being circular.

and sufficient conditions for a's being a part of b, for a's being between b and c, for a's being a member of b. But it doesn't follow that these equivalences provide *analyses* of a, b, and c being thus-and-so. Don't forget that ($>$), (L), and ($\in$) also provide necessary and sufficient conditions for everything that overlaps a to overlap b, for every line segment that overlaps both y and z to overlap x, and for a to overlap b and there be something of the same rank as b that overlaps everything of the same rank as a. Obviously it's not enough to be entitled to adopt an equivalence as an analysis merely to establish that the equivalence allow us to state necessary and sufficient conditions. It needs to be established that one side of the equivalence, the one intended to serve as the analysis, is logically prior to the other. In order to paraphrase away commitment to the non-symmetric relations of part–whole, between and set-theoretic membership it needs to be established that the right-hand-sides of ($>$), (L), and ($\in$) have logical priority over their left-hand-sides.

If Armstrong and Dorr had indeed demonstrated that commitment to non-symmetric relations is inherently suspect that would indeed provide us with a credible motivation for assigning priority to the left-hand sides of these equivalences – because if there are no non-symmetric relations then the predicates on the right-hand side can hardly pick them out and must bear some other significance, if Dorr is right delineated by their right-hand-sides. But Armstrong and Dorr's arguments have failed to demonstrate that commitment to non-symmetric relations is inherently toxic. It might be suggested that the right-hand sides of ($>$), (L), and ($\in$) have priority over their left-hand sides because theories that employ only the vocabulary employed on their right-hand sides are more economical or simpler than theories that employ only vocabulary that appears on their left-hand sides. But it's far from evident that this is the case. What is certain is that this cannot be established by isolated inspection of ($>$), (L), and ($\in$) but only by appreciation of whole theories and how they compare. And even if it were successfully shown that the right-hand side of these equivalences enjoy priority over their left-hand sides it would be difficult to avoid the suspicion that a non-symmetric, so to speak, meta-relation had been presupposed, the non-symmetric relation expressed by the predicate 'has priority over.' More generally, non-symmetric logical relations are the elephant in the room in contemporary discussions of relations (MacBride 2011: 273–75).

Dorr's suggestion about how to use ($\in$) to paraphrase away the member-ship relation confronts especial difficulties. Dorr introduces the symmetric predicates 'overlap set-theoretically' and 'are of the same rank' on the basis of our prior understanding of established non-symmetric vocabulary of set theory that appears on the right-hand side of ($D1$) and ($D2$), including the non-symmetric predicate 'is a member of.' It is only because 'overlap set-theoretically' and 'are of the same rank' are so understood in terms of the established language of set theory that we can add these definitions to set theory and get ($\in$) to follow – otherwise the novel vocabulary introduced will hang aloof from the established vocabulary of set theory and nothing significant will result from their union. But when Dorr proposes that we read ($\in$) as an analysis of 'is a member of' he requires us to take a logical somersault: to understand 'is a member of' in terms of 'overlap set-theoretically' and 'are the same rank.' But we only understand these symmetric predicates because they were introduced in terms of established non-symmetric vocabulary including 'is a member of.' It follows that we cannot rely upon ($\in$) to provide a basis for paraphrasing away commitment to the membership relation because the symmetric vocabulary that appears on the right-hand side of ($\in$) presupposes the non-symmetric vocabulary that appears on the left-hand side.

The foreseeable response: avoid the alleged circularity by interpreting (D1) and (D2) as respective analyses of a's being a member of b, and a and b's being members of exactly the same ranks. So even though epistemologically or cognitively we only achieve an understanding of 'overlap set-theoretically' and 'are of the same rank' via the established use of 'is a member of,' the ontological situation is the reverse. When we describe the world using statement of the forms that appear on the right-hand sides of (D1) and (D2) our descriptions are grammatically misleading. The same content is perspicuously captured by statements of the forms that appear on the left-hand sides of (D1) and (D2). But always remember that it's never enough to have some equivalence before us – the privilege has to be earned to read the equivalence as an analysis, assigning priority to one side rather than another.

There's another difficulty that besets this proposal to avoid circularity. Let's focus on (D2): Two things *are of the same rank* iff they are members of exactly the same ranks. It's important to bear in mind here that the symmetric predicate introduced here that features on the left-hand side of (D1) has no internal structure. It is simply introduced *en bloc* as having the same significance as the predicates that feature on the right-hand side. So the logical structure of the left-hand side is simply *aRb*. It follows that if the left-hand side of (D2) has priority over the right-hand side then the grammatical structure of what appears on the right-hand side must be logically misleading. Instances of the right-hand side appear to require quantification over ranks but if (D2) is taken an analysis that proceeds from right to left, then the appearance of quantification on the right-hand side must be logically misleading. In fact statements of the left-hand-side form

('x and y are members of exactly the same ranks') cannot involve genuine quantification over ranks at all because, the analysis leads us to appreciate, we are only saying that x and y satisfy the unanalyzable predicate 'are of the same rank' – we are *not* saying that there is some rank that they both share.

It's already been remarked that (D2) cannot be harnessed up to established set theory to help yield ($\in$) unless the vocabulary of set theory bears the same significance as the right-hand-side vocabulary of (D2). But this means, if priority is assigned to the left-hand side of (D2), that quantification over ranks in established set theory must be a logical sham too, at least where it assumes the form of the right-hand side of (D2) – no matter how mathematicians may have thought they understood the structure of such statements, i.e. as involving quantification over ranks. There may be the grammatical appearance of quantification over ranks in such set-theoretic contexts but if (D2) is to be understood as providing the basis of a reductive paraphrase, the grammar of set theory must, at least in such contexts, be deemed logically misleading as well. But bear in mind that there are statements about ranks in set theory that *don't* assume the form of the right-hand side of (D2). Obviously these statements cannot be reduced by assigning priority to the left-hand side of (D2) because they don't assume the form of its right-hand side. But now the difficulty is that the reduced contexts have nothing semantically in common with the contexts that cannot be reduced this way and this threatens to block the derivation of ($\in$) from (D1) and (D2) via set theory when the routine logical relations between set-theoretic statements of different forms about ranks have been disrupted. And, of course, the general problem remains that it seems far more probable that there is something awry with this analysis for paraphrasing away commitment to non-symmetric relations in set theory than that the scientific and mathematical communities should have been so fundamentally misled concerning the basic quantificational structure of their own lingua franca.[9]

---

[9] I am grateful to the audience at an Eidos conference in Varano Borghi where a version of this chapter was delivered, and the participants in an earlier seminar on relations at the Scuola Normale Superiore in Pisa that helped push forward my understanding of the subject. I would also like to thank Philipp Blum, Cian Dorr, Kit Fine, Jane Heal, Gabriele Galluzzo, Nick Jones, Frédérique Janssen-Lauret, Kevin Mulligan, Stephan Leuenberger, E. J. Lowe, and Alan Weir for discussion.

CHAPTER 9

States of affairs and the relation regress

Anna-Sofia Maurin

The following three theses together comprise a view that has been proposed by quite a few contemporary metaphysicians (the foremost of whom is D. M. Armstrong): There are universals and there are substrates.[1] Universals and substrates obey what Armstrong (1978: vol. 1) calls the Principle of Instantiation (PI) and the Principle of the Rejection of Bare Particulars (PRB):

(PI)   A universal, if it exists, must be instantiated in some substrate.
(PRB) A substrate, if it exists, must exemplify some universal.

When a universal is instantiated in a substrate (when a substrate exemplifies a universal) there exists, besides (yet somehow constituted by) the universal and the substrate, a state of affairs.[2]

But why, if there are universals and substrates, and universals and substrates depend generically on one another in the way prescribed by (PI) and (PRB), do we need to posit states of affairs as well? In this chapter, I consider and criticize one influential answer to that question.[3]

[1] The arguments in this chapter would be of equal relevance to someone (like e.g. C. B. Martin 1980) who construes states of affairs as in part constituted by tropes rather than by universals. There are, however, strong reasons for thinking that these arguments ought to be of *special* interest (not to mention, the cause of special concern) to a universal realist. For, although trope-theory could most probably be developed *without* recourse to states of affairs (cf. Maurin 2014a), the same is arguably not true of universal realism (cf. Armstrong 1978: vol. 1, 91–96 for an argument to this effect).

[2] This is hence a kind of *constituent ontology* in the sense of Loux, van Inwagen, and Garcia (this volume). That is, it is a view which metaphysically explains (or *grounds*) the existence of familiar things and their properties in the existence and nature of entities belonging to more fundamental ontological categories.

[3] I would like to thank the editors of this book, Nils-Eric Sahlin, Johannes Persson, Ingar Brinck, Göran Hermerén, and two anonymous referees for helpful comments and criticisms. I am especially grateful to Johan Brännmark for his help in all matters – practical as well as theoretical. This chapter was completed with financial support from *Riksbankens Jubileumsfond* and *Vetenskapsrådet*.

1. The problem of unity

According to the view presently under investigation, one (quite probably the main) reason for positing states of affairs in addition to their constituent substrates and universals is that states of affairs are needed to solve a serious philosophical problem: *the problem of unity*. To see how, suppose that (at least) contingent truths are made true by entities in the world,[4] and suppose that distinct truths, i.e. truths with (at least asymmetrically) independent truth-values, must have different truthmakers.[5] Remember that according to the view presently under investigation, although universals and substrates depend *generically* for their existence on one another, if *a* exemplifies F-ness, *a* could have existed and exemplified some universal other than F-ness, and F-ness could have existed instantiated in some substrate other than *a*. This means that the constituents of a state of affairs have an existence that is independent of the existence of the state of affairs they happen to be the constituents of.[6] And this means that the following two situations (or 'worlds'), are both possible:[7]

A: *a* and F-ness exist; $<a$ and F-ness exist$>$ is true; $<a$ is F$>$ is true
B: *a* and F-ness exist; $<a$ and F-ness exist$>$ is true; $<a$ is F$>$ is false

Now, both $<a$ and F-ness exist$>$ and $<a$ is F$>$ are contingent truths and so must, if true, be made true by something. And as the former proposition can be true while the latter is false, their truthmakers may at most be overlapping. Something *besides* or *other* than whatever exists in B, must in other words exist in A. But *what*?

---

[4] For the purposes of the discussion conducted here it is enough if we accept this truthmaker principle for atomic propositions of the forms $<a$ exists$>$ and $<a$ is F$>$. This should make the principle acceptable to more or less everyone who accepts that there are truthmakers to begin with. In particular, it should make it acceptable to defenders and critics of so-called 'truthmaker maximalism' alike. For an overview, cf. MacBride (2014).

[5] This assumption is entailed given Truthmaker Necessitarianism (TN): the assumption that the existence of a truthmaker necessitates the truth of some particular proposition. Whether or not TN should be accepted is hotly debated. It is at least an open question if the assumption made in this chapter is not only entailed by, but also requires the truth of TN. For more on TN cf. Cameron (2005).

[6] This does *not* mean that the existence of the constituents of a state of affairs exist independently of the existence of *some* state of affairs. Nor does it entail that given a specific state of affairs, *it* could have been differently constituted. That the constituents of a state of affairs are existentially independent of the state of affairs they happen to constitute is, in other words, fully compatible with (although it does not require) that the state of affairs has its constituents essentially (*cf.* Maurin 2011: 76f.).

[7] Throughout this chapter anything surrounded by '$<$' and '$>$' is a *truthbearer*. I will talk as if truthbearers are propositions, but that they are is most likely not essential to anything I will argue here.

An immediately attractive answer, or so the story goes, is one that says that in A, but not in B, something which 'unifies' *a* and F-ness – a relation, a connection, a tie, a nexus – exists. This seems right, but to be satisfactory this answer needs some supplementation. What is the nature of this unifier, and how does its addition turn situation B into situation A?

Most would agree that relations which hold between, and so unify, distinct relata, are either *internal* or *external* to them. Suppose our unifier is internal to its relata. Then, it and its relata symmetrically depend for their existence (and nature) on one another: necessarily, if *a* and F-ness exist (and 'are what they are'), so does their unifier. But this cannot be right. For then every situation in which *a* and F-ness exist will be a situation in which *a* is F, thus ruling out situation B.

To make room for situation B we must therefore assume that our unifier is *external* to its relata, and so such that it, *a*, and F-ness, could exist without *a* being F. But now, it seems, our unifier can no longer do the work for which it was introduced. For, if it is not 'by its nature' such that it *must* relate *a* and F-ness, the following two situations are both possible:

C: *a*, F-ness, unifier exist; <*a*, F-ness, unifier exist> is true; <*a* is F> is true

D: *a*, F-ness, unifier exist; <*a*, F-ness, unifier exist> is true; <*a* is F> is false

Again, something must 'make' the difference between the two situations. Using the same logic which led us from A to C we could add yet another unifier, in this case to situation C, and say that in C, but not in D, *a*, F-ness, and the unifier exist unified. But then, for the same reasons as those set out above, we must say that this unifier is external to that which it supposedly unifies, which means that new problematic pairs of situations will be generated. And so on, *ad infinitum*.[8] This is the problem of unity.[9]

---

[8] This regress is often called the 'Bradley regress,' in honor of the argument once presented by F. H. Bradley (1897) (cf. also Maurin 2012). So as not get stuck in interpretive issues, I prefer to refer to it with the more neutral 'relation regress.' To Bradley, this regress was just one part of a more comprehensive argument aimed at proving that pluralism in general is false. If Bradley was right about just how serious this problem is, and if it turns out that states of affairs can solve what Bradley thought was unsolvable, this would speak highly in favor of their introduction. A circumstance which makes a critical investigation of the 'states-of-affairs-solution' all the more relevant.

[9] But what if our unifier is *not* either symmetrically dependent or symmetrically independent of its relata, but rather depends *a*symmetrically on them (what if it, given that it exists must relate the relata it does, even though those relata might exist and not be related by it)? In Maurin (2010) and (2011), I argue that a unifier thus understood solves the problem of unity (although it does so by forcing its proponents to accept at least some tropes). Here, this alternative will be ignored and so it will be assumed (given reasons stated above) that the unifier-solution (in its

2.   States of affairs to the rescue

The idea is now that the introduction of states of affairs solves the problem of unity. In Armstrong's words (1989a: 88):[10]

> Why do we need to recognize states of affairs? Why not recognize simply particulars, universals (divided into properties and relations), and, perhaps, instantiation? The answer appears by considering the following point. If *a* is F, then it is entailed that *a* exists and that the universal F exists. However, *a* could exist, and F could exist, and yet it fail to be the case that *a* is F (F is instantiated, but instantiated elsewhere only). *a*'s being F involves something more than *a* and F. It is no good simply adding the fundamental tie or nexus of instantiation to the sum of *a* and F. The existence of *a*, of instantiation, and of F does not amount to *a*'s being F. *The something more must be a's being F – and this is a state of affairs* [italics added].

And again (1997b: 116):

> We are asking what in the world will ensure, make true, underlie, serve as the ontological ground for, the truth that *a* is F. The obvious candidate seems to be the state of affairs of *a's being F*. In this state of affairs (fact, circumstance) *a* and F are brought together.

This sounds promising. If the difference between situation A and situation B, is the presence in A (but not in B) of the state of affairs *that a is F*[11] we seem to have the means finally to account for the truth of $<a$ is F$>$ in a way that does not land us in vicious infinite regress. For the existence of the state of affairs *that a is F* is clearly *in*compatible with the falsity of $<a$ is F$>$, which means that no new problematic pairs of situations result from its introduction. Problem solved?

3.   What are states of affairs?

To be able to judge if the introduction of states of affairs solves the problem of unity, it is not enough simply to say that in A there is the state of affairs *that a is F* whereas in B there is not. For what does that mean exactly? It must mean more than simply that in A, *a* and F-ness exist united

---

traditional – symmetric – guise) fails. This is because what interests me here is not if there is any *need* for states of affairs to begin with, but rather whether, if there is such a need, states of affairs manage to solve the problem for which they were introduced.

[10] Cf. also Armstrong (1978: vol. I, 1997b, 2004). Armstrong calls this the 'truthmaker argument' for the existence of states of affairs. Molnar (2003) introduced the term 'master argument' for it (a title that is rather fitting in view of its standing among proponents of states of affairs).

[11] In what follows (worldly) states of affairs will be referred to using italics.

whereas in B they don't, or to introduce states of affairs would just be to introduce another way of talking about a still unresolved and unexplained phenomenon.[12] What we need is a substantial and non-circular account of the nature of that which exists in A but not in B, i.e. we need an account of the nature of states of affairs. Only given such an account can we then go on to judge if states of affairs constitute a viable solution to the problem of unity and if, as a consequence, the role played by states of affairs in relation to this problem can be used as an argument for their existence.

Now, we know that, since B is a possible situation, whatever a state of affairs is, it isn't reducible to a and F-ness, or to a, F-ness, and a unifier, or to a, F-ness, and an infinity of unifiers of increasing order. This was the lesson learnt from the relation regress. States of affairs are *irreducible*. But what exactly should this be taken to entail?

There are two main options: Either states of affairs are irreducible and ontologically simple or they are irreducible and ontologically complex. Below I investigate these options in turn, only to find that neither is acceptable, at least not to the traditional proponent of states of affairs.

4.   States of affairs as irreducible and ontologically simple

According to Armstrong, states of affairs 'come first' and bare particulars (substrates) and uninstantiated universals are 'vicious abstractions from what may be called states of affairs: this-of-a-certain-nature' (1997a: 110). But what does it mean to say of the state of affairs that it 'comes first' or that bare particulars and uninstantiated universals are 'vicious abstractions' from it? For states of affairs to be able to solve the problem of unity, it must mean something more than just that a and F-ness are generically dependent on one another for, as we have seen, to say this does not prevent you from ending up in vicious infinite regress (but cf. Armstrong 1997a: 110). Still, it must mean something less than that a and F-ness depend specifically on one another, or the existence of the state of affairs *that a is F*, and hence the truth of $<a$ is F$>$ would follow necessarily simply given the existence of a and F-ness (thus ruling out situation B). A radical interpretation of Armstrong's pronouncements is one which takes his talk of *vicious* abstraction very seriously. Literally, on this suggestion, a and F-ness do not exist. All there is are states of affairs. 'a' and 'F-ness' may

---

[12] Somewhat like you cannot explain the sleep-inducing properties of opium by saying that they stem from a 'virtus dormitiva.'

still be said to have referential force, but their referent will be the state of affairs, for that is all there is.[13] States of affairs are our rock-bottom.

This is certainly not an answer favored by Armstrong or, for that matter, by proponents of states of affairs generally. Yet, if this suggestion is adopted, the problem of unity disappears. For if there is no a and no F-ness, then there is no situation in which a exists but does not exemplify F-ness, or where F-ness exists but is not instantiated in a. Instead there are only states of affairs, and to say that a and F-ness are only contingently united, is another way of saying that although this is a situation in which the state of affairs *that a is F* exists, there are also situations in which it does not but where e.g. the states of affairs *that a is G* and *that b is F* exist.

Against this suggestion we may, however, raise at least two objections. First, if states of affairs are irreducible and ontologically simple, then realism is in effect traded for nominalism. For if what exists are ontologically simple – 'blobby' – states of affairs, and if states of affairs are (as Armstrong would take them to be) concrete particulars, then, on this suggestion, the world is a world of simple concrete particulars. Bad news indeed for anyone who thinks there are properties. Second, and relatedly, although on this suggestion, the problem of unity is certainly *dis*solved, we cannot really say that it is *solved*. For if states of affairs are ontologically simple, the problematic kind of complex whole does not exist, which means that there is no problem of unity. But if there is no problem of unity, then there is nothing that the introduction of states of affairs can be used to solve. If states of affairs are irreducible and ontologically simple, therefore, the (non-existent) role they play in relation to the (non-existent) problem of unity is not a reason to think that they exist (cf. Dodd 1999: 151 for a similar objection).

5.   States of affairs as irreducible and ontologically complex

If states of affairs cannot be irreducible and ontologically simple, they must be irreducible yet ontologically complex. This means that, when the state of affairs *that a is F* exists, so does the substrate a and the universal F-ness. PI and PRB still prevent a and F-ness from existing except as the constituents of *some* state of affairs, but on the present suggestion the fact that a and F-ness must constitute some state of affairs does not mean that a

---

[13] Perhaps we could even say that they refer to different 'aspects' of the state of affairs. But then we must take care so that talk of 'aspects' does not (re)introduce substrates and universals as distinct categories.

and F-ness cannot count as some of the (perhaps *the*) ultimate constituents of the world.

What the relation regress teaches us is that the state of affairs *that a is F* cannot be reduced to the pair of *a* and F-ness. This means that the way *a* and F-ness make up the state of affairs *that a is F*, on the present suggestion, cannot be one of the ways in which *a* and F-ness constitute a complex whole simply by existing. This entails, more specifically, that the state of affairs *that a is F* cannot be either (merely) a mereological whole with *a* and F-ness as parts,[14] or a set with *a* and F-ness as members. According to Armstrong therefore, and as far as I can tell this is the common view among defenders of states of affairs generally, we must conclude that 'states of affairs hold their constituents together in a *non-mereological mode of composition* [italics added]' (Armstrong 1997b: 118).

For this to mean something more substantial, the special kind of non-mereological composition characteristic of the state of affairs needs some more flesh on the bones. How, on this suggestion, is situation A, in which there exists a non-mereologically composed whole consisting of *a* and F-ness, different from situation B, in which those same constituents at most make up a mereological whole? Again, there are two options. Either A is different from B because something exists in A that does not exist in B, or A is different from B, but this difference is brute and cannot be traced back to some difference in what, in particular, exists in either A or B.

If the difference is brute, situation A and B are *just* different, i.e. they are different, but there is no particular thing which *makes* this difference. According to Vallicella, this is unintelligible. He argues (2000: 248):

> It is unintelligible to suppose that two distinct *complexes* [the mereological sum *a* + F-ness, and the state of affairs *that a is F*] just differ as a matter of brute fact. A fact and the sum of its constituents are distinct complexes; hence there is need of a ground of their difference.

This seems right to me, but need not convince everyone.[15] Suppose therefore, and *pace* Vallicella, that to say that there is a difference but that nothing *makes* this difference is intelligible. Then it is still unclear in what way saying this in any way substantially solves the problem of unity. In Dodd's words (1999: 151–52):

> [If the difference between the non-mereologically composed state of affairs *that a is F* and the mereological whole *a* + F-ness is brute] the familiar

---

[14] Assuming that we accept David Lewis' (1991) principle of unrestricted mereological composition.
[15] It certainly didn't convince one of this text's referees.

question remains unanswered: how can something with just a particular and a universal as constituents be a unity? How is it possible for a and F to be 'brought together' to form a unified entity which exists just in case a is F? Such a 'bringing together' of a and F is not by means of an instantiation relation; and, as we have seen, it can be neither set-theoretical nor mereological. We are left with no idea of how a and F are combined to form a genuinely unified state of affairs. Given this state of play, Armstrong's invention of states of affairs amounts to philosophical wish-fulfillment.

If, on the other hand, something does exist in A to make the difference between this situation and a situation in which a and F-ness, but not the state of affairs *that a is F*, exist, we are in trouble. For what could turn an a and F-ness situation into an *a is F*-situation without vicious infinite regress? It does not help to say, as Armstrong does, that what exists when the state of affairs does is a *non-relational* tie or nexus (1997b: 118). A non-relational tie must either *not* be an addition to A in comparison to B, which means that, again, A and B are *just* different; an option that we are henceforth treating (with good reason) as essentially flawed. Or, it must *be* an addition to A; but then, again, we seem to be left in the dark as to what kind of addition it is or, for that matter, how adding it is supposed to provide unity yet not lead to the vicious infinite regress. At one point, Armstrong could be interpreted as addressing this latter concern. He argues (1997b: 118):

> *even if a 'relation' is conceded*, the regress is harmless. The thing to notice is that, while the step from constituents to state of affairs is a contingent one, all the further steps in the suggested regress follow necessarily . . . once noticed, may it not be argued that the sole truthmaker required for each step in the regress *after the first* (the introduction of the fundamental tie) is nothing more than the original state of affairs? Many truths if you like, but only one truthmaker.

This 'explanation' is arguably unsatisfactory. For, it is hardly the relation which is added to a and F-ness in the presumably benign regress' first step that is what accomplishes their unity (which is precisely what the relation regress set out above proves). Instead it must be the special togetherness (the 'non-mereological mode of composition') of the state of affairs as a whole that does this. Here it does its magic one step further up the regress-ladder than if we disallowed any type of relational constituent to occur in the state of affairs. But it (whatever it is) does its magic nevertheless. And all our original questions still remain: *What* does the magic? *How* does it do it?

6. An impossible dilemma

According to Vallicella, the irreducible nature of states of affairs (what he calls 'the nonreductionist conception of states of affairs') is *incoherent*. He argues (2000: 247):

> a nonsupervenient state of affairs is a whole of parts (insofar as it is complex) that is not a whole of parts (insofar as it is more than its constituents), and is thus a self-contradictory structure.

A more cautious way of putting the matter is in terms of a dilemma: States of affairs are either reducible or irreducible. They cannot be reducible or you end up in vicious infinite regress. If irreducible, on the other hand, states of affairs are either irreducible and ontologically simple or they are irreducible and ontologically complex. But, again, at least if you count universals (or tropes for that matter) among the world's basic constituents, and if you believe that the contribution states of affairs make to the solution to the problem of unity is a (strong) reason for thinking that they exist, states of affairs can be neither.

7. A third option?

Have we exhausted all possibilities? Perhaps not. So far it has been implicitly assumed that if *something* makes the difference between situation A and situation B, then it must be internal to the state of affairs itself. But what if the state of affairs *that a is F* (in A) and the aggregate consisting of *a* and F-ness (in B), are both constituted by (just) *a* and F-ness? What if they *just* differ, but this difference is not left unaccounted for, but is metaphysically explained – or grounded – in the existence of something *external* to the state of affairs itself, something which exists in A, but not in B, and makes *a* and F-ness into a complex unity? This option is explicitly endorsed by Vallicella. He argues (2000: 249–50):

> But there is a third possibility, namely, that the unity of a state of affair's constituents is due to an external unifier. For it does not straightaway follow from a fact being more than its (primary and secondary) constituents that it is a connectedness without a connector or unifier. The unifier might be external to the fact and its constituents. If sense can be made of this, we can retain the attractive view that a fact is not an entity distinct from its constituents (which is the element of truth in the reductionist approach) while also accounting for the undeniable unity of the fact's constituents. Just as contingently true sentences have need for states of affairs to make them true, contingent states of affairs have need of an external unifier to

connect their constituents and so make them exist. The external unifier is the 'existence-maker' of states of affairs.

To be able to judge if this suggestion can give us what we need, it must be supplemented with an account of the nature of this external unifier. Vallicella does provide us with the requisite supplementation by reasoning from analogy (2000: 252):

> Suppose I judge that *a* is F, and suppose further that the contents of acts of judging are not Fregean propositions, but items that cannot exist apart from the act of judging. In judging that *a* is F I create mentally a complex content composed of a subject-constituent and a predicate-constituent. This complex is a unity of constituents. On the one hand, the judgmental content is nothing more than its constituents. But on the other hand, the judgmental content is something more than its constituents insofar as it is the latter actually united to form a content capable of being either true or false – in the way in which neither the constituents taken by themselves, nor any list, set or sum of them is capable of being either true or false. But how can the judgmental content be something more than its constituents without being a further entity irreducible to them? The only way to resolve this tension is by positing an external unifier, an external ground of the unity of the judgmental content. In this case it is the judging consciousness that brings about the content's unity. Without recourse to such an external ground, we would be stuck with the tension.

According to Vallicella, whatever our external unifier is, it must be an *active* force, an agent (or, more neutrally put, an ontological operator), something which 'do[es] something to the primary constituents to unify them' (2000: 250). This agent, Vallicella believes, cannot be an individual human being, or a finite consciousness, as '[t]hat would be to embrace an intolerable idealism' (2000: 252). The only option is to regard the external unifier as a transcendental consciousness of some kind. As a theist, Vallicella has a good candidate in mind (2000: 252): 'God has His uses. God can play the role of external unifier or 'existence-maker' for all contingent states of affairs.'

But (how) does God manage to unify the states of affairs without vicious infinite regress? The short answer is that in and of himself, he doesn't. For, if God is what externally unifies *a* and F-ness in A, nothing seems to prevent God from existing also in B (some would say that nothing *could* prevent this, as God's existence is necessary). As a purposive agent, God (or whatever we choose to call this transcendental consciousness) could have opted for not uniting *a* and F-ness. But then it is not the existence of God that makes the difference between A and B after all. Suppose instead that it is *a unifying act of God* which does this. Now, even if a unifying act of God can hardly exist without God existing, and even if God could not exist without acting in one way or another, God could certainly exist without acting in a way that makes the state of affairs *that a is F* exist (proof of which is situation B). In order for God to be able to play the role of 'existence-maker' for which he was introduced, therefore, his acts would have to be more finely individuated. The difference between situations A and B, we would have to say, is the existence in A, of the (Godly) act of *unifying a and F-ness*.[16] This act, it seems, is a good candidate for something which makes the difference between A and B without vicious infinite regress. But now the proponent of states of affairs must ask herself whatever remains of the role for which states of affairs were introduced. On the present account, it is God, or perhaps rather, God's purposive – and rather finely individuated – act, that solves the problem of unity. And if God is the solution to the problem of unity, then that problem can no longer be used to justify positing states of affairs in ontology.[17]

8. States of affairs as externally unified by states of affairs

But what if the unity of the state of affairs was accomplished by *another* state of affairs, external to the first? This is Orilia's view (2006: 229):

> What makes F*a* [the state of affairs *that a is F*] an entity that exists over and above F and *a* is the state of affairs E²F*a*, understood as different from F*a*, in that E² is taken to be the really attributive constituent of the former, whereas F is taken to be the really attributive constituent of the latter.

On this suggestion, the state of affairs *that a is F* exists and guarantees the unity of *a* and F-ness as well as the truth of <*a* is F> *because* a higher-order state of affairs, the state of affairs *that a, F-ness, and a unifier unified* exists. If successful, this suggestion, apart from being compatible with a healthy naturalism, avoids the difficulty encountered by Vallicella. If states of affairs are externally unified by states of affairs, then states of affairs are relevantly involved in a solution to the problem of unity, and so the existence of states of affairs can be justified with reference to the role they play in relation to this problem.

---

[16] As this act essentially involves the constituents of the state of affairs it is supposed to unify, one might complain that it is not a truly *external* unifier after all (and one might wonder what difference that makes to the suggestion's chances of solving the problem of unity). Here I leave discussion of this particular complaint for another occasion.

[17] Vallicella (2000: 256) disagrees. However, as far as I can see, he can only do this if he takes 'state of affairs' to *mean* 'the solution to the problem of unity'; a strategy I would advise against.

But can states of affairs be externally unified by higher-order states of affairs without infinite regress? Sadly, no. For if the possible existence of the state of affairs *that a is F* (or F*a*, to borrow Orilia's formalism) *requires* the existence of the higher order state of affairs that *a, F-ness, and a unifier are unified* (E²F*a*) then it would seem that the latter state of affairs needs a still higher order state of affairs to ensure its possible existence; the state of affairs *that a, F-ness, a unifier and a 2nd order unifier are unified* (E³(E²(F*a*))). But now it is easy to see that this state of affairs also stands in need of something to guarantee its existence; a yet higher order state of affairs. Et cetera, *ad infinitum.*

9.   External vs. internal infinite regress

Perhaps surprisingly, proponents of the view now under consideration – the 'infinitists' – gladly accept the regress generated above. In fact, the infinite regress to which their view commits them is not only one that they are prepared to live with, it rather forms an integral part of their solution to the problem of unity; it is *because* rather than *in spite of* this infinite regress, that the state of affairs *that a is F* exists.[18]

Now, the infinitists do not dispute that the infinite regress described in the beginning of this paper viciously prevents us from grounding the truth of <*a* is F>. But then the regress to which they themselves are committed must be importantly different from that one. To be able to judge if the infinitist can successfully solve the problem of unity, we must therefore make sure, first, *that* the regress to which infinitism gives rise really is importantly different from the regress described in the beginning of this chapter and, second, that it is different in a way that is of relevance to the question of viciousness.

Now, *that* the two regresses are substantially different is easily demonstrated. For, whereas in the original regress, what exists at each step can be regarded a corrective expansion of, and so identical with, that which is supposed to exist in the regress's previous step, this is not true of the infinitist's regress. To the contrary, in the infinitist's regress, each step is distinct from, though related to, each other step in the regress. Given the

---

[18] This view is defended by Orilia (2006) and (2009) (a similar view is proposed by Gaskin 2008 and 2010, cf. also Maurin (2013b) for a critical discussion of both Orilia's and Gaskin's views). An early precursor to Orilia is Segelberg. Segelberg published exclusively in Swedish, but thanks to a relatively speaking recent translation (by Hochberg and Ringström Hochberg, see Segelberg 1999), his complete works are now available in English. For more on Segelberg's views, cf. Hochberg (1999) and Maurin (2014b).

original regress, therefore, the result is one infinitely complex whole which, because at no step is this a *unified* whole, contradicts the existence of the state of affairs *that a is F*. Given the infinitist's regress, on the other hand, the result is instead an infinity of finitely complex and unified wholes or states of affairs. This means that whereas the original regress envelops *inside* the would-be state of affairs *that a is F*, the infinitist's regress rather develops *given* and so *outside* this state of affairs. The two regresses are therefore clearly different. To capture this difference we can say, with Orilia, that the original regress is 'internal' whereas the infinitist's regress is 'external.' The difference can be depicted as follows (using Orilia's 'E' for 'unifier'):

Internal Regress	**External Regress**
$F - a$	Fa
$F - E^1 - a$	$E^1(Fa)$
$F - E^2 - E^1 - E^2 - a$	$E^2(E^1(Fa))$
$F - E^3 - E^2 - E^3 - E^1 - E^3 - E^2 - E^3 - a$	$E^3(E^2(E^1(Fa)))$
$\ldots$	$\ldots$
∞	∞

But what, if anything, is it about this difference that should make us judge the internal regress vicious yet the external regress benign?

Fortunately, to be able to answer that question no theory on what distinguishes a vicious from a benign regress generally needs to be formulated (but cf. Gratton 2010 and Maurin 2013a). Instead we can make do with an account of what would constitute a failure to answer the particular questions posed in this chapter. Those questions, remember, were, first: 'What makes it the case that in A, but not in B, is it true that $<a$ is F$>$?' And, second, given that we have opted for answering the first question with 'The state of affairs *that a is F*': 'What makes it the case that the state of affairs *that a is F* exists?' What we are looking for is what we might call the *ontological ground* for, or *metaphysical explanation* of, both the existence of the state of affairs *that a is F* and, as a consequence, for the truth of $<a$ is F$>$; something the existence of which *guarantees* the existence of the state of affairs.[19] Any regress preventing us from producing this ground is therefore a vicious regress.

---

[19] A distinctively metaphysical explanation, I assume, is an explanation such that, if x metaphysically explains y (if y *in virtue of x*) then not only does x necessitate y, or makes y exist/obtain, but it does so in virtue of being what y (mereologically or non-mereologically) consists of or, at least, by being the base on which y supervenes or from which y emerges. This is of course only a first stab at an account of the distinctively metaphysical explanation, but it will have to do for now. Cf. also e.g. Betti (2010), Schaffer (2010), and Wieland and Weber (2010).

It is now easy to see why the internal relation regress is a vicious regress. In this regress, each step contains something that is compatible both with the truth and falsity of $<a$ is F$>$ and with both the existence and non-existence of the state of affairs *that a is F*, which means that at *no* step are we given something which guarantees *that a is F*. Unfortunately, not every regress is as easily evaluated, and the external relation regress is a case in point.

A quick look at the external relation regress should make us think that this is an unproblematic regress. After all, our explanatory task is completed already given this regress's first step. For, given the existence of the state of affairs *that a is F*, both the truth of $<a$ is F$>$ and, trivially, the existence of the state of affairs *that a is F*, is guaranteed. But then, whatever happens next in the regress should make no difference to the end-result. As Armstrong (1997b: 119) puts it when exploring a similar alternative: '[m]any truths if you like, but only the one truthmaker.'

This is not how the infinitist wants us to understand the regress she endorses. For, if the regress is unproblematic in this way, then the state of affairs *that a is F* is *not* metaphysically explained by what comes next in the regress. But that it is, is however exactly what the infinitist wants to claim. According to the infinitist, although a quick look at this regress might make us think that whatever it contains after its first step depends for its existence on what exists at this first step, the existential dependence relations are actually the other way around; whatever exists in any step in the regress (including the first) has its existence guaranteed – is metaphysically explained – by whatever succeeds it in the regress. According to the proponent of infinitism, since the regress is infinite, at no step will there be anything that isn't metaphysically grounded in what succeeds it. And since everything is grounded in what succeeds it, *everything* is grounded, period. Therefore, this regress is benign.

Critics of infinitism tend to disagree. Now, interestingly, this is not a disagreement over what makes a regress vicious. Proponents and critics of infinitism alike agree that the regress is vicious if it prevents the regress' first step from constituting a metaphysical explanation of the existence of the state of affairs *that a is F*. Instead, this is a disagreement over whether or not it is a problem that no step in the infinitist's regress could constitute the requisite explanation were it not for the existence of the next step in the regress. That is, this is a disagreement, not so much over what makes a regress vicious, but rather over what it takes for something to be a metaphysical explanation in the first place. More specifically, this is a disagreement over whether or not (metaphysical) explanation must ground out.

10.   Must explanation ground out?

The principle over which proponents and critics of infinitism disagree is the following (Cameron 2008: 8):

> [W]hen there is an infinite chain of entities $e_1, e_2, e_3, \ldots$, or an infinite chain of facts $f_1, f_2, f_3, \ldots$, then while e_2 may ontologically depend on e_1, and e_3 on e_2, etc., and while f_2 may obtain in virtue of f_1 and f_3 in virtue of f_2, etc., it is impossible for e_1 to be ontologically dependent on e_2, and e_2 ontologically dependent on e_3, etc., or for f_1 to obtain in virtue of f_2 and f_2 in virtue of f_3, etc. There must be a metaphysical ground, a realm of ontologically independent objects, and a realm of basic facts which provide the ultimate metaphysical grounding for all the derivative facts.

If this principle – which we, following Orilia (2009) may call *Ontological Well-Foundedness* (WF) – is accepted, infinitism must fail to provide us with the requisite metaphysical explanation. For to hold that the existence of the state of affairs *that a is F* can metaphysically explain the truth of $<a$ is F$>$ in virtue of it being, in turn, metaphysically explained by what comes next in the regress, etc. *ad infinitum*, is basically to do precisely what WF forbids.

Intuition is certainly on the side of WF.[20] Although he wants to reject the principle, even Orilia is prepared to admit as much (2006: 232):

> intuitively it seems correct to say that we have an explanation for P only insofar as there is, so to speak, an increase in our knowledge/understanding, when we contemplate P. But, one could argue, if in an attempt to explain P I begin an explanatory task wherein at every stage I must presuppose a succeeding stage, then there is no increase. For any such increase is an approximation to the final stage and if there is no such stage, then there is no explanation. And thus there cannot be infinite explanatory chains.

Now, intuitions may be misleading and, in this case, the infinitist must argue that they are. And if Orilia is right, and the intuitiveness of WF stems from ideas about how explanation must result in an increase in our knowledge and understanding, it does seem as if the infinitist may have good cause to be critical. Metaphysical explanations, after all, are *very* different from everyday explanations. To give a metaphysical explanation of *x* is to metaphysically ground *x*. Whether or not our understanding of *x* thereby increases doesn't seem to have anything to do with whether or not this is a successful explanation, but can at most constitute a coincidental,

---

[20] WF's historical precursor can be said to be *the principle of sufficient reason*, first explicitly discussed by Spinoza and then by Leibniz, but probably 'as old as philosophy itself.' Recent arguments based on WF include, e.g., Schaffer's (2010) argument for 'Priority Monism' (discussed by Cameron 2008: 5f.).

albeit be it very likely, side-effect of such success. If Orilia is right, and this is the main reason why people tend to think that explanation must ground out, it may therefore turn out that we have *no* reason to think that explanation must ground out as long as it is metaphysical explanation that we are talking about.

But is this our only justification for so strongly believing that explanation must ground out? I don't think so. The more important reason for the principle's strong standing is, rather, a very different sort of belief. As put by Cameron (2008: 3):

> [If] there are infinitely many levels of facts, the obtaining of each depending on the facts at the next level . . . it is hard to see how things could get off the ground in the first place.

Or, in Schaffer's words (2010: 62):

> Being would be infinitely deferred, never achieved.

So, perhaps it is not that we think that unless explanation grounds out can it result in an increase in our understanding, but that unless it grounds out can anything (begin to) exist. This is a reason of more obvious relevance to the sort of explanation that interests us here. However, arguably, just as we may think that metaphysical explanation must ground out because we think that 'being' needs some base in order to get off the ground; we think that 'being' needs some base in order to get off the ground because we think that metaphysical explanation must ground out. This belief can therefore at most be used to explain our strong belief in WF, it cannot be used to justify it.

Cameron concludes that it is futile to try to give a metaphysically principled defense of WF. Instead we must just accept that WF is a bedrock principle; it is the starting- rather than the end-point of argumentation. The principle, he believes, can still be defended, although not with reference to some even more basic metaphysical principle. Instead, WF should be defended on methodological rather than on metaphysical grounds. To justify WF, we should therefore see how this principle (and its opposite) fares in relation to our most treasured methodological principles. In this particular case Cameron suggests that we evaluate WF (and its opposite) with the following 'unificationist' methodological principle in mind (2008: 12):

> If we seek to explain some phenomena, then, other things being equal, it is better to give the same explanation of each phenomenon than to give

separate explanations of each phenomenon. A unified explanation of the phenomena is a theoretical benefit.

And this principle, Cameron argues, seems to provide some evidence for WF, for (2008: 12):

> if there is an infinitely descending chain of ontological dependence, then while everything that needs a metaphysical explanation (a grounding for its existence) has one, there is no explanation of everything that needs explaining. That is, it is true for every dependent x that the existence of x is explained by the existence of some prior object (or set of prior objects), but there is no collection of objects that explains the existence of every dependent x.

Whether or not this really is a reason to accept WF can and has been disputed (cf. Orilia 2009). Here we need not decide either way. It is enough if we agree that, as a fundamental metaphysical principle, WF is, in spite of its prominence in our (philosophical) thinking, hard to justify in a way that is likely to convince our opponents. What it comes down to is theoretical cost.

A theoretical cost seldom appears in isolation. To solve the problem of unity, as we have seen, some are willing to add states of affairs to their ontology. This is what we may call a theoretical cost of an ontological kind. If you are not willing to pay that price, proponents of states of affairs argue, you will have to pay another one: the price of not being able to distinguish situation A from situation B. A cost most would regard as unacceptable. Now, suppose that explaining how A differs from B requires, not only that we posit states of affairs but also that for every state of affairs we posit, we automatically posit infinitely many states of affairs. This is a further ontological cost. Suppose next that our addition, as it turns out, can only solve the problem of unity if a principle that guides much of our philosophical thinking and which most of us take for granted, is given up. This is a big cost. It should be taken to count against the suggestion but may, on balance, be acceptable. It all depends, I guess, on how much one wants to solve the problem of unity and, of course, it depends on if there are any cheaper alternative solutions available. Either way, from pointing out that accepting infinitism brings with it the admittedly high cost of having to give up WF, it does not follow that infinitism cannot successfully solve the problem of unity.[21]

---

[21] Perhaps infinitism is even *compatible* with a slightly modified version of WF. For, given infinitism, it is not simply because every step of the regress is explained by what succeeds it that the existence of the state of affairs is metaphysically explained; it is also important, for the suggestion to be successful,

11.   The wrong kind of explanation

Does this mean that the infinitist can solve the problem of unity? No. And the reason why not, ironically enough, is precisely the reason why, so far, she has managed so much better than her rivals. With recourse to the external relation regress, remember, the infinitist can distinguish situation A from situation B:

A: a, F-ness, Fa, E^2(Fa), E^3(E^2(Fa)), etc. *ad infinitum*, exist; $<a$ and F-ness exist$>_{\text{true}}$; $<a$ is F$>_{\text{true}}$.

B: a, F-ness, exist; $<a$ and F-ness exist$>_{\text{true}}$; $<a$ is F$>_{\text{false}}$.

According to the infinitist, it is *because* E^2(Fa) . . . exist in A that Fa exists in A, and it is *because* Fa exists in A that $<a$ is F$>$ is true in A. Given this account of the difference between A and B, moreover, no new problematic pairs of situations are generated. In particular, there can be no situation in which E^2(Fa) . . . exists yet it is false that $<a$ is F$>$. Why not? This may sound like a stupid question as the answer should be obvious. E^2(Fa) . . . cannot exist in a world in which it is false that $<a$ is F$>$ because E^2(Fa) . . . cannot exist in a world in which Fa does not exist.

But then, just as the existence of the state of affairs *that a is F* is guaranteed by the existence of what we find at the next step of that regress, so is the existence of what exists after the first step in the regress guaranteed to exist by the existence of the state of affairs *that a is F*. Existential dependence, in the external relation regress, is in other words symmetric not asymmetric.[22]

To see why this is problematic, note that the question 'What makes it the case that the state of affairs *that a is F* exists?' is ambiguous. If disambiguated, two distinct questions can now be formulated:

> HOW can there be a situation in which the state of affairs *that a is F* exists?
> WHAT makes this a situation in which the state of affairs *that a is F* exists?

Here the how-question is supposed to capture the sense in which we, when asking for a metaphysical explanation of the existence of the state of affairs *that a is F*, are asking for that which makes the state of affairs *possibly* exist,

---

that there are *infinitely many* such steps. But does this not, in a sense, mean that explanation, even on this account, grounds out *in infinity* (cf. Cameron 2008, for a similar discussion). I think we can conclude that whether or not the combination of infinitism with WF, thus modified, could be defended, the fact that infinitism can only metaphysically explain the existence of states of affairs if WF (in its original form) is discarded, does not mean that infinitism cannot explain the existence of states of affairs, period.

[22] Some might even think that if dependence, and so (metaphysical) explanation, must be taken as symmetrical, this in itself shows that the account fails (cf. e.g. Schaffer 2010). I leave a discussion of this objection for another occasion.

given the existence of F-ness and *a*, whereas the what-question is meant to convey the sense in which that same question can be used to ask, *of the state of affairs that a is F*, what exists when it, and not just F-ness and *a*, does. This is a fine distinction indeed, and for most purposes we can overlook it. For the infinitist, however, the distinction makes all the difference in the world.

As we have just seen, the infinitist explains the existence of the state of affairs *that a is F* with reference to something (the regressively generated infinity of increasingly complex states of affairs) which has *its* existence grounded in the existence of the state of affairs *that a is F*. Explanation goes both ways. But this means that, although the explanation offered by the infinitist can certainly do very well as an answer to the what-question, it will not do as an answer to the how-question. After all, you cannot explain the *possible* existence of the state of affairs *that a is F* by introducing the relevant regress into an F-ness and *a* situation. Because, in order to get the regress you have to already be in a situation in which *a* is F. The possible existence of the state of affairs *that a is F* is, in other words, presupposed by your explanation.

Now, *must* we answer the how-question in order to be able to solve the problem of unity? Unfortunately, yes. The infinitist's external relation regress can only guarantee the existence of unity in complexity if there is unity in complexity. This is however not the problem of unity. The problem of unity is rather a problem that arises when we try to understand *how* there can be unity in complexity. Therefore, although the infinitist does manage to explain WHAT exists when the state of affairs *that a is F* exists, she does not manage, appearances perhaps to the contrary, to meet the more fundamental challenge, which was to explain HOW there can be a situation in which the state of affairs *that a is F* exists in the first place.

12. States of affairs and the relation regress: taking stock

According to proponents of states of affairs, one important reason for holding that states of affairs exist is that states of affairs can solve the problem of unity. In this chapter I have argued that only if the nature of states of affairs can be substantially and non-circularly spelled out, can we even begin to evaluate that claim. The account of the nature of states of affairs that comes closest to giving us what we want is the infinitist's. But, as it turns out, even though the infinitist manages to spell out the nature of states of affairs in one way, this is nevertheless not the account of their nature we need in order for states of affairs to be able to function as a solution the problem of unity. I conclude, therefore, that we have very little reason to think that states of affairs can solve the problem of unity. Consequently, we have very little reason to think that the role played by states of affairs in relation to that problem constitutes a reason to think that they exist.[23]

---

[23] When Armstrong in his (2005, 2006) surprisingly changes his mind (only to change it right back shortly after) and argues that instantiation is necessary, thereby automatically dissolving the problem for which his states of affairs were originally introduced, he is careful to point out that other reasons still exist for accepting the existence of states of affairs. This means that even if the argument set out in this paper succeeds in demonstrating that one important reason for positing states of affairs fails, this at most substantially weakens the case for the existence of states of affairs.

References

Ackrill, J. L. 1963. *Aristotle. Categories and De Intepretatione.* Oxford University Press.

Ademollo, F. 2013. 'Plato's Conception of the Forms: Some Remarks,' in Chiaradonna and Galluzzo (eds.), 41–85.

Albritton, R. 1957. 'Substance and Form in Aristotle,' *Journal of Philosophy* 54: 699–708.

Allaire, E. 1963. 'Bare Particulars,' *Philosophical Studies* 14: 1–8.

Almog, J. 1991. 'The What and the How,' *Journal of Philosophy* 88: 225–44.

Armstrong, D. M. 1975. 'Towards a Theory of Properties: Work in Progress on the Problem of Universals,' *Philosophy* 50: 145–55.

1978. *Universals and Scientific Realism,* 2 vols. Cambridge University Press.

1983. *What is a Law of Nature?* Cambridge University Press.

1989a. *Universals: An Opinionated Introduction.* Boulder: Westview Press.

1989b. *A Combinatorial Theory of Possibility.* Cambridge University Press.

1993a. 'Reply to Forrest,' in J. Bacon, K. Campbell, and L. Reinhardt (eds.), *Ontology, Causality and Mind: Essays in Honour of D. M. Armstrong.* Cambridge University Press, 62–77.

1993b. 'The Identification Problem and the Inference Problem,' *Philosophy and Phenomenological Research* 53: 421–22.

1996. 'Reply to Martin,' in T. Crane (ed.), *Dispositions: A Debate.* New York: Routledge, 88–104.

1997a. 'Against "Ostrich" Nominalism: A Reply to Michael Devitt,' in D. H. Mellor and A. Oliver (eds.), *Properties.* Oxford University Press, 101–11. Originally published in *Pacific Philosophical Quarterly* 61 (1980): 440–49.

1997b. *A World of States of Affairs.* Cambridge University Press.

2004. *Truth and Truthmakers.* Cambridge University Press.

2005. 'How Do Particulars Stand to Universals?,' in D. W. Zimmerman (ed.), *Oxford Studies in Metaphysics,* Vol. 1, 139–54.

2006. 'Particulars Have Their Properties of Necessity,' in P. F. Strawson and A. Chakrabarti (eds.), *Universals, Concepts and Qualities: New Essays on the Meaning of Predicates.* Aldershot: Ashgate, 239–47.

Bacon, J. 1995. *Universals and Property Instances: The Alphabet of Being*. Oxford: Blackwell.

2008. 'Tropes,' in E. N. Zalta (ed.), *Stanford Encyclopedia of Philosophy*. http://plato.stanford.edu/archives/spr2008/entries/tropes/.

Baker, R. 1967. 'Particulars: Bare, Naked, and Nude,' *Noûs* 1: 211–12.

Barnes, J. 1984. *The Complete Works of Aristotle*, 2 vols. Princeton University Press.

Beebee, H., Effingham, N., and Goff, P. 2011. *Metaphysics: The Key Concepts*. London and New York: Routledge.

Bergmann, G. 1967. *Realism*. Madison, WI: University of Wisconsin Press.

Betti, A. 2010. 'Explanation in Metaphysics and Bolzano's Theory of Ground and Consequence,' *Logique et Analyse* 211: 281–316.

Bird, A. 2005. 'The Dispositionalist Conception of Laws,' *Foundations of Science* 10: 353–70.

2007. *Nature's Metaphysics: Laws and Properties*. Oxford: Clarendon Press.

2012. 'Are any Kinds Ontologically Fundamental?', in Tahko (ed.), 94–104.

Black, M. 1952. 'The Identity of Indiscernibles,' *Mind* 61: 153–64.

Bradley, F. H. 1897. *Appearance and Reality* (2nd edn.). London: George Allen & Unwin.

1927. *Ethical Studies* (2nd edn.). Oxford University Press.

Brody, B. A. 1972. 'Towards an Aristotelian Theory of Scientific Explanation,' *Philosophy of Science* 32: 20–31.

1973. 'Why Settle for Anything Less Than Good Old-Fashioned Aristotelian Essentialism?,' *Noûs* 7: 351–65.

Cameron, R. 2005. 'Truthmaker Necessitarianism and Maximalism,' *Logique et Analyse* 48: 43–56.

2008. 'Turtles All the Way Down: Regress, Priority and Fundamentality,' *Philosophical Quarterly* 58: 1–14.

Campbell, K. 1981. 'The Metaphysics of Abstract Particulars,' *Midwest Studies in Philosophy* 6: 477–88.

1990. *Abstract Particulars*. Oxford: Blackwell.

Cartwright, N. 1989. *Nature's Capacities and Their Measurement*. Oxford: Clarendon Press.

1999. *The Dappled World: A Study of the Boundaries of Science*. Cambridge University Press.

Castañeda, H. 1975. 'Identity and Sameness,' *Philosophia* 5: 121–50.

1974. 'Thinking and the Structure of the World,' *Philosophia* 4: 3–40.

Casullo, A. 1988. 'A Fourth Version of the Bundle Theory,' *Philosophical Studies* 54: 125–39.

Chakravartty, A. 2007. *A Metaphysics for Scientific Realism: Knowing the Unobservable*. Cambridge University Press.

Charles, D. 2000. *Aristotle on Meaning and Essence*. Oxford University Press.

Chiaradonna, R. and Galluzzo, G. (eds.) 2013. *Universals in Ancient Philosophy*. Pisa: Edizioni della Scuola Normale.

Chisholm, R. 1976. *Person and Object*. LaSalle, IL: Open Court.

Code, A. 1984. 'The Aporematic Approach to Primary Being in Aristotle's Meta-physics Z,' in Pelletier and King-Farlow (eds.), 1–20.

1986. 'Aristotle: Essence and Accident,' in R. Grandy and R. Warner (eds.), *Philosophical Grounds of Rationality: Intentions, Categories, Ends*. Oxford: Clarendon Press, 411–39.

Cohen, S. M. 1978. 'Essentialism in Aristotle,' *Review of Metaphysics* 31: 387–405.

Cottingham, J., Stoothoff, R., and Murdoch, D. (trans.) 1984. *The Philosophical Writings of Descartes*, vol. 2. Cambridge University Press.

Cover, J. A. and O'Leary-Hawthorne, J. 1999. *Substance & Individuation in Leibniz*. Cambridge University Press.

Daly, C. 1997. 'Tropes,' in D. H. Mellor and A. Oliver (eds.), *Properties*. Oxford University Press, 140–59.

Davidson, D. 1970. 'Events as Particulars,' *Noûs* 4: 25–31.

Demos, R. 1948. 'Note on Plato's Theory of Ideas,' *Philosophy and Phenomenological Research* 8: 456–60.

Descartes, R. 1641. 'Reply to Points that May Cause Difficulty to Theologians,' in Cottingham et al. (1984), 172–78.

Devitt, M. 1980. 'Ostrich Nominalism or "Mirage Realism"?,' *Pacific Philosophical Quarterly* 61: 433–49.

Dodd, J. 1999. 'Farewell to States of Affairs,' *Australasian Journal of Philosophy* 77: 146–60.

Donagan, A. 1963. 'Universals and Metaphysical Realism,' *The Monist* 47: 211–46.

Dorr, C. 2005. 'Non-Symmetric Relations,' *Oxford Studies in Metaphysics* 1: 155–92.

Driscoll, J. 1981. 'ΕΙΔΗ in Aristotle's Earlier and Later Theories of Substance,' in D. O'Meara (ed.), *Studies in Aristotle*. Washington DC: The Catholic University of America Press, 129–59.

Ehring, D. 1997. *Causation and Persistence*. Oxford University Press.

1999. 'Tropeless in Seattle: The Cure for Insomnia,' *Analysis* 51: 19–24.

2011. *Tropes: Properties, Objects, and Mental Causation*. Oxford University Press.

Ellis, B. 2001. *Scientific Essentialism*. Cambridge University Press.

Erismann, C. 2007. 'Immanent Realism: A Reconstruction of an Early Medieval Solution to the Problem of Universals,' *Documenti Studi Sulla Tradizione Filosofica Medievale* 18: 211–29.

Feynman, R., Leighton, R. B., and Sands, M. 1963–65. *The Feynman Lectures on Physics*, 3 vols. Reading, MA: Addison-Wesley.

Fine, K. 1989. 'The Problem of De Re Modality,' in J. Almog, J. Perry, and H. Wettstein (eds.), *Themes from Kaplan*. New York: Oxford University Press, 197–272.

1994a. 'Essence and Modality,' *Philosophical Perspectives* 8: 1–16.

1994b. 'Senses of Essence,' in W. Sinnott-Armstrong, D. Raffman, and Nicholas Asher (eds.), *Modality, Morality and Belief: Essays in Honor of Ruth Barcan Marcus*. Cambridge University Press, 53–73.

1995. 'Ontological Dependence,' *Proceedings of the Aristotelian Society* 95: 269–90.

2000. 'Neutral Relations,' *Philosophical Review* 109: 1–33.

Forrest, P. 1993. 'Just Like Quarks,' in J. Bacon, K. Campbell, and L. Reinhardt (eds.), *Ontology, Causality and Mind: Essays in Honour of D. M. Armstrong*. Cambridge University Press, 45–65.

2010. 'The Identity of Indiscernibles,' in E. N. Zalta (ed.), *Stanford Encyclopedia of Philosophy*. http://plato.stanford.edu/entries/identity-indiscernible/.

Frede, M. 1987a. 'Individuals in Aristotle,' in M. Frede, *Essays in Ancient Philosophy*. Oxford University Press, 49–71.

1987b. 'Substance in Aristotle's Metaphysics,' in M. Frede, *Essays in Ancient Philosophy*. Oxford University Press, 72–80.

Frede, M. and Patzig, G. 1988. Aristoteles, *Metaphysik Z, Text, Übersetzung und Kommentar*, 2 vols. Munich: Beck.

Galluzzo, G. 2013. 'Universals in Aristotle's Metaphysics,' in Chiaradonna and Galluzzo (eds.), 209–53.

Galluzzo, G. and Mariani, M. (eds.) 2007. *Aristotle's Metaphysics, Book Zeta. The Contemporary Debate*. Pisa: Edizioni della Scuola Normale.

Garcia, R. 2009. 'Nominalist Constituent Ontologies: A Development and Critique', PhD dissertation, University of Notre Dame.

2010. 'Tropes and Tropers,' unpublished paper.

2014a. 'Bare Particulars and Constituent Ontology,' *Acta Analytica* 29: 149–59.

2014b. 'Bundle Theory's Black Box: Gap Challenges for the Bundle Theory of Substance,' *Philosophia* 42: 115–26.

2014c. 'Tropes and Dependency Profiles: Problems for the Nuclear Theory of Substance,' *American Philosophical Quarterly* 51: 167–76.

MS a. 'Tropes as Character-Grounders.'

MS b. 'Two Ways to Particularize a Property.'

Gaskin R. 2008. *The Unity of the Proposition*. Oxford University Press.

2010. 'Précis of the Unity of the Proposition,' *Dialectica* 64: 259–64.

Goodman, N. 1966. *The Structure of Appearance* (2nd edn.). Indianapolis: Bobbs-Merrill.

Gratton, C. 2010. *Infinite Regress Arguments*. Dordrecht: Springer.

Heil, J. 2003. *From an Ontological Point of View*. Oxford: Clarendon Press.

2005. 'Real Tables,' *The Monist* 88: 493–509.

2009. 'Relations,' in R. Le Poidevin and R. Cameron (eds.), *The Routledge Companion to Metaphysics*. London: Routledge, 310–21.

2010. 'Powerful Qualities,' in A. Marmodoro (ed.), *The Metaphysics of Powers: Their Grounding and their Manifestations*. London: Routledge, 58–72.

2012. *The Universe as We Find It*. Oxford: Clarendon Press.

2015. 'Cartesian Transubstantiation,' in J. Kvanvig (ed.), *Oxford Studies in Philosophy of Religion*. Oxford University Press, 138–57.

Heller, M. 1990. *The Ontology of Physical Objects*. Cambridge University Press.

Hochberg, H. 1999. *Complexes and Consciousness*. Stockholm: Thales.

Hoffman, J. and Rosenkrantz, J. S. 2005. 'Platonist Theories of Universals,' in M. J. Loux and D. Zimmerman (eds.), *The Oxford Handbook of Metaphysics*. Oxford University Press, 46–73.

Hume, D. 1739. *A Treatise of Human Nature*, ed. L. A. Selby-Bigge and P. H. Nidditch (2nd edn.). Oxford University Press, 1978.

James, W. 1904. 'A World of Pure Experience,' *Journal of Philosophy* 1: 52–76.

Kant, I. 1768. 'On the First Ground of the Distinction of Regions in Space,' Academy Edition, vol. 2. Berlin: De Gruyter.

    1783. *Prolegomena to Any Future Metaphysics*, trans. L. W. Beck. Indianapolis: Bobbs-Merrill, 1950.

Keinänen, M. 2011. 'Tropes: The Basic Constituents of Powerful Particulars?,' *Dialectica* 65: 419–50.

Koslicki, K. 2008. *The Structure of Objects*. Oxford University Press.

    2012. 'Essence, Necessity and Explanation,' in Tahko (ed.), 187–206.

Küng, G. 1967. *Ontology and the Logistic Analysis of Language*. Dordrecht: Reidel.

Kung, J. 1977. 'Aristotle on Essence and Explanation,' *Philosophical Studies* 31: 361–83.

LaBossiere, M. 1994. 'Substances and Substrata,' *Australasian Journal of Philosophy* 72: 360–70.

Leibniz, G. W. 1715. *Leibniz–Clarke Correspondence*, trans. M. Morris and G. H. R. Parkinson, in G. H. R. Parkinson (ed.), *Leibniz: Philosophical Writings*. London: J. M. Dent and Sons, 1973.

Levinson, J. 1978. 'Properties and Related Entities,' *Philosophy and Phenomenological Research* 39: 1–22.

    1980. 'The Particularization of Attributes,' *Australasian Journal of Philosophy* 58: 102–15.

    2006. 'Why There Are No Tropes,' *Philosophy* 81: 563–79.

Lewis, D. 1983. 'New Work for a Theory of Universals,' *Australasian Journal of Philosophy* 61: 343–77.

    1986a. *On the Plurality of Worlds*. Oxford: Blackwell.

    1986b. 'Against Structural Universals,' *Australasian Journal of Philosophy* 61: 343–77.

    1986c. *Philosophical Papers*, vol. 2. New York: Oxford University Press.

    1991. *Parts of Classes*. Oxford: Basil Blackwell.

Lewis, F. 1982. 'Accidental Sameness in Aristotle,' *Philosophical Studies* 42: 1–36.

    1984. 'What is Aristotle's Theory of Essence?,' in Pelletier and King-Farlow (eds.), 89–131.

    1991. *Substance and Predication in Aristotle*. Cambridge University Press.

Loux, M. 1978. *Substance and Attribute*. Dordrecht: Reidel.

    1991. *Primary Ousia. An Essay on Aristotle's* Metaphysics Z and H. Ithaca: Cornell University Press.

    2002. *Metaphysics* (2nd edn.). London: Routledge.

    2004. 'Aristotle on Matter, Form, and Ontological Strategy,' *Ancient Philosophy* 25: 81–123.

2006a. 'Aristotle's Constituent Ontology,' in D. W. Zimmerman (ed.), *Oxford Studies in Metaphysics*, vol. 2. Oxford University Press, 207–49.

2006b. *Metaphyisics: A Contemporary Introduction*. New York and London: Routledge.

2007a. 'Substance, Coincidentals, and Aristotle's Constituent Ontology,' in Shields, 371–99.

2007b. 'Perspectives on the Problem of Universals,' *Documenti e studi sulla tradizione filosofica medievale* 18: 601–21.

2009. 'Aristotle on Universals,' in G. Anagnostopoulos (ed.), *A Companion to Aristotle*. Oxford: Wiley-Blackwell, 186–96.

Lowe, E. J. 1987. 'What is the Problem of Induction?,' *Philosophy* 62: 325–40.

1989. *Kinds of Being: A Study of Individuation, Identity, and the Logic of Sortal Terms*. Oxford: Blackwell.

1995. 'The Metaphysics of Abstract Objects,' *Journal of Philosophy* 92: 509–24.

1998. *The Possibility of Metaphysics: Substance, Identity, and Time*. Oxford University Press.

2002a. *A Survey of Metaphysics*. Oxford University Press.

2002b. 'Metaphysical Nihilism and the Subtraction Argument,' *Analysis* 62: 62–73.

2005. 'Individuation,' in M. J. Loux and D. Zimmerman (eds.), *The Oxford Handbook of Metaphysics*. Oxford University Press, 75–95.

2006. *The Four-Category Ontology: A Metaphysical Foundation for Natural Science*. Oxford University Press.

2009. *More Kinds of Being: A Further Study of Individuation, Identity and the Logic of Sortal Terms*. Malden, MA and Oxford: Wiley-Blackwell.

2010. 'Ontological Dependence,' in E. N. Zalta (ed.), *Stanford Encyclopedia of Philosophy*. http://plato.stanford.edu/archives/spr2010/entries/dependence-ontological/.

MacBride, F. 1999. 'Could Armstrong Have Been a Universal?,' *Mind* 108: 471–501.

2005. 'Lewis's Animadversions on the Truthmaker Principle,' in H. Beebee and J. Dodd (eds.), *Truthmakers: The Contemporary Debate*. Oxford University Press, 117–40.

2007. 'Neutral Relations Revisited,' *Dialectica* 61: 25–56.

2011. 'Relations & Truthmaking,' *Proceedings of the Aristotelian Society* 111: 161–79.

2013a. 'How Involved Do You Want To Be in a Non-Symmetric Relationship?,' *Australasian Journal of Philosophy* 92: 1–16.

2013b. 'The Russell–Wittgentein Dispute: A New Perspective,' in M. Textor (ed.), *Judgement and Truth in Early Analytic Philosophy and Phenomenology*. Basingstoke: Palgrave Macmillan, 206–41.

2014. 'Truthmakers,' in E. N. Zalta (ed.), *Stanford Encyclopedia of Philosophy*. http://plato.stanford.edu/archives/spr2014/entries/truthmakers/.

Macdonald, C. and Macdonald, G. 2006. 'The Metaphysics of Mental Causation,' *Journal of Philosophy* 103: 539–76.

Manley, D. 2002. 'Properties and Resemblance Classes,' *Noûs* 36: 75–96.

Mariani, M. 2013. 'Universals in Aristotle's Logical Works,' in Chiaradonna and Galluzzo (eds.), 185–208.

Martin, C. 1980. 'Substance Substantiated,' *Australasian Journal of Philosophy* 58: 3–10.

2008. *The Mind in Nature*. Oxford University Press.

Matthews, G. B. 1990. 'Aristotelian Essentialism,' *Philosophy and Phenomenological Research* Suppl. Vol. 50: 251–62.

Matthews, G. B. and Cohen, S. M. 1968. 'The One and the Many,' *Review of Metaphysics* 21: 630–55.

Maurin, A.-S. 2002. *If Tropes*. Dordrecht: Kluwer Academic Publishers.

2010. 'Trope Theory and the Bradley Regress,' *Synthese* 175: 311–26.

2011. 'An Argument for the Existence of Tropes,' *Erkenntnis* 74: 69–79.

2012. 'Bradley's Regress,' *Philosophy Compass* 7: 794–807.

2013a. 'Infinite Regress Arguments,' in C. Svennerlind, J. Almäng, and R. Ingthorsson (eds.), *Johanssonian Investigations*. Heusenstamm: Ontos Verlag, 421–38.

2013b. 'Exemplification as Explanation,' *Axiomathes* 23: 401–17.

2014a. 'Tropes,' in E. N. Zalta (ed.), *Stanford Encyclopedia of Philosophy*. plato.stanford.edu/archives/fall2014/entries/tropes/.

2014b. 'Segelberg on Unity and Complexity,' in H. Malmgren, T. Nordin, and C. Svennerlind (eds.), *Botany and Philosophy: Essays on Ivar Segelberg*. Stockholm: Thales, 36–54.

Mellor, D. 1991. *Matters of Metaphysics*. Cambridge University Press.

Merricks, T. 2001. *Objects and Persons*. Oxford University Press.

Mertz, D. W. 1996. *Moderate Realism and its Logic*. New Haven: Yale University Press.

Minio-Paluello, L. 1949. *Aristotle's Categoriae et Liber De Interpretatione*. Oxford University Press.

Molnar, G. 2003. *Powers: A Study in Metaphysics*. Oxford University Press.

Moore, G. E. 1919. 'External and Internal Relations,' *Proceedings of the Aristotelian Society* 20: 40–62. Reprinted in G. E. Moore, *Philosophical Studies*. London: Routledge & Kegan Paul, 1922, 276–309.

1922. *Philosophical Studies*. London: K. Paul, Trench, Trubner & Co.; New York: Harcourt, Brace & Co.

Moreland, J. P. and Pickavance, T. 2003. 'Bare Particulars and Individuation: Reply to Mertz,' *Australasian Journal of Philosophy* 81: 1–13.

Morrison, J. S. 1977. 'Two Unresolved Difficulties in the Line and the Cave,' *Phronesis* 22: 212–31.

Newton, I. 1729. *Mathematical Principles of Natural Philosophy*, trans. A. Motte, revised F. Cajori. Berkeley and Los Angeles: University of California Press, 1934.

Oderberg, D. S. 2007. *Real Essentialism*. Abingdon and New York: Routledge.

O'Leary-Hawthorne, J. and Cover, J. A. 1998. 'A World of Universals,' *Philosophical Studies* 91: 205–19.

Orilia, F. 2006. 'States of Affairs: Bradley vs. Meinong,' in V. Raspa (ed.), *Meinongian Issues in Contemporary Italian Philosophy*, vol. 2. Heusenstamm: Ontos Verlag, 213–38.

2009. 'Bradley's Regress and Ungrounded Dependence Chains: A Reply to Cameron,' *Dialectica* 63: 333–41.

Parsons, J. 1999. 'There is No "Truthmaker" Argument Against Nominalism,' *Australasian Journal of Philosophy* 77: 325–34.

2009. 'Are There Irreducibly Relational Facts?,' in E. J. Lowe and E. Rami (eds.), *Truth and Truth-Making*. Stocksfield: Acumen Press, 217–26.

Paul, L. A. 2002. 'Logical Parts,' *Noûs* 36: 578–96.

2004. 'The Context of Essence,' *Australasian Journal of Philosophy* 82: 170–84.

2006a. 'Coincidence as Overlap,' *Noûs* 40: 623–59.

2006b. 'In Defense of Essentialism,' in J. Hawthorne (ed.), *Philosophical Perspectives*, vol. 20: *Metaphysics*. Oxford: Blackwell, 333–72.

2012a. 'Building the World from its Fundamental Constituents,' *Philosophical Studies* 158: 221–56.

2012b. 'Metaphysics as Modeling: The Handmaiden's Tale,' *Philosophical Studies* 160: 1–29.

forthcoming. 'A One Category Ontology,' in J. A. Keller (ed.), *Freedom, Metaphysics, and Method: Themes from van Inwagen*. Oxford University Press.

Pelletier, J. and King-Farlow, J. (eds.) 1984. *New Essays on Aristotle*. Guelph, Ontario: Canadian Association for Publishing in Philosophy.

Pickavance, T. 2014. 'Bare Particulars and Exemplification,' *American Philosophical Quarterly* 51: 95–108.

Quine, W. V. O. 1954. 'On What There Is,' in W. V. O. Quine, *From a Logical Point of View*. Cambridge, MA: Harvard University Press, 1–19. Originally published in *Review of Metaphysics* 2 (1948): 21–36.

1960. *Word and Object*. Cambridge, MA: MIT Press.

Rea, M. (ed.) 2008. *Critical Concepts in Philosophy: Metaphysics, Vol. 5*. London and New York: Routledge.

Robb, D. M. 1997. 'The Properties of Mental Causation,' *Philosophical Quarterly* 47: 178–94.

2005. 'Qualitative Unity and the Bundle Theory,' *Monist* 88: 466–92.

Rodriguez-Pereyra, G. 2004. 'The Bundle Theory is Compatible with Distinct but Indiscernible Particulars,' *Analysis* 64: 72–81.

Ross, W. D. 1924. *Aristotle's Metaphysics*, 2 vols. Oxford University Press.

1936. *Aristotle's Physics*. Oxford University Press.

1949. *Aristotle's Prior and Posterior Analytics*. Oxford University Press.

1958. *Aristotle's Topica et Sophistici Elenchi*. Oxford University Press.

Russell, B. 1903. *The Principles of Mathematics*. Cambridge University Press. Reprinted London: Routledge, 2010.

1925. 'Logical Atomism,' in J. H. Muirhead (ed.), *Contemporary British Philosophy*. London: Allen & Unwin, 359–83.

1940. *An Inquiry into Meaning and Truth*. London: Allen & Unwin.

Santayana, G. 1930. *The Realm of Matter*. New York: Charles Scribner's Sons.

Schaffer, J. 2001. 'The Individuation of Tropes,' *Australasian Journal of Philosophy* 79: 247–57.
2010. 'Monism: The Priority of the Whole,' *Philosophical Review* 119: 31–76.
Seargent, D. A. J. 1985. *Plurality and Continuity*. Dordrecht: Martinus Nijhoff.
Segelberg, I. 1999. *Three Essays in Phenomenology and Ontology*, trans. H. Hochberg and S. Ringström Hochberg. Stockholm: Thales.
Sellars, W. I. 1957. 'Substance and Form in Aristotle,' *Journal of Philosophy* 54: 688–99.
1963a. *Science, Perception and Reality*. London: Routledge & Kegan Paul.
1963b. 'Abstract Entities,' *Review of Metaphysics* 16: 627–71. Reprinted in Sellars, *Philosophical Perspectives*. Springfield, IL: Charles C. Thomas, 1967, 229–69.
Shields, C. (ed.) 2012. *The Oxford Handbook of Aristotle*. Oxford University Press.
Shoemaker, S. 1980. 'Causality and Properties,' in P. van Inwagen (ed.), *Time and Cause*. Dordrecht: D. Reidel, 109–35.
1998. 'Causal and Metaphysical Necessity,' *Pacific Philosophical Quarterly* 79: 59–77.
Sider, T. 2006. 'Bare Particulars,' *Philosophical Perspectives* 20: 387–97.
Simons, P. 1994. 'Particulars in Particular Clothing,' *Philosophy and Phenomenological Research* 54: 553–75.
Stout, G. F. 1921. 'The Nature of Universals and Propositions,' *Proceedings of the British Academy* 10 (1921–23): 157–72. Reprinted in Stout (1930), 384–403.
1930. *Studies in Philosophy and Psychology*. London: Macmillan.
1936. 'Universals Again,' *Proceedings of the Aristotelian Society*, Suppl. Vol. 15: 1–15.
Strawson, P. and Grice, P. 1956. 'In Defense of a Dogma,' *Philosophical Review* 65: 141–58.
Swoyer, C. 1982. 'The Nature of Natural Laws,' *Australasian Journal of Philosophy* 60: 203–23.
Tahko, T. E. (ed.) 2013. *Contemporary Aristotelian Metaphysics*. Cambridge University Press.
Vallicella, W. F. 2000. 'Three Conceptions of States of Affairs,' *Noûs* 34: 237–59.
Van Cleve, J. 1985. 'Three Versions of the Bundle Theory,' *Philosophical Studies* 51: 95–107.
Van Fraassen, B. C. 1989. *Laws and Symmetry*. Oxford: Clarendon Press.
1993. 'Armstrong, Cartwright and Earman on Laws and Symmetry,' *Philosophy and Phenomenological Research* 53: 431–44.
2002. *The Empirical Stance*. New Haven and London: Yale University Press.
Van Inwagen, P. 1981. 'The Doctrine of Arbitrary Undetached Parts,' *Pacific Philosophical Quarterly* 62: 123–37.
1986. 'Two Concepts of Possible Worlds,' *Midwest Studies in Philosophy* 11: 185–213.
1990. *Material Objects*. Ithaca and London: Cornell University Press.
2006. 'A Theory of Properties,' in D. W. Zimmerman (ed.), *Oxford Studies in Metaphysics*, vol. 1. Oxford University Press, 107–38.

2007a. 'Impotence and Collateral Damage: One Charge in van Fraassen's Indictment of Analytical Metaphysics,' *Philosophical Topics* 35: 67–82.

2007b. 'A Set of Accidents,' *Times Literary Supplement*. December 21 and 28.

2009. 'The New Anti-Metaphysicians,' *Proceedings and Addresses of the American Philosophical Association* 83: 45–61.

2012. 'What is an Ontological Category?' in L. Novák, D. D. Novotný, P. Sousedík, and D. Svoboda (eds.), *Metaphysics: Aristotelian, Scholastic, Analytic*. Heusenstamm: Ontos Verlag in cooperation with Studia Neoaristotelica, 11–24.

2014. *Existence: Essays in Ontology*. Cambridge University Press.

Wedin, M. V. 1984. 'Singular Statements and Essentialism in Aristotle,' in Pelletier and King-Farlow (eds.), 67–88.

Wieland, J. W. and Weber, E. 2010. 'Metaphysical Explanatory Asymmetries,' *Logique et Analyse* 211: 345–65.

Wiggins, D. 1980. *Sameness and Substance*, Cambridge, MA: Harvard University Press.

2001. *Sameness and Substance Renewed*. Cambridge University Press.

Williams, D. 1953. 'The Elements of Being, I,' *Review of Metaphysics* 7: 3–18.

1954. 'Of Essence and Existence in Santayana,' *Journal of Philosophy* 51: 31–42.

1959. 'Universals and Existents,' paper delivered to the Yale Philosophy Club, published posthumously in *Australasian Journal of Philosophy* 64 (1986): 1–14.

1966. *Principles of Empirical Realism*. Springfield, IL: Charles C. Thomas.

Williamson, T. 1985. 'Converse Relations,' *Philosophical Review* 94: 249–62.

Wittgenstein, L. 1922. *Tractatus Logico-Philosophicus*, trans. C. K. Ogden, introd. B. Russell. London: Routledge & Kegan Paul.

Wolterstorff, N. 1970a. 'Bergmann's Constituent Ontology,' *Noûs* 4: 109–34.

1970b. *On Universals*. University of Chicago Press.

1991. 'Divine Simplicity,' *Philosophical Perspectives* 5: 531–52.

Index

Lightning Source UK Ltd.
Milton Keynes UK
UKHW02f0453100318
319168UK00010B/137/P